sculpture

Penelope Curtis

Published for the Paul Mellon Centre for Studies in British Art
by Yale University Press • New Haven and London

open

closed

sculpture

vertical

horizontal

contents

This book is about four key qualities of sculpture and how together they build the larger spaces that we know and experience. Each of the first four chapters identifies a quality - the vertical, the horizontal, the closed and the open – as being central to sculpture, and explores it through a range of examples. One might well read the first two chapters as forming a pair, followed by another. I have on occasion likened this project to a table, with four legs supporting a top and making up a whole, and as it turned out tables had more than passing relevance to the subject more generally. The book has not set out to identify or analyse all the qualities of sculpture, but rather to suggest a framework that underlies sculpture as a whole.

The fifth and last chapter suggests that when the four qualities pull together we end up with the kinds of ensemble that have become closely associated not only with the sculptural experience, but also with the special qualities of ceremonial or commemorative space. This chapter suggests more particularly that when we enter this kind of space – when we step over the threshold – we step inside sculpture. The threshold then, is both conceptual and physical, and I want to thread together those moments when the one seems to announce the other.

In many ways the threshold is the invitation to apprehend that moment of transition, that moment of 'becoming sculpture'. The argument of the book often invokes the physical position of the spectator: the relationship between standing (or walking) and looking, between the feet and the eyes, the ground and the wall. The threshold is also closely connected to the representation of the passage from life to death. Most sculpture historians are used to the fact that much of their material is funereal, but here I intimate a deeper link between sculpture and death, and with it a vocabulary that continues to this day, even if less overtly.

The way in which the forms and positions that I deal with here convey their meaning is also closely allied to the elements: to earth, air, fire and water. These elemental associations recur throughout the chapters of this book. I want to suggest the porousness of many sculptural forms, and the way they hover between one state and another. Thus the notion of metamorphosis – more or less tightly connected to Ovid – is frequently present, as sculpture seems to present itself as the place where the elements perform and bring about change.

A trajectory that involves isolating primary qualities, their association with the elements, and with change, implicitly also describes the shift from the functional to the representative. A lot of the objects I choose to talk about have had a function: most often as markers or containers. Even semi-decorative pieces, like mirrors or fireplaces, had important functions that added meaning to the stories elaborated by the artists who designed them. Part of my argument is that those very functions persist today in the forms and meanings of sculpture.

Because of the fact that the lecture series on which this book is based required a specifically British focus, the examples I choose to discuss and illustrate are largely drawn from the British environment. More importantly, perhaps, they are known to me personally, and the personal aspect of the project is part of its wider import. My argument is that, though my specimens are specific to me (echoing as they do places I have known, works I have seen, artists with whom I have worked), they have sufficient validity to be effectively interchangeable with others.

I want to convey the qualities that underlie sculpture more generally, and to suggest that they are so embedded as often to be forgotten. This then is at once an attempt to name, and thus to reanimate, but also an acknowledgement of the persistence of forms and meanings whether or not they are named, or now go under other names and guises.

Penelope Curtis
2017

vertical

i

vertical

1

By way of introduction I want to go back a century or more, to a lecture given in 1907, in Dresden, and then again in Prague, by the poet Rainer Maria Rilke. Rilke told his audience:

> my purpose is to awaken memories in you which are not yours, which are older than you; to restore connexions and renew relationships which lie in the distant past.[1]

My aim is to do something similar, and we shall return to Rilke at the end. For the moment, however, you might hold his words, along with those sleeping half-remembered connections and relationships, in your memory.

- - -

London is anchored by Trafalgar Square, with, at its centre, **Nelson's Column**. Nelson's Column might be seen as the quintessential statue, but I would like to think as much about its verticality as its figuration, drawing as such on a lineage of markers as much as on a lineage of statues. In this, I want to suggest, it is inherently sculptural.

...

vertical

1. William Railton and Edward Hodges Baily, Nelson's Column, 1840–43

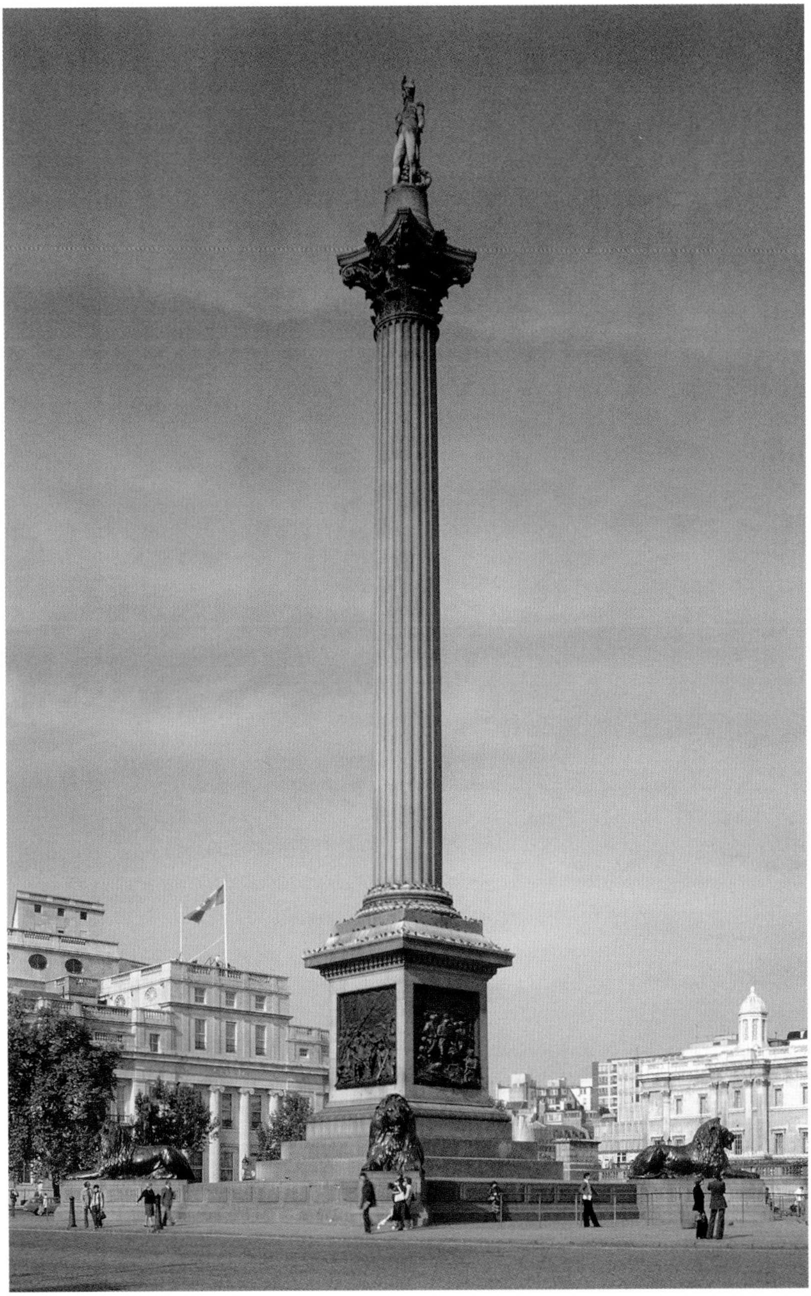

3

Glasgow, Dublin and Great Yarmouth had Nelson columns before London.[2] Another, earlier, marker, **Nelson Monument** in Portsmouth, was facilitated by the very fact that it really was a marker, a Seamark, and was soon appearing on maps, painted in red and white stripes. (This monument, known as a column, but in fact an obelisk, was modelled not so much on a classical obelisk as on the monument at **Axum** in Ethiopia.[3])

Nelson's death, combined with his role at sea, made for a peculiarly fecund terrain in terms of the erection of commemorative monuments that also served as coastal markers, their functional role thus securing any less concrete feelings of commemorative respect. The commemorated hero, juxtaposed with the sea, becomes a monument. The sea might even be understood as acting as the ground against which Nelson rises, surveying its horizon, warding off danger.

I would like to suggest that it is, in part, the very verticality of Nelson's Column that makes us think of it as sculptural, and that the custom of putting an upright figure on a column is in many ways a kind of doubling of the statue itself.[4] Nelson's Column follows the tradition of conjoining column and plinth to make a vertical whole that is neither quite figurative nor quite architectural. Whereas Roman precedents[5] conjoin different regimes and periods, those in Britain are largely homogenous, or simultaneous.

Statues 'en pied', or literally 'on their feet', increased exponentially in the years after this column was erected, largely as a result of a new civic piety, their verticality a testament to their subjects' exemplary nature and a call to emulation, and to their very status as statuary. However, those rather fewer statues on columns take on a much richer urbanistic symbolism.[6]

Nelson's Column might be seen to represent not just himself but also the centre of the city, and in many ways seems thus to assume into itself the notion of epicentre. It is not, however, the official centre or 'kilometre zero' of London, though we do not have to go much farther to find the spot that is.

- - -

2. John Groves, Nelson Monument, 1807–8

3. Obelisk of Axum, c.3rd–4th century

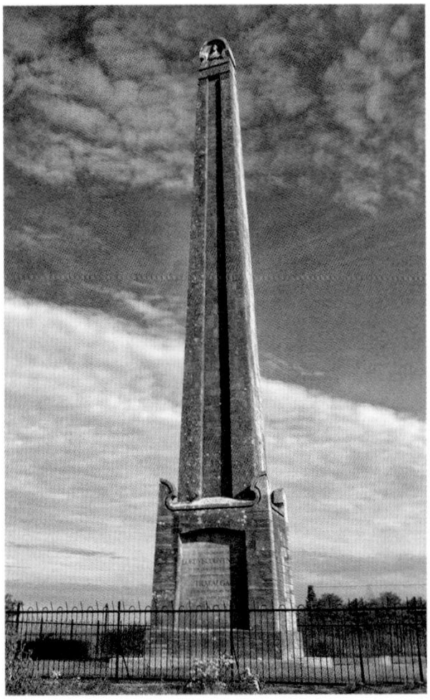

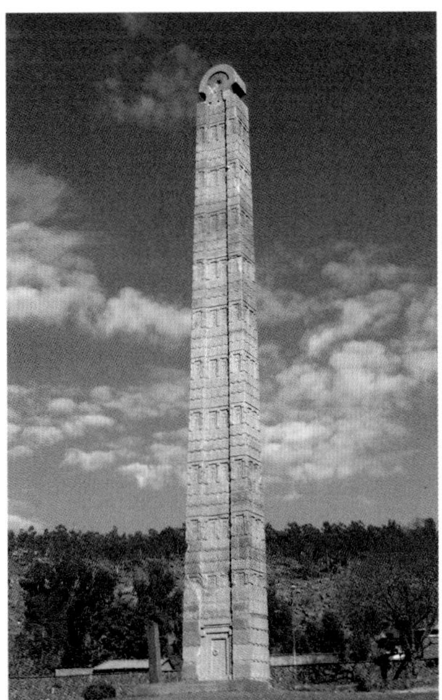

5

The body of Queen Eleanor of Castile was laid at the point that now marks the centre of London, before its burial in Westminster Abbey. A plaque now indicates the spot, but it was previously marked by the last of twelve crosses that commemorated the daily pauses of the Queen's funeral cortège from Harby near Lincoln, where she had died in 1290.

Of the original crosses[7] that marked the repose of the royal body, only three survive, at **Hardingstone**, **Waltham Cross** and **Geddington**. In Geddington the so-called cross is distinguished by the monolithic character of its base, with densely worked decoration wrapping its triangular stem before giving onto the three figures of the Queen above. Despite its name, this cross is actually much more of a column.

...

4. Queen Eleanor's Cross, Hardingstone, c.1290/92

5. Queen Eleanor's Cross, Waltham Cross, c.1290/92

6. Queen Eleanor's Cross, Geddington, c.1290/92

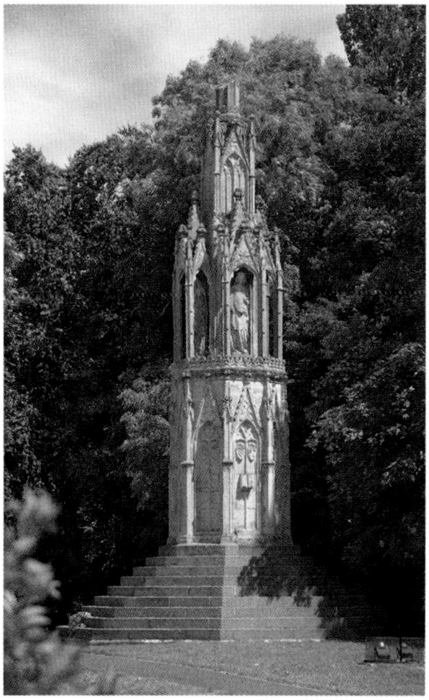

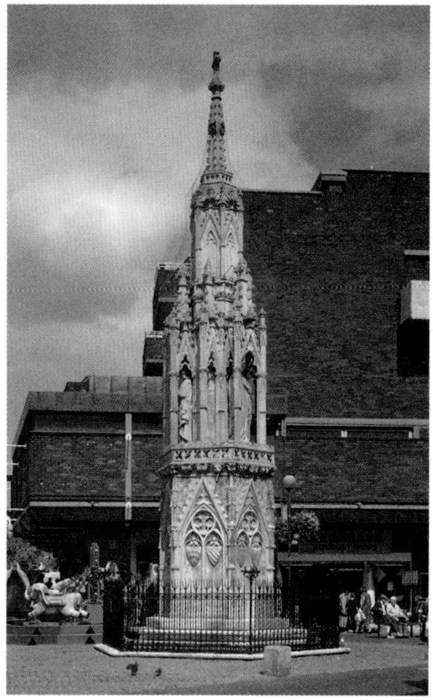

7

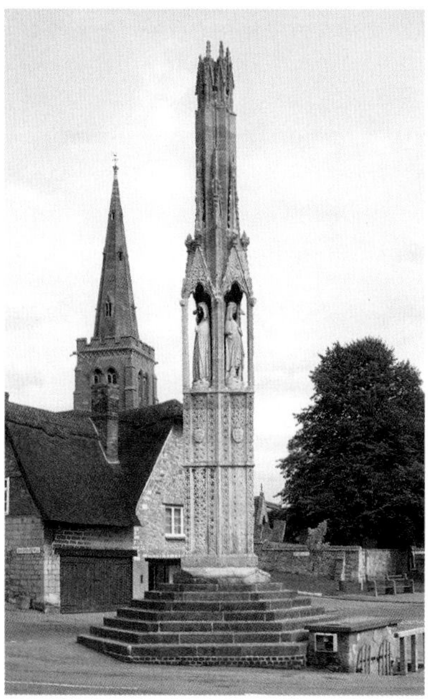

Crosses in general, and the Cheapside version in particular, were notably subject to the Civil War-period Committee for the Demolition of Monuments of Superstition and Idolatry (1643), though Charing Cross survived another four years. It had come to serve as a marker of place[8] and of distance – the centre of London and the point from which distances were measured – and when it was finally dismantled, in 1647, by order of the House of Commons, the story went that people lost their way:

> Undone, undone, the lawyers are,
> They wander about the towne,
> Nor can find the way to Westminster,
> Now Charing-cross is downe:
> At the end of the Strand, they make a stand,
> Swearing they are at a loss,
> And chaffing say, that's not the way,
> They must go by Charing-cross.[9]

vertical

Some of the Charing Cross stones were used to pave Whitehall and its fate might be compared to the London Stone, which has suffered as much, if not more than, the Eleanor Crosses. The **London Stone**, which is probably at least a century earlier than the Eleanor Crosses, now survives as a mutilated stump within a protective grille at 111 Cannon Street, but it was already a marker on late twelfth-century maps.[10] These two different centrepoints remind us of the two parts of London, respectively under the jurisdictions of St Peter and St Paul, the 'west minster' and the 'east minster' of the City.

7. London Stone, late 12th century

In the sixteenth century the London Stone was outside St Swithin's, but when that church was rebuilt by Christopher Wren after the Great Fire, he incorporated the stone within a larger one. The church was again destroyed by fire during the Blitz, and the stone was again rescued and placed in its current location.

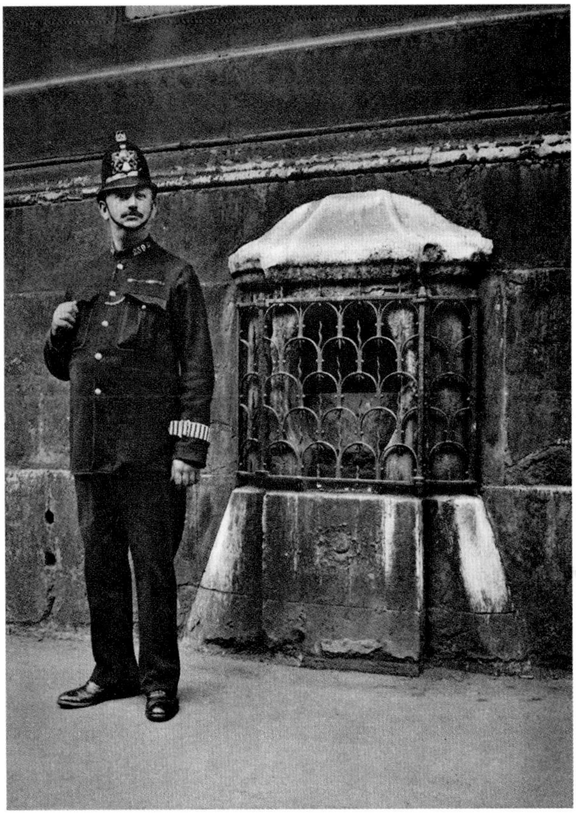

6

Wren is probably better known as the architect of another column that marked a spot, and in its name at least this column lays claim to its full and purposeful status. This is the Monument, London's **Monument**, and remains so to this day. Its height measures the distance from the spot where the Great Fire began, and, like the antique Victory Columns, it is not just an object to be seen but one to be entered and one that affords a view of the surroundings that it had, as it were, conquered. (In this it is akin to the continental Plague Columns, usually erected to a saint or the Virgin to express thanks for delivery from the plague.) As with the Roman precedents, Wren had proposed a figurative statue at the top of the column, but his estimate for the figure of Charles II[11] was found to be too costly, and so the gilt flames, which had in fact been part of his first design (along with an orb), were the part that was chosen and that survives to this day. The **flames** of the Monument enhance its quality as a marker; at once warning of fire, it is itself presented as a beacon, and Wren described it as a 'Pillar in Flames',[12] and Defoe spoke of it as resembling a candle.

- - -

8. Christopher Wren, Monument to the Great Fire of London, 1671–7

9. Christopher Wren, Monument to the Great Fire of London, detail showing the gilt f ames, 1671–7

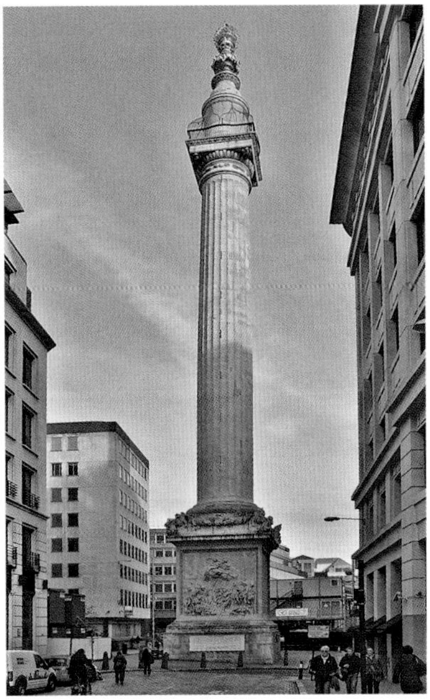

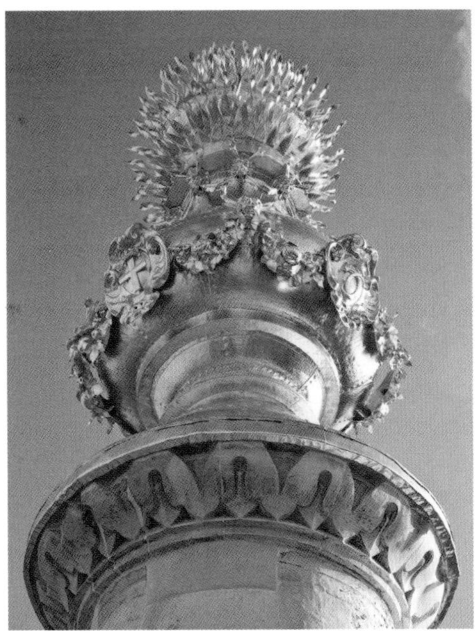

Another early design proposed by Wren for the Monument had featured a phoenix, but this was judged ill-suited to high winds[13]. Wren's proposal brings us to another type of monument, representing in a different way the power of heat and light: the sundial pillar. An early example is the **Turnbull sundial** of 1581 at Corpus Christi College, Oxford, which is also surmounted by a resurgent bird, in this case a pelican. The pelican, preparing to feed its young with its own blood, echoes the planetary cycle and the idea of rebirth, which is similarly embedded in the phoenix.[14]

The sundials made in central and north-east Scotland, principally after the Union of the Crowns in 1707 and up to c.1730, are exceptional (see, for example, that of **Kelburn** Castle, Ayrshire), with their polyhedral heads and their lectern- or obelisk-type supports.[15] The **Glamis** sundial in the castle's dial garden had an impressive twenty-four faces, but was superseded by others with even more. They were originally painted and gilded. The stonemasons involved in these works appear to have been Scottish, which is surprising, and may perhaps speak to the intimate masonic symbolism of the production.[16]

Other eighteenth-century Scottish sundials more simply commemorate family unions, with hearts, initials and coats of arms. In this sense they are 'achievements'; durable signs of family hierarchy and often visible only to the family and its guests, within the privy garden. Even if such remarkable sundials are more about ostentation than about the sun, they are still markers, and sanctioned by the measurement of time, which is regulated by the sun. Their upright form is premised upon light and upon their role, even if only notional, as constant markers of time's passage.

Many Scottish sundials are based upon the **obelisk** form, representing as it does the idea of parity[17]– having equal sides and no clear front or back; in this the upright sundial can be compared to the obelisk not only as commemorative marker but as a central point against which several distances can be measured out.

...

10. Charles Turnbull, Pelican Sundial, 1581

11. Kelburn Castle sundial, 1707

12. Glamis Castle sundial, 1671

13. John Mylne, Drummond Castle obelisk sundial, 1630

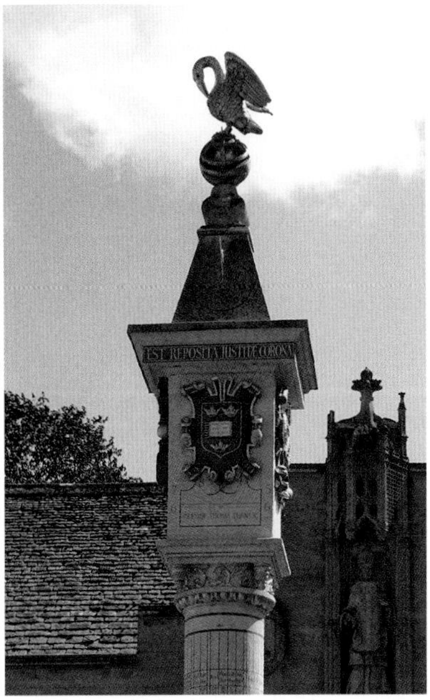

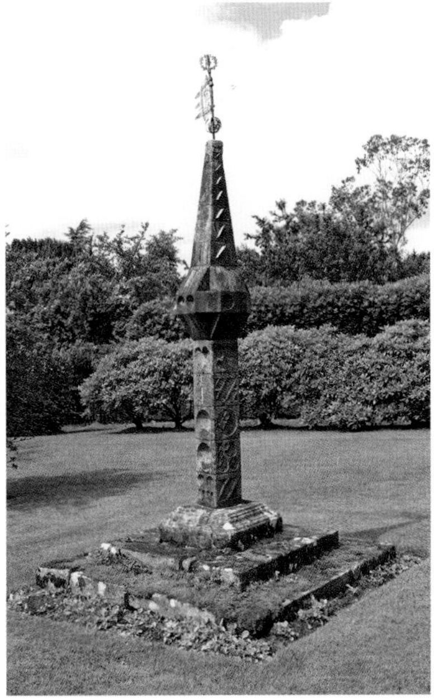

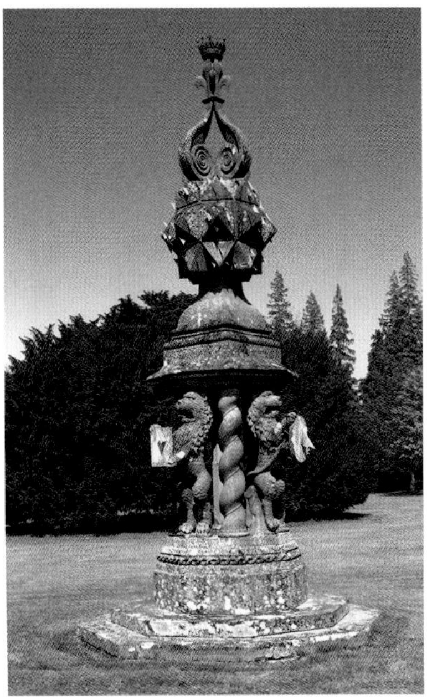

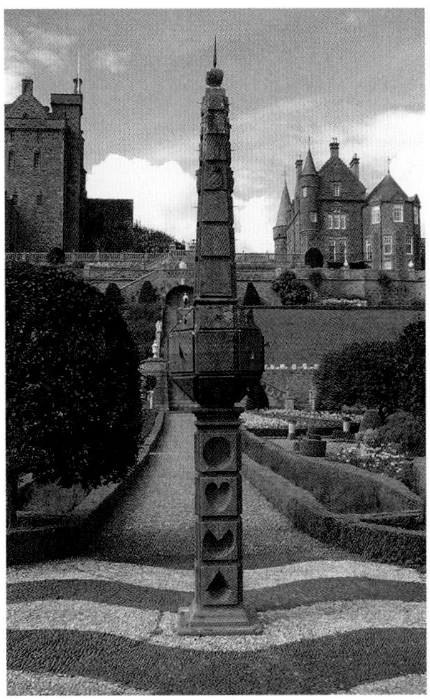

The earliest known post-Roman sundial in Britain is in fact engraved upon the **Bewcastle Cross** in Cumbria, and distinguished also by the fact that, as a sundial, it is free-standing. (Most sundials are found on the southern wall of churches.[18]) We know that crosses in medieval Britain served as markers of many kinds: as boundary markers, as burial markers, and above all, as markers of the routes that were taken by saints, or by their bodies. They marked translation and progression. They mark space and time.

- - -

vertical

14. Sundial (detail from the Bewcastle Cross), late 7th century

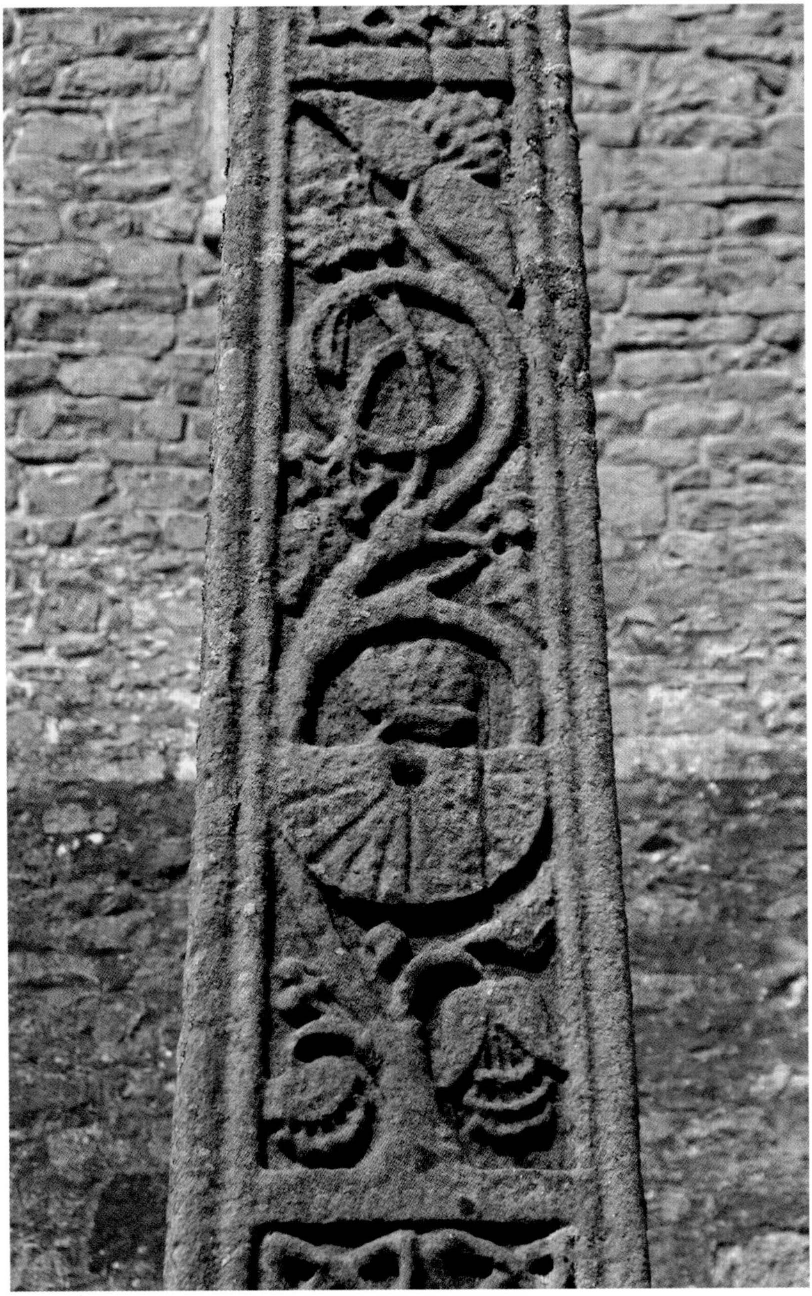

15

Some crosses have less of a religious function and, instead, act more as landmarks – objects that people know and use as reference points. Such markers also take the form of obelisks, like that at **St George's Circus**, Southwark, built to honour the Lord Mayor Brass Crosby, and measuring one mile from or to Palace Yard, Westminster Hall. The **milestone obelisk** on Richmond Bridge, erected a few years later on what was a new bridge, gives the distances to various local towns and places of significance. These obelisks, unlike Roman milestones, might be seen as radial rather than sequential. Their equal faces unite a range of places around their centre.

...

15. Robert Mylne, St George's Circus obelisk, 1771

16. Milestone obelisk, late 18th century

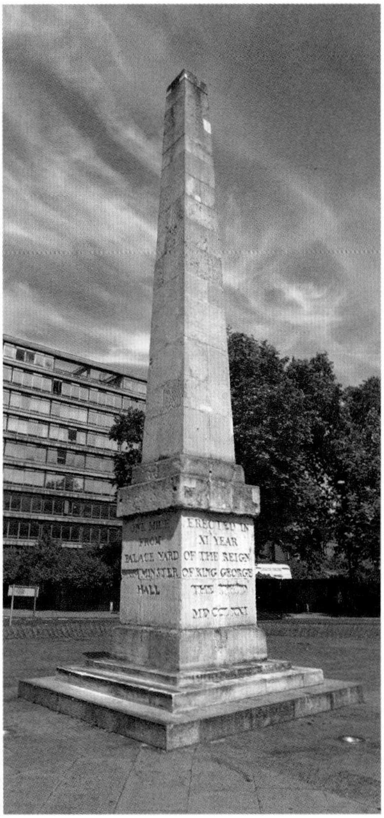
FROM
PALACE YARD
HALL
XI YEAR
OF THE REIGN
OF KING GEORGE

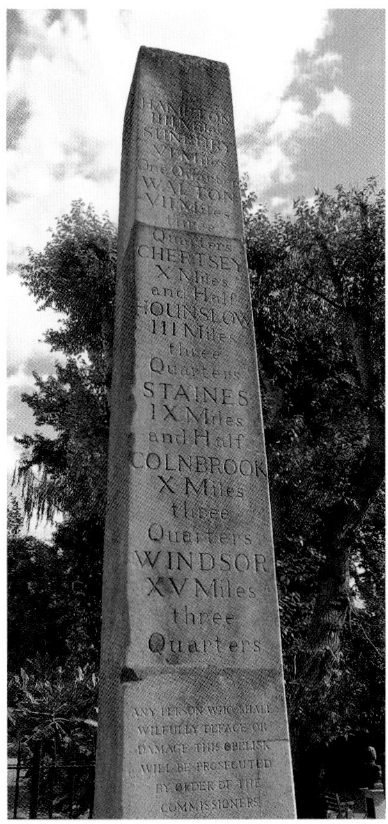
CHERTSEY
X Miles
and Half
HOUNSLOW
III Miles
three
Quarters
STAINES
IX Miles
and Half
COLNBROOK
X Miles
three
Quarters
WINDSOR
XV Miles
three
Quarters
ANY PERSON WHO SHALL
WILFULLY DEFACE OR
DAMAGE THIS OBELISK
WILL BE PROSECUTED
BY ORDER OF THE
COMMISSIONERS

The form of the sundial, functioning through sunlight, approaches the anthropomorphic, and especially so in the case of some **Scottish examples**. Their role as markers of family status also links them to the markers that are used to demarcate land, as can still be found on the **Yorkshire moors** (overleaf). More than mere milestones, these stones represent ownership, as indeed did early milestones on the roads owned by the Turnpike Trusts.[19] This kind of simple verticality, across the empty, largely horizontal landscape, is immediately reminiscent of the Neolithic monoliths whose purpose remains unclear. Nonetheless, they are perhaps, of all upright stones, the ones that feel most familiar. Menhir or monolith, these standing stones might well be seen as the precursor of all kinds of signal, whether they measure time in miles or in hours, marking proximity or distance, as a warning or a welcome, to come in or keep out.

- - -

The close relation between the milestone or marker and the headstone is signalled by the common employment of the same masons and materials. Swithland slate was prized across the North Midlands for all kinds of purposes, but notably for milestones and headstones, on which numbers and letters could be durably inscribed.[20] Before the advent of cast iron markers, mile-stones were indeed made of stone; the **Markham Moor** stone being an unusual survivor.[21]

...

17. Pittodrie House sundial, 17th century

18. Markham Moor milestone, Markham Moor, Nottinghamshire

← 19. Stone boundary marker, Urra Moor, Yorkshire

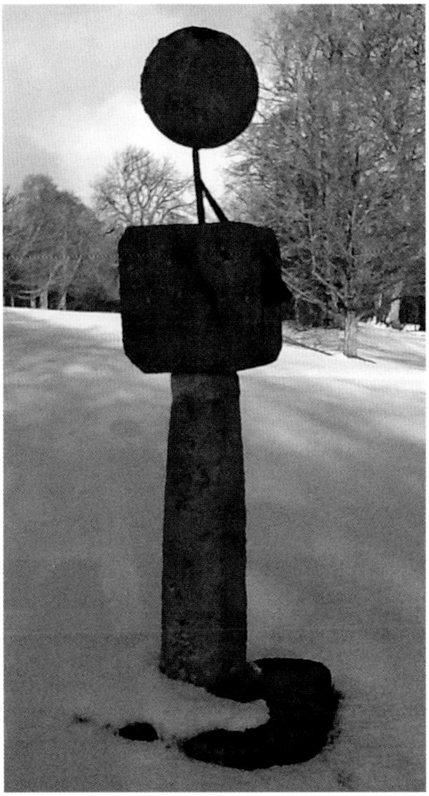

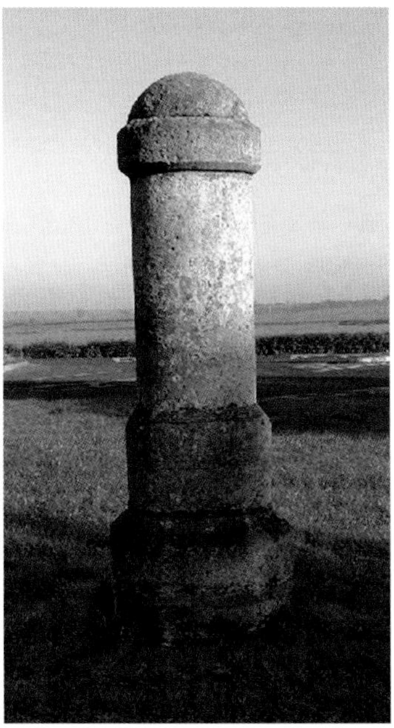

The strange and memorable amalgam of road and tomb is most resonant of, and goes back to, the Roman **Via Appia**, especially the section between the fourth and the sixth milestone. It was at the fifth that Rome traditionally gave way to Latium. On either side of the flat basalt paving stones are lined the tombs of ancient Romans, in various shapes and sizes; in the form of houses, altars, temples, cylinders and pyramids.[22] The cautionary aspect of the Roman tomb, combined with the demonstrative aspect of the family shrine, fed into the dynastic imagery of British commemoration.[23]

Some of the grander nineteenth-century metropolitan cemeteries, and above all the avenues of honour created by the **Commonwealth War Graves Commission** in the twentieth century, echo this ancient combination of walking and remembering; pacing out the commemorative process.

...

20. Tombs along the Via Appia, Rome

21. Tyne Cot Commonwealth War Graves Cemetery, Belgium

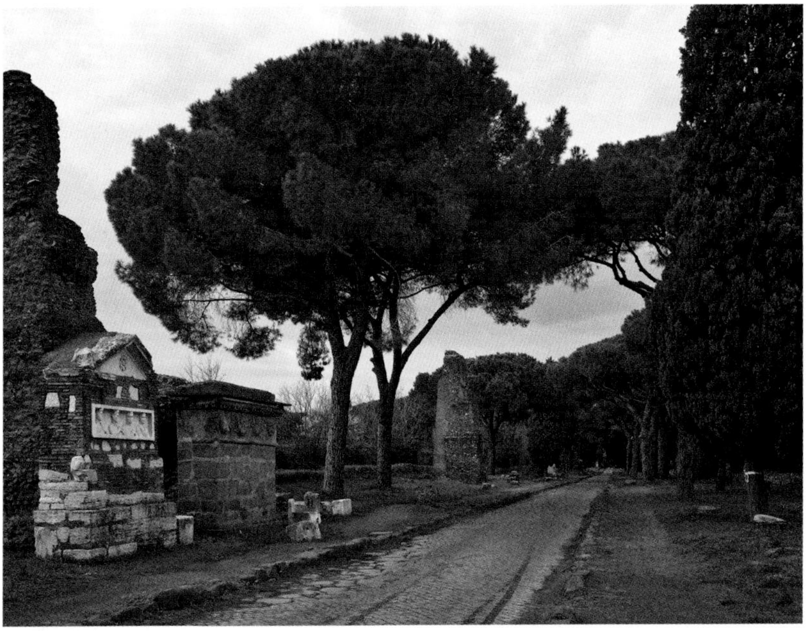

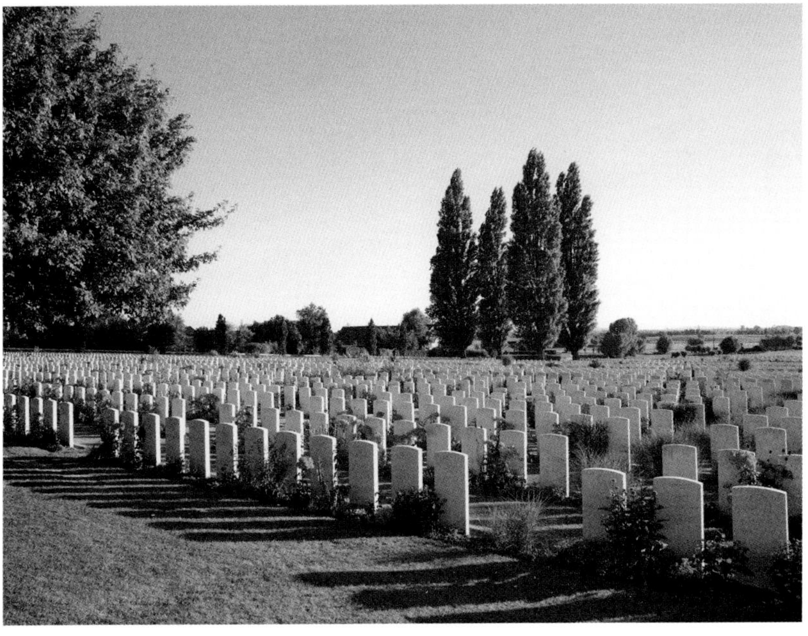

23

Gilbert Ledward's 1936 sculpture ***Monolith*** has notably subtle carving and continuity of surface. It reminds us of the symbolism of the obelisk, column or other simple geometric form in its essential parity of plane. This was thought fitting for commemorative work, especially when the commemorated were many, nameless and essentially equal, as in the wars of the twentieth century.[24]

There was a tendency in Britain in the inter- and post-war periods to emphasise the archaic form. Barbara Hepworth, like Ledward, used the same simple title, ***Monolith***, for a major carving of 1953, and added the qualifying term 'Empyrean' (or heavenly).[25] The heavenly stone might indeed be the sundial or Neolithic monolith, which is so closely related and which takes us back to the sun, and the shadow.

- - -

The upwards tendency of the column is well suited to Eric Kennington's signpost for the **Comet Inn** at Hatfield, with its model of a Comet aeroplane made by the local company de Havilland. It seems to echo both the notion of a village maypole and a sundial, while suggesting a new industrial age in the sky overhead.

...

22. Gilbert Ledward, *Monolith*, 1936

23. Barbara Hepworth, *Monolith – Empyrean*, 1953

24. Eric Kennington, signpost for Comet Inn at Hatfield, 1936

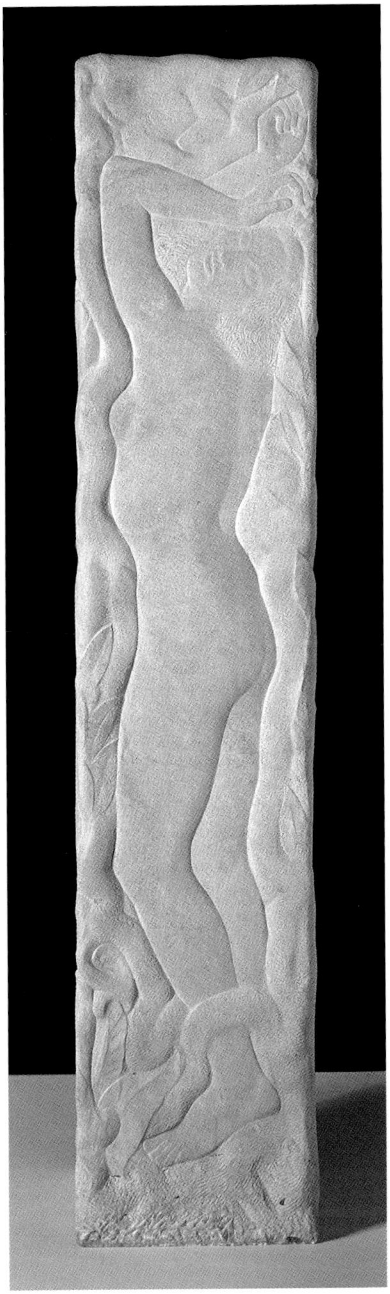

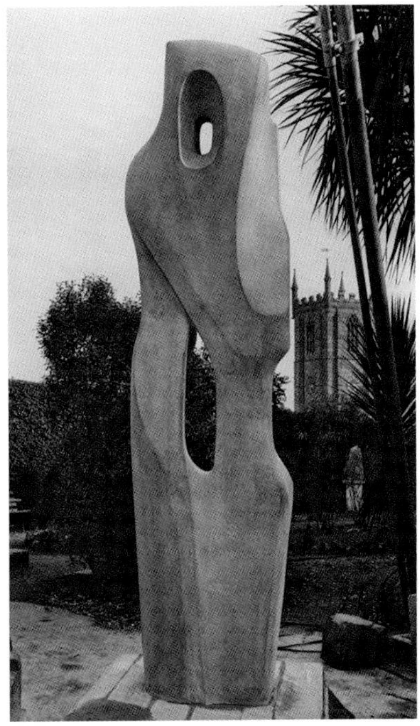

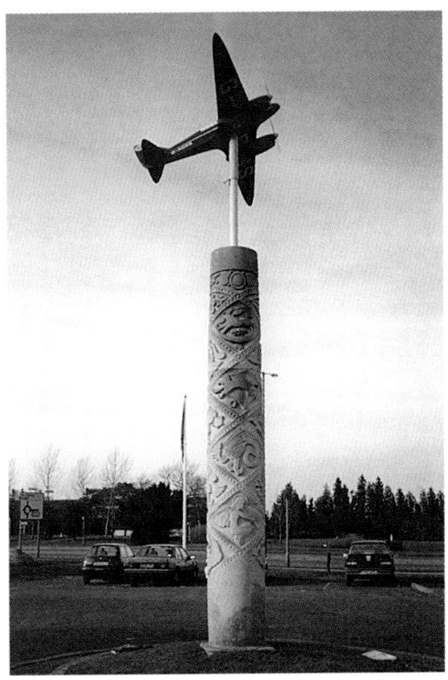

The vertical marker is integral to sculpture in general and to statuary in particular. It is a beacon. **Beacons** are embedded in British topography, prevalent especially in times of danger, created to facilitate communication by means of space and light. Most are found around the coast. Even when erected away from the coast, vertical markers frequently commemorated naval victories or marked tree-planting undertaken for naval purposes.[26]

...

25. William Ashurst, Ashurst Beacon, 1798

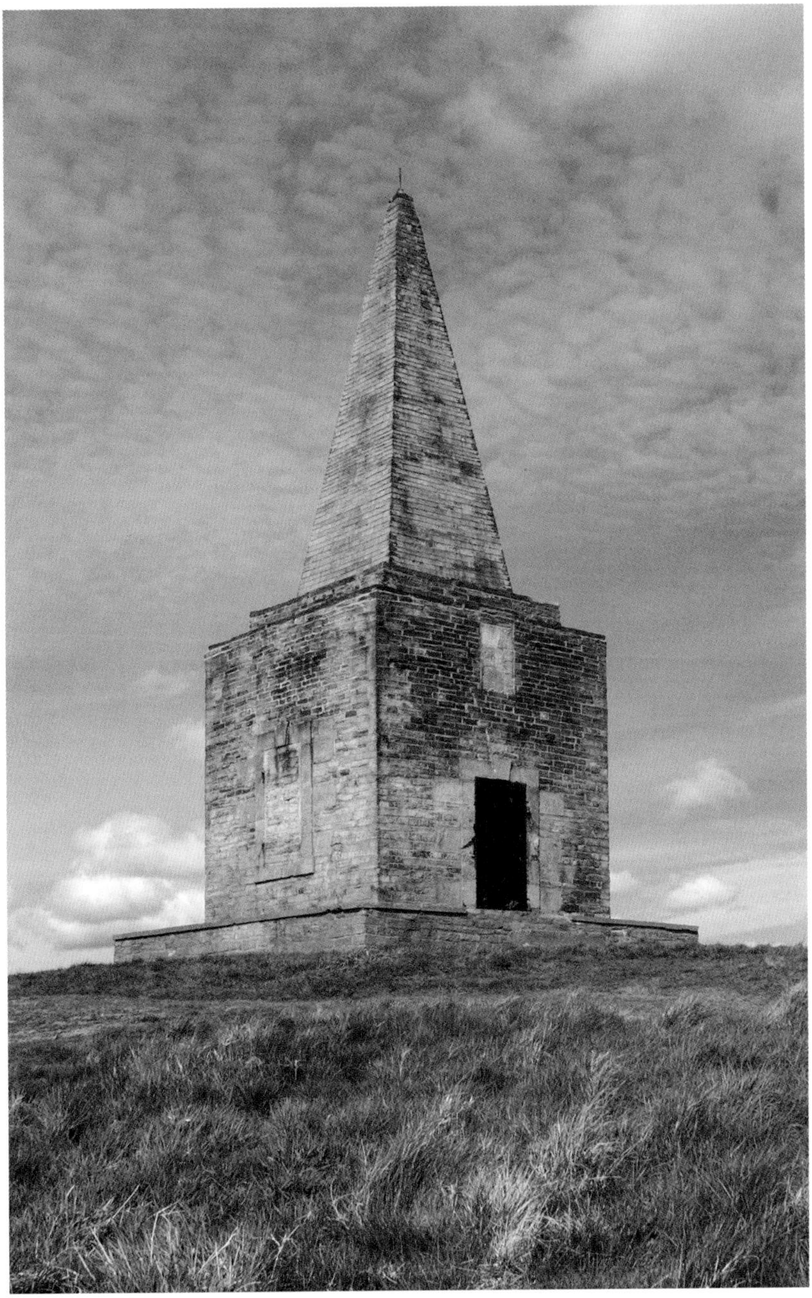

A beacon for modern times was proposed by Reg Butler in his winning submission for the monument to the ***Unknown Political Prisoner***, its site nominally West Berlin, but its meaning resonant to anyone who had lived through the aerial warfare of the Second World War and now grappling with a new Cold War.

In this sense, modern sculptors like Henry Moore and Barbara Hepworth integrate such functional verticality into the meaning of their sculpture. A good example is Moore's ***Three Standing Figures***, which has been sited at Battersea Park since 1948, just a year after it was made.[27] The sense that these figures are watching and waiting, anxiously looking up, reminds us of the war-time threat from the skies, a recurrent trope in English sculpture of this period. These sculptures are both figures and markers, pieces of stone that oscillate from one to the other.

To a degree Moore's Battersea figures are reminiscent of the **herms** of classical tradition, in which a piece of stone terminates in a face, or even with a Janus-face that looks two ways. Stone starts to live, to suggest the human figure, but also to suggest the beacon. Stone looks for us, acting for our eyes.

- - -

26. Reg Butler, final maquette for *The Unknown Political Prisoner*, 1951–2

28. Herm, c.510 BC

27. Henry Moore, *Three Standing Figures*, 1947–8

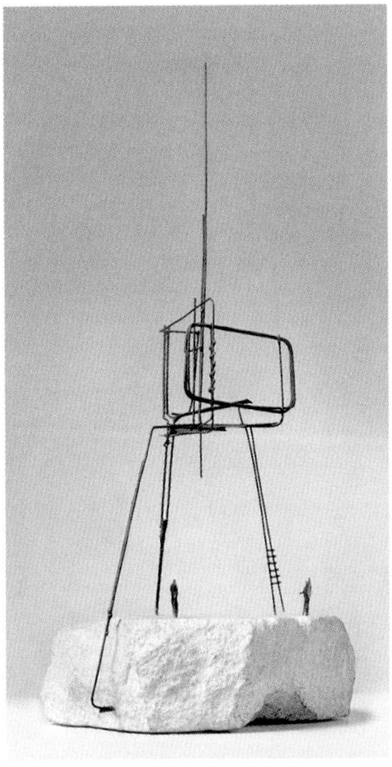

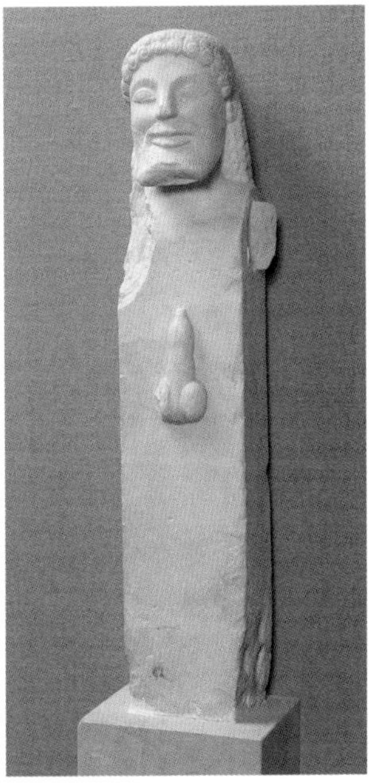

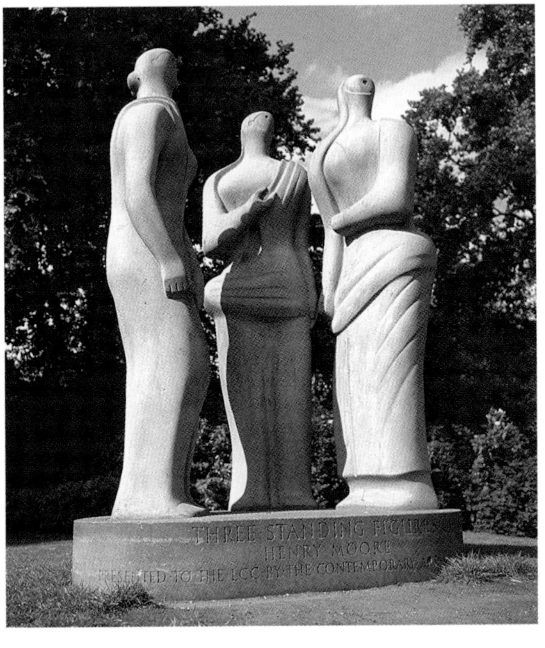
HENRY MOORE

The monolith, or single stone, reminds us then of the alternative to wood. Hepworth's titles are like gentle reminders of the transformation wrought by the artist, from sedimentary limestone bed to upright sculpture. Far from being the natural choice, stone brings with it a concomitant superiority because of its very lack of normalcy. Limestone does not usually come in large, upright, single blocks, whereas trees are vertical by nature.

Because verticality is counter-instinctive in stone, it is perhaps easy to forget how germane verticality is to sculpture, and to forget its original kinship to the tree. Trees are standards; they bear flags, signs, lights. They are ludic as well as salutary. They are maypoles, flagpoles, beacons, liberty trees and scaffolds.[28] They carry the trophies taken in battle. They are masts, and an incidental, but apposite, footnote to Nelson's story adds that his coffin was made from his tallest mast. The hero is felled, laid to rest. Here the passage from life to death is very clearly marked by the move from vertical to horizontal. The Tyburn Martyrs remind us of the original **Tyburn Tree**, the gallows that stood close to today's Marble Arch.

Trees, poles and standards represent the absent body, and mark the power of those who hold them. Most obviously, the figure of **Black Rod** is named for his ebony rood, or rod, and his ceremonial function, like that of the Sergeant of Arms, reminds us of how the staff has integral importance, echoed in other instruments such as the mace, which have shifted from a wartime to a ceremonial function.[29] They are instruments of power that stand in for the body. When vertical they are active, when horizontal, at rest, or indeed markers of death.

- - -

29. Scene at Tyburn showing crowds gathered to watch a hanging, 1696

30. The Gentleman Usher of the Black Rod at the State Opening of Parliament, 4 June 2014

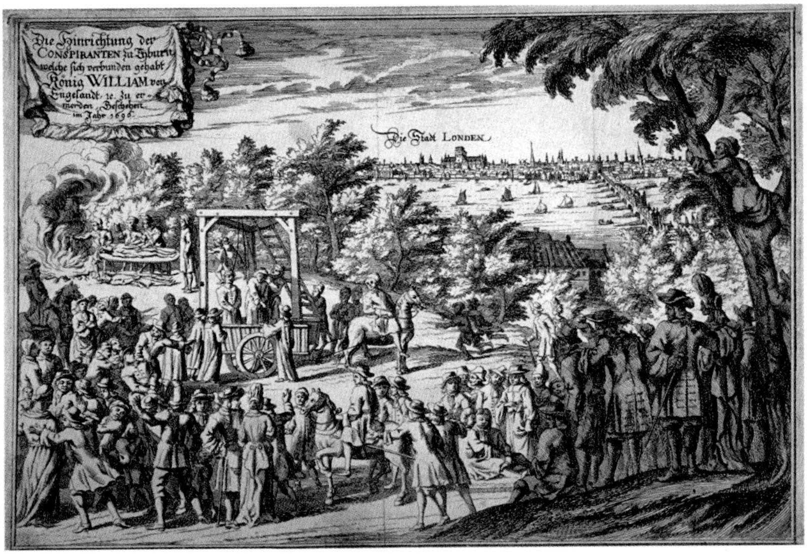
Die Hinrichtung der
CONSPIRANTEN zu Tyburn
welche sich verbunden gehabt
König WILLIAM von
Engelandt. rc. zu er-
morden. Geschehen
im Jahr 1696.
Die Stadt LONDEN

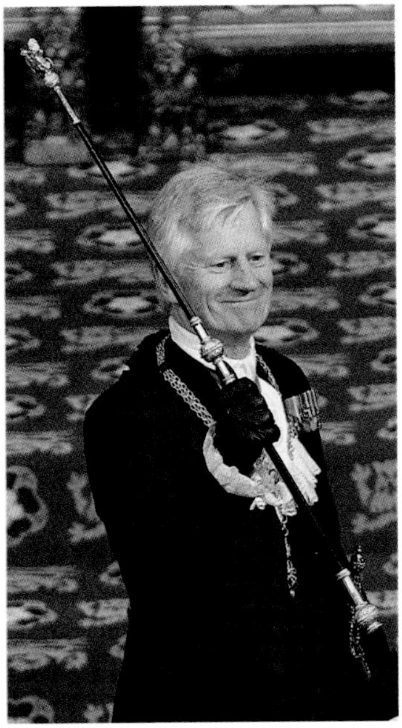

Such associations between the tree and the human figure are also contained within the column, well-illustrated by Shute, in ***The First and Chief Groundes of Architecture*** of 1563, with its diagrams in which the various orders are paired with standing men or women.[30] They are perhaps more evident in the caryatid, in which the original wooden pillar is effectively transposed into a carved draped female figure. A famous example in London, based on the Erechtheion, is the tribune of **St Pancras Church** on London's Euston Road. That shift from tree to figure remains present in the columns themselves, with their fluting suggestive of drapery. When columns support the porch through which we pass, so the body seems to enter the building, transformed first into wood and then into stone.

...

31. John Shute, folio from *The First and Chief Groundes of Architecture*, 1563

32. William Inwood, St Pancras Church caryatid porch, 1822

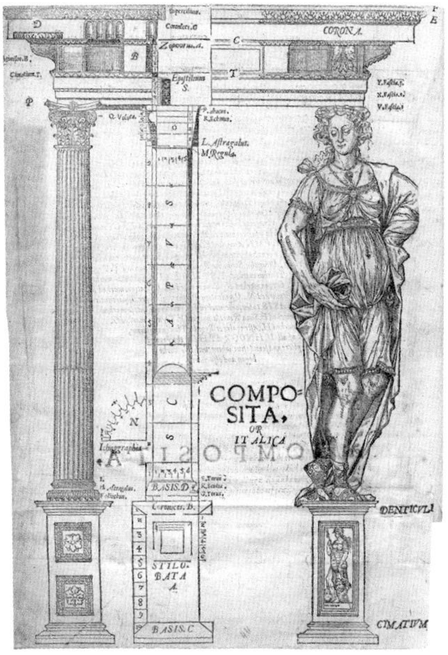
CORONA
COMPO-
SITA,
OR
ITALICA
BASIS.D
STILO-
BATA
A.
BASIS.C
DENTICULI
CIMATIUM

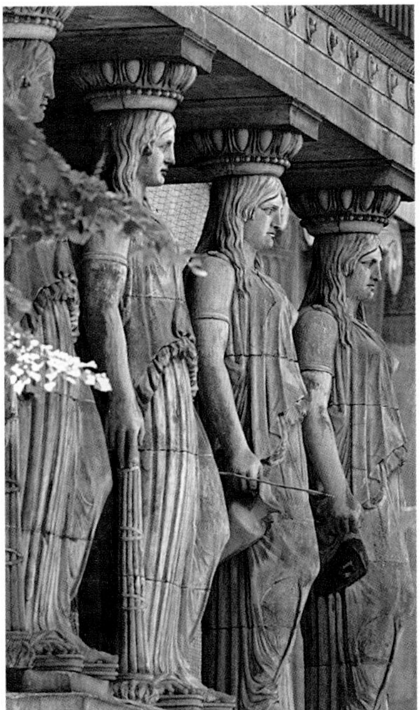

There is an analogous resonance in representations of the martyrdom of Saint Sebastian, which similarly elide tree and column. The saint's body can effectively be caught between the two and supersede both. The shift from body to tree to stone is illustrated in painting with the jump from **Memling** to **Mantegna**. In sculpture the elision is both more and less effective, being both literal and functional, with the tree literally supporting the body. Pierre **Puget**'s figure in Sta Maria Assunta di Carignano, Genoa, is part of a formal tradition leading us up to the Chapman brothers' *Great Deeds against the Dead* (see p. 279).[31]

- - -

33. Hans Memling, *Martyrdom of Saint Sebastian*, c.1475

34. Andrea Mantegna, *Saint Sebastian*, 1481

35. Pierre Puget, *Saint Sebastian*, 1663–8

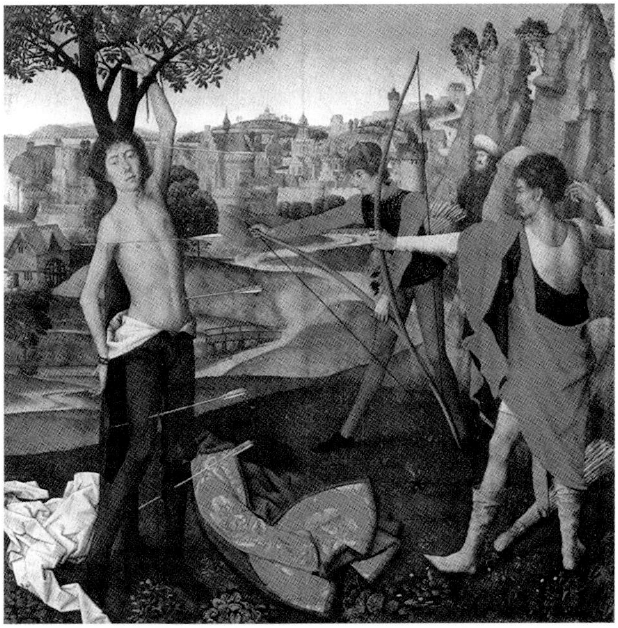

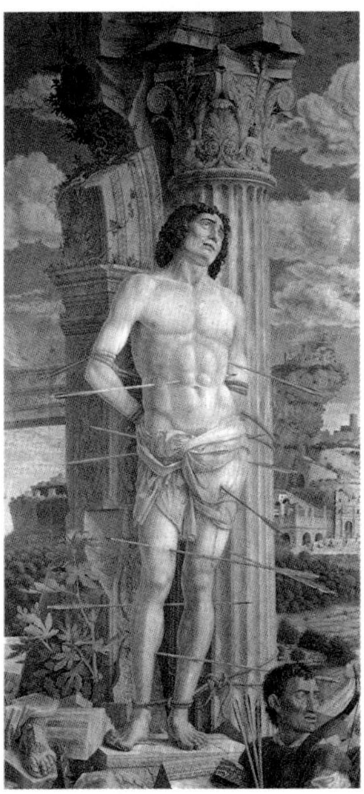

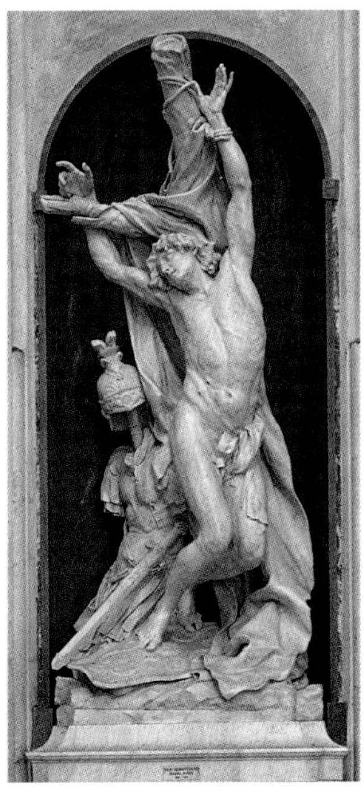

Hepworth was unusual in her early works by allowing the trunk to seep through the sculpture, but to be as much body as support, as it is in early figure works such as the **torso** in Manchester's Whitworth Art Gallery. In this respect the figure is not only the tree but also the support, the trunking reminding us of the original rod or rood.

The **Single Form**, which Hepworth elaborated throughout her career, came to its apogee in the 1961 version that was to commemorate the United Nations Secretary General Dag Hammarskjöld, shot down from the skies. Poised between sculpture and memorial, 'stone' and marker, this was the conjunction of modern sculpture with its ancient antecedents and remains so to this day, in the plaza of the UN in New York. Hammarskjöld never knew this piece, but already had his own *Single Form*, made by Hepworth in 1937–8, in wood, as were the others in this series.

A notebook of Hammarskjöld's poetry, later published in English in a version by W. H. Auden, was found by his bedside after his death.[32] 'Single Form' was one of those poems. It seems to reflect Hammarskjöld's ascetic spiritualism and has often been seen also as a foreboding of his own death:

> Shall my soul meet
> This curve, as a bend in the road
> On her way to form?

It is probably not going too far to suggest that we might see Hammarskjöld's *Single Form* in religious terms, but it may well be too much to see it as the cross. Indeed, I want here to continue to think of the tree in terms of the single form or figure, and as a marker, and not as a crucifix or cruciform structure.

…

36. Barbara Hepworth, *Torso*, 1930

37. Barbara Hepworth, *Single Form*, 1961–4

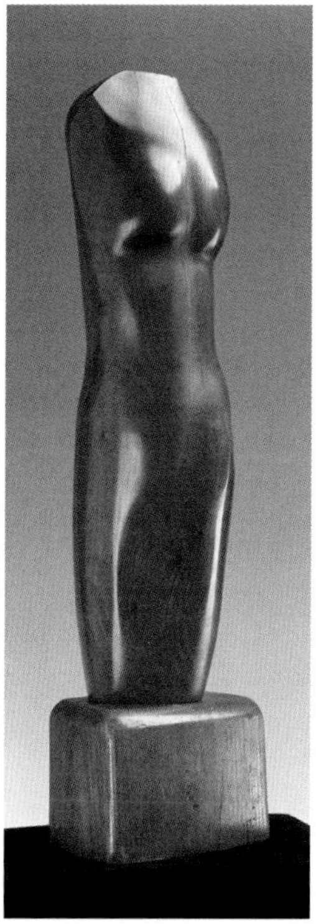

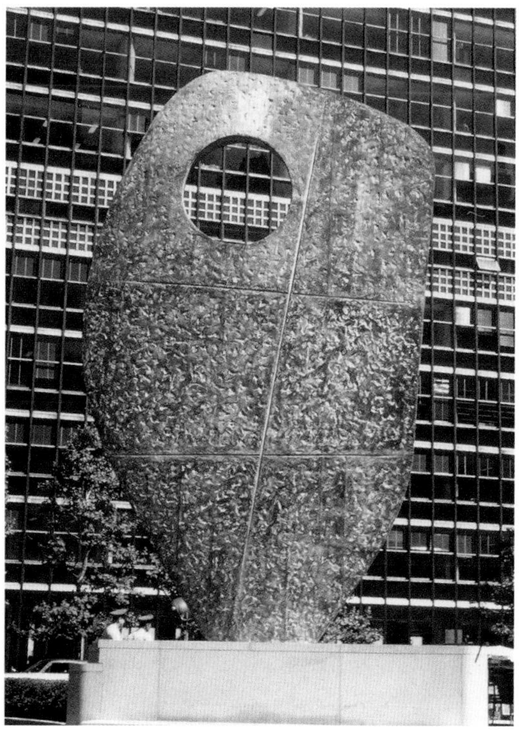

In the Anglo-Saxon poem 'The Dream of the Rood' the rood describes how it was 'cut down from the edge of the forest, removed from my foundation', carried away and set on a hill, how it was pierced with 'dark nails', from which it bears the scars, but later resurrected and adorned with precious metals:

> Hear while I tell about the best of dreams
> Which came to me the middle of one night
> While humankind were sleeping in their beds.
> It was as though I saw a wondrous tree
> Towering in the sky suffused with light,
> Brightest of beams; and all that beacon was
> Covered with gold.[33]

Some lines from this poem,[34] which dates back to between the seventh and ninth centuries, are found on the **Ruthwell Cross**, thus enabling, then, and since their almost contemporaneous rediscovery in the early nineteenth century, a strong degree of reciprocal interpretation.[35]

vertical

The Ruthwell Cross, as it is commonly called, was, however, most probably originally a column, which only later became a cross,[36] and should be called a **monument**. Indeed, the account by the Reverend Duncan of 1833 describes, very nicely, 'the remarkable monument in the shape of a cross', and his chosen words have supported modern scholars in their proposition that the Ruthwell Cross should properly be styled a monument, comprising both a column and a cross. In itself the column might refer to Roman victory columns in Britain and elsewhere (it was, after all, in an area of Roman encampment) and also to obelisks and pyramids.[37] This works for my purposes, because it is its columnar, and monolithic, quality that I want to emphasise here.

---

38. Runic alphabet and drawings of the Ruthwell Cross, c.1832

39. Drawn by Rev. Dr Duncan and engraved by W. Penny, *Runic Monument in the garden belonging to Ruthwell Manse*, c.1832

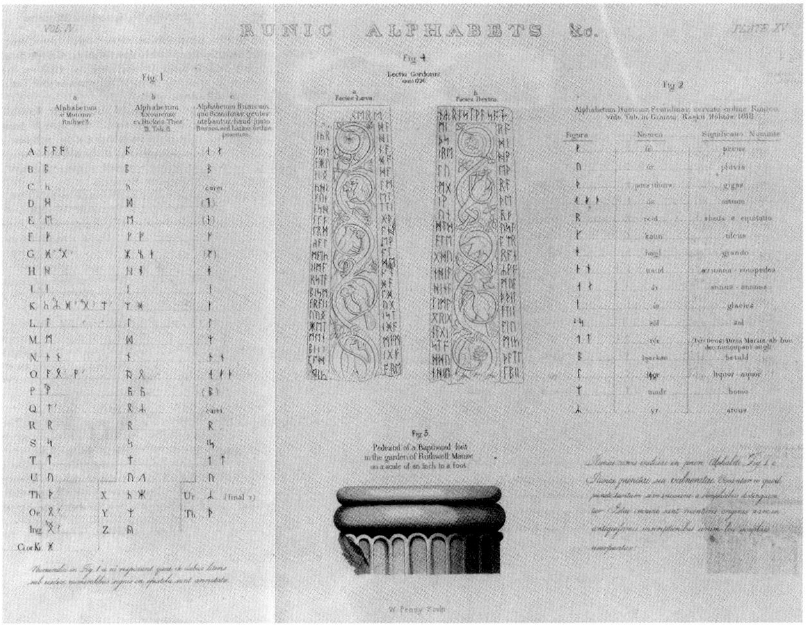
Vol. IV
RUNIC ALPHABETS &c.
PLATE XV
Fig 1
Fig 4
Lectio Gordonis
Faciei Laeva
Facies Dextra
Fig 2
Fig 3
Pedestal of a Baptismal font
in the garden of Ruthwell Manse
on a scale of an inch to a foot
W. Penny Sculpt

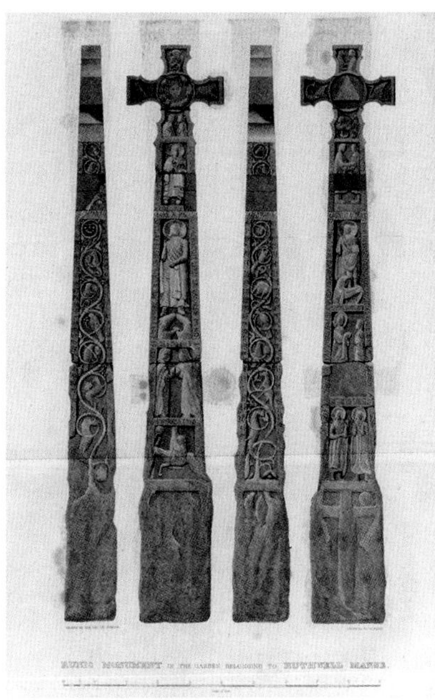
RUNIC MONUMENT IN THE GARDEN BELONGING TO RUTHWELL MANSE.

A few years after making his Battersea group, Henry Moore abstracted from it to make another, more essentialist grouping, *Upright Motives*. These motives were reminiscent of totem poles, and thus, if implicitly, of the tree. There is a subtle and complex series of metamorphoses here, in which tree turns into sculpture, sculpture into tree, tree into body. Indeed it was apparently a poplar tree at the first site, at the Olivetti complex in Milan, that 'convinced' Moore that the piece would work, even if its component parts drew on his earlier drawings of bombs.[38] Another intriguing transition is the way the title allows the 'motif' to become the 'motive'.

One of the 'motives' was gradually transformed into the individual piece that became known as the **Glenkiln Cross**, from the site where it stood in Scotland. In this one might think back to Moore's Battersea figures and see them as the three figures at the base of a Crucifixion; watching and waiting. Given that Moore was a trustee at the Tate when Francis Bacon's *Three Figures* was acquired, this seems more than plausible, especially given the arrangement of the ***Three Upright Motives*** at the Kröller-Müller Museum. The relationship between the victim and those who look on now extends beyond the mourner.

...

40. Henry Moore, *Upright Motive No. 1: Glenkiln Cross*, 1955–6

41. Henry Moore, *Three Upright Motives*, 1955–6, cast 1965

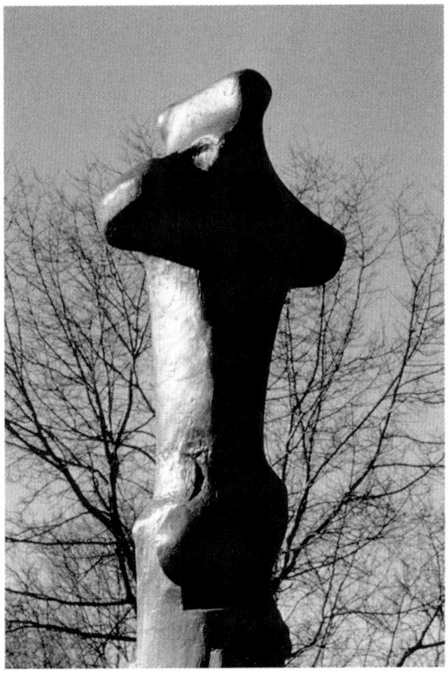

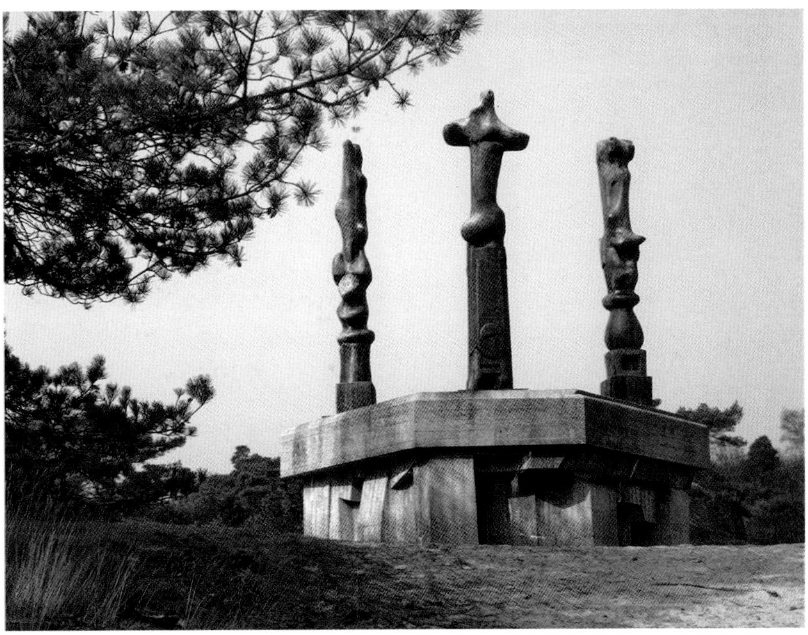

The gaze of the figure, up, ahead or downwards, links it to the sky or to the earth. The grieving figure normally looks to the ground, standing watch over the body, a vertical guardian of the effigy below, but with a gaze that bridges one world and the other. A good example of this connectedness is François Dieussart's great monument to **Charles Morgan** in the Great Church of Bergen op Zoom, in which the looking reinforces the play of the elements and draws the viewer in. Dieussart's Roman period suggests his likely familiarity with antique stele, while his service to the Earl of Arundel, for whom he restored antique works, means that he knew stele such the one to **Philista**, now in the Ashmolean.[39]

- - -

The relationship between the tomb and its mourners is part of the nexus of sculptural vocabulary, even if the part that endures may be singular and bereft of those who originally accompanied the body on its journey and supplied its meaning. Crosses and markers were at first made simply of wood, and the translation of the Eleanor Crosses into stone reminds us of the Cenotaph, another 'temporary', if more abstract, marker of loss and of respect. The process of translation was remarkably similar, seven centuries later, for the Cenotaph, and took place only a few hundred metres further south from the original Charing Cross.

...

42. François Dieussart, monument to Charles Morgan, 1645–6

43. Philista Stele, 2nd century BC

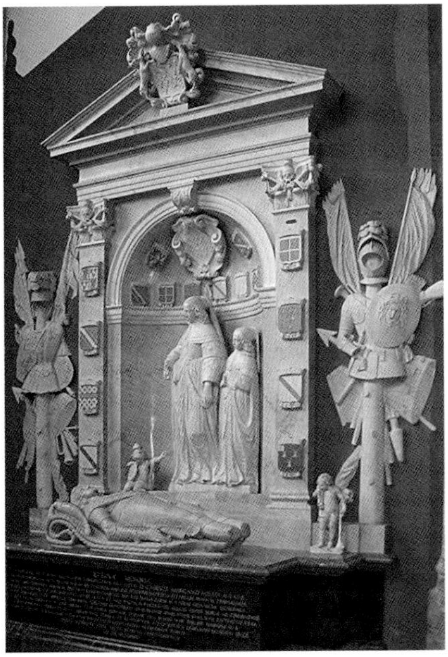

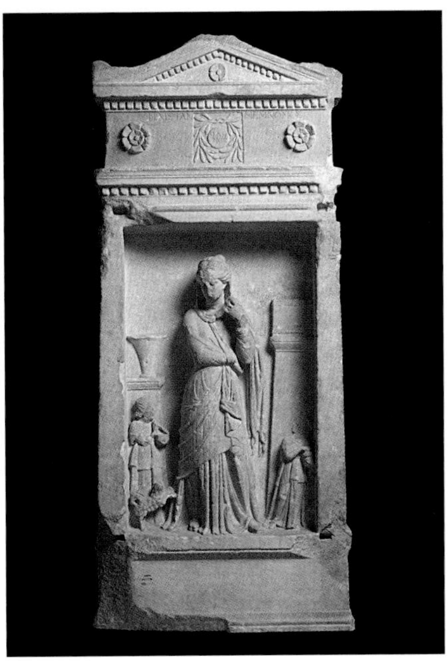

On London's Whitehall, a monument hugs the ground, acting more or less as its own plinth. The address is frontal, but non-hierarchical. Each side has an essential equality. The monument is not representative; it is only itself, and as such commands our attention. Edwin Lutyens was asked by the Ministry of Works, almost literally, to knock something up that would allow the British at least to equal the French in their earlier procession towards the tomb of the unknown soldier. Lutyens's hastily penned sketches were realised for him by the Ministry of Works. Lutyens looked for the right word to describe the form he envisaged; the French catafalque – a temporary wooden construction that represents a tomb or monument – was in many ways very accurate, but the monument that we now know in Whitehall was to be christened the **Cenotaph**, or empty tomb. Made in wood to act as a focal point for a new ceremony, this empty tomb was so thoroughly consecrated by the salutes and tributes of soldiers and mourners that it was turned into stone before the year was out. Its translation into masonry came about exactly because it was felt that the wooden structure had worked so effectively, and represented so resonantly the war dead, that it had to be made permanent. This was effected as if in private, behind hoardings, so that the temporary structure was apparently turned into stone.

vertical

One can insist upon the essential verticality of the Cenotaph, without underestimating the importance of its other features: the way in which it hugs the ground, its quality of enclosure and its conceptual emptiness. These are qualities integral to the next three chapters, but for the present I want to focus on the remarkable frontal relationship between the viewer and the monolith, clearly articulated in a work by artist Michael Dean, in his address to the Cenotaph, entitled *The Array of Rain* (overleaf).[40]

44. Edwin Lutyens, Cenotaph, 1919

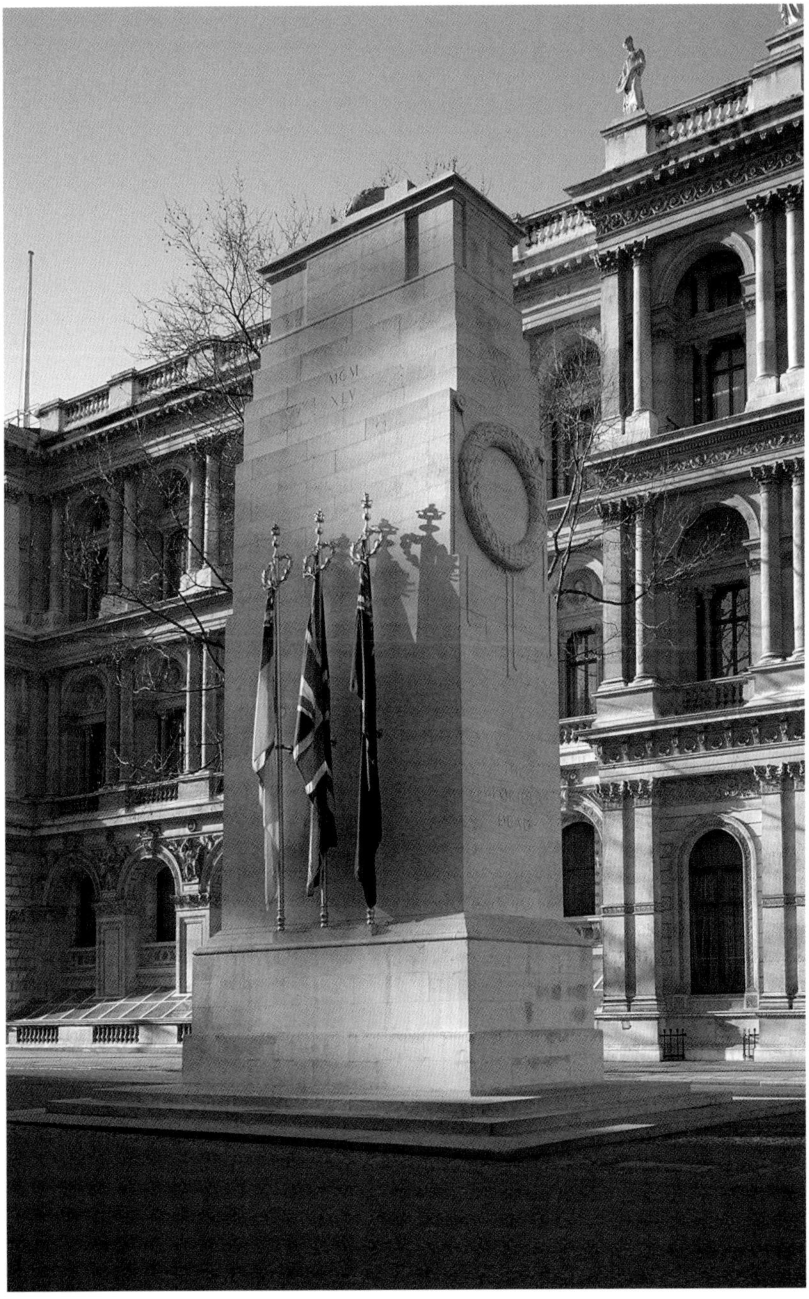

Curtain

VOICE
Distances forest.

VOICE
And then address.

VOICE
The single
distance of these features resembled in distances.

VOICE
The
distance of these distances described by the parallel
and equivalence of this throat and these shoulders
to this.

VOICE
The again of this to the left arm.

VOICE
The
resemblance and parallel of this wrist to this.

Curtain
Curtain

VOICE
Permanence forests.

VOICE
Pause and arrest, then in
impermanent analogue to permanence, address.

VOICE
Out
of analogue and then arrest and address the new again of
this to the right arm and the resemblance and parallel of this
hand and inside leg to this.

Curtain
Curtain

VOICE
The stone same to the ribbon difference.

VOICE
The off and
soft next to stay straight.

VOICE
The away and weakness meets
these straights easily and repeats proximity about this stone
stay with soft differences.

VOICE
Or like
likeness.

VOICE
Still

VOICE
In still correspondence.

VOICE
The away
raise and soft faltering piece of cloth of a flag.

VOICE
Raise
easy away solt falter return and stone.

VOICE
Raise easily
away and softly falter to repeat in any number of returns
to nearness.

VOICE
Though awake at stone sleep.

VOICE

Meet

and approximate permanence or keep this easy physique
and soft replica of proximity.

VOICE

We return and

meet to repeat proximity.

VOICE

The parallel address of the cloth

standards soft differences to stone.

VOICE

The proximate

addition of differences in softness and curves. The
context of our physical address.

VOICE

To return and

meet we repeat proximity.

VOICE

Falter in correspondence and

with any amount of softness, curve and fall in imitation and
difference to permanence.

VOICE

The backs

of these arms and pylons.

VOICE

The architecture of a mothers

arms. The architecture of a fathers arms.

VOICE

The

difference of our softness that can close in and out of
imitating stone

VOICE

The parallel address in the

softness of cloth.

VOICE

The difference of our happening

softness to stone in the parallel address of the happening
cloth of a standard.

Curtain
Curtain

VOICE

This standards softness and differences in our absence.

VOICE

Then when we return and repeat with the

context of our physical address all the approximate
correspondence of our impermanence to permanence.

VOICE

How we weather stone with the soft context of

our physical address.

Curtain
Curtain

VOICE

Left in the array of rain.

VOICE

Left to slowly motion ruin

away

VOICE

Littered in leaving.

VOICE

The staying disarray of

remaining in leaves left to leave, slowly motioning ruin.

Curtain

horizontal

ii

horizontal

When the body (and heart) of **Queen Eleanor of Castile** had made its journey to London from Harby, Nottinghamshire, each stage marked by a cross, it was laid to rest in Westminster Abbey.[1] Her tomb was raised in Edward the Confessor's chapel, and was marked by a gilt bronze effigy cast by the goldsmith William Torel in 1291.[2] This was, quite literally, where Eleanor's (eviscerated) body came to rest, and so it was laid down. Moreover, it has stayed here, undisturbed, ever since, unlike the majority of the Eleanor Crosses, which were cut down during the Commonwealth.

Torel's bronze casts are remarkable for their size, representing as they do the fully clothed body of the deceased who lies beneath, within the tomb chest itself. In this sense they are the empty, if physical, reminders of those who were once alive, and might be seen as being akin to those casts made from the actual body, whether alive or dead, which faithfully replicate its particular 'proportions', to use the contemporary term.[3]

...

horizontal

45. William Torel, effigy of Eleanor of Castile, 1291

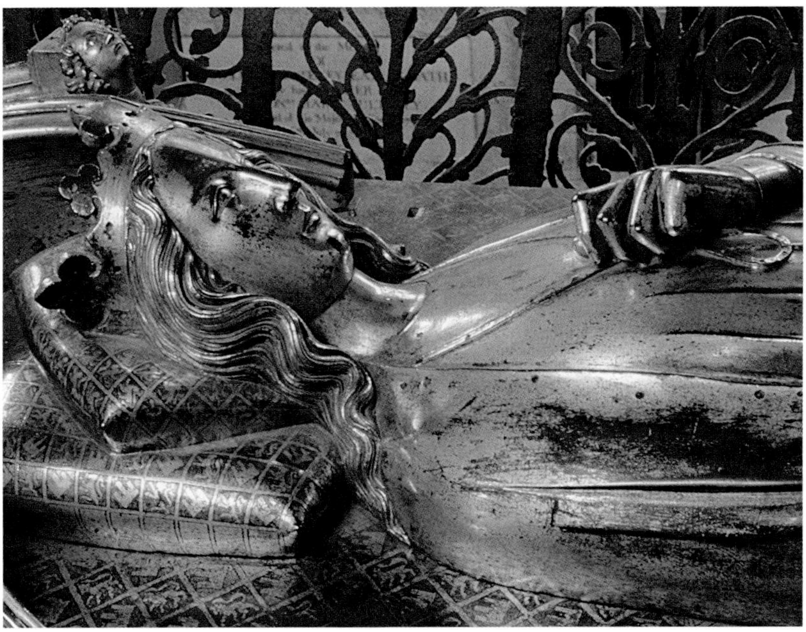

For around three centuries, effigies were the standard way in which to commemorate the affluent dead.[4] Effigies from the fourteenth century represent the figure ambiguously, between life and death. Those wooden effigies that represented the real (and royal) body during a lengthy funeral procession are even more ambiguous. That which stood in for **Edward III**, for example, in 1377, was used at the funeral held two weeks after he died.[5] Even if sleep is the state with which we would most readily associate such figures, in fact (as with the **d'Isigny** family at Norton Disney), the male figures are generally ready for battle, while the female partner prays.[6]

...

horizontal

46. Effigy of Edward III, 1377

47. D'Isigny family effigy, late 13th century

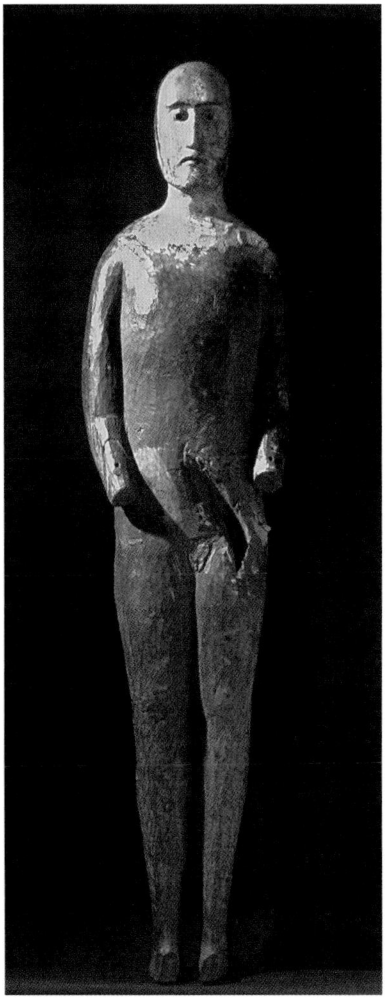

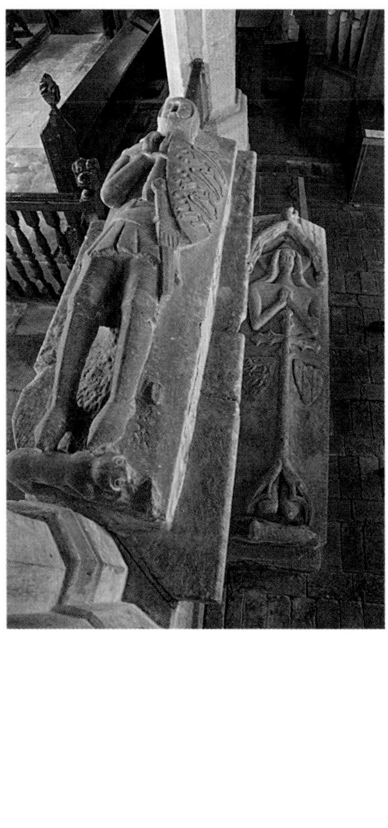

Later effigies make death plainer: the early seventeenth-century tomb to **Anne Bruce of Kinlosse** retains the medievalising effigy on top of a classical chest, but plays in a sophisticated fashion with its realistic treatment of the shroud, making the figure closer to death than to life. A few years later **Lady Abigail Sherard** commissioned effigies from an unknown sculptor to commemorate her husband and herself. Already by mid-century we see a more playful mixing of life and death: the monument to **Sir Roger Smith** varies the register; he is definitively dead, while his two wives seem closer to life.

...

horizontal

48. Tomb to Anne, wife of Lord Bruce of Kinloss, 1627

49. Effigy of Lady Abigail Sherard and her husband, 1640

50. Monument to Sir Roger Smith, 1655

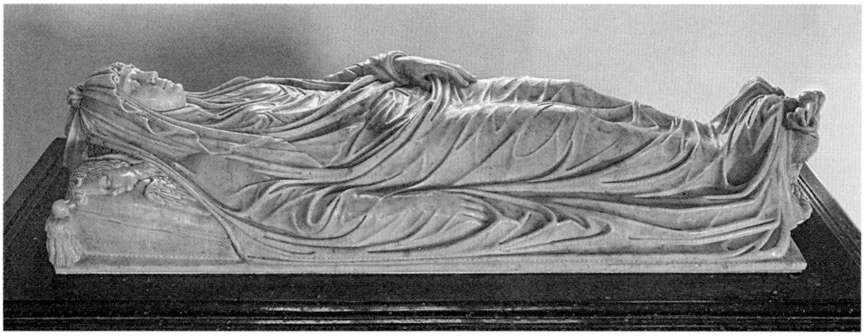

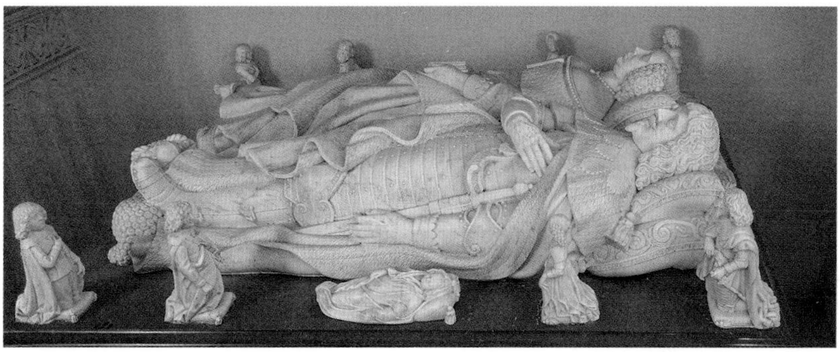

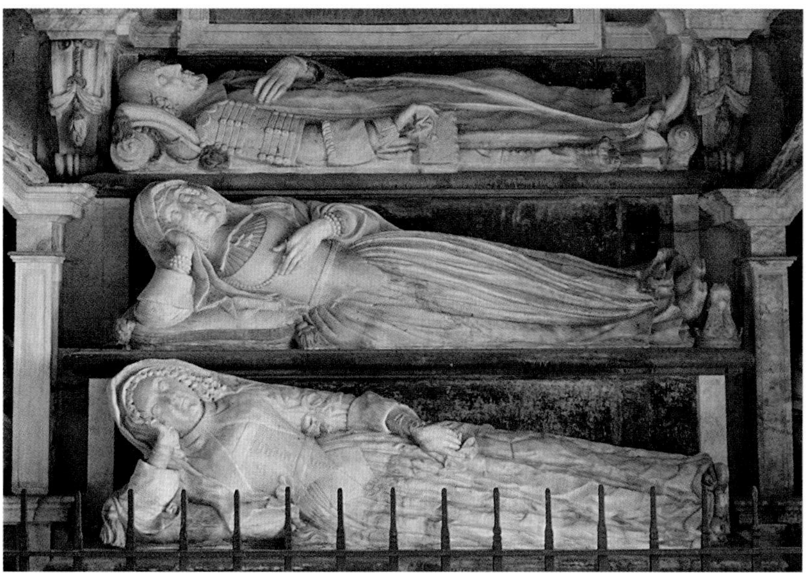

During the eighteenth and nineteenth centuries, it was the walls of the church that were more likely to commemorate the departed, whether in text or in figurative form, partly because of a lack of space, but also because of the greater pictorialism that was a component of the neo-classical. However, towards the end of the nineteenth century a renewed interest in the medieval spawned a fashion for the effigy, notable especially within the patronage of the royal family and of the church itself.

Good examples can be found within the private chapels of the royal family, and these were followed by the aristocracy and the newly ennobled. The effigies to **Queen Victoria and Prince Albert** in the Frogmore Mausoleum at Windsor by Carlo Marochetti were laid on a granite sarcophagus and represent the thorough acceptance of the form at this period. Victoria was greatly affected by the effigy of her husband and found solace in visiting and touching it.[7]

...

horizontal

51. Carlo Marochetti, effigies of Queen Victoria and Prince Albert, 1867

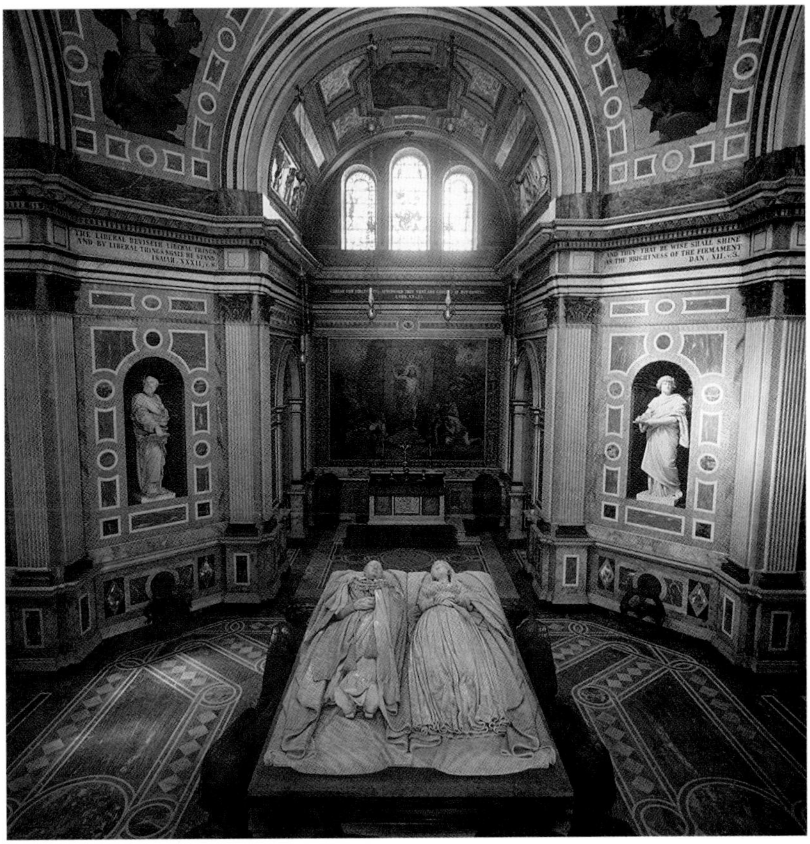
THE LIBERAL DEVISETH LIBERAL THINGS
AND BY LIBERAL THINGS SHALL HE STAND
ISAIAH XXXII
AND THEY THAT BE WISE SHALL SHINE
AS THE BRIGHTNESS OF THE FIRMAMENT
DAN. XII. v3.

A good example of juvenile aristocratic commemoration is at Lanercost Priory, Cumbria, where **Elizabeth Howard**, the infant daughter of the Earl of Carlisle is laid out by Sir Edgar Boehm as if for a nap. This equivocal treatment seems fitting for a child whose parents are the chief mourners. William Goscombe John's effigies in Llandaff (1900) and Westminster Abbey (1912) inspired the commission for the **Leverhulme tombs** at Port Sunlight, sculpted by John for his long-standing patrons. Other late examples flourish in historicising building projects such as Gilbert Scott's Anglican Cathedral in Liverpool, where the tombs of **Bishop Ryle** and the Earl of Derby are marked by effigies designed in the inter-war years.

52. Edgar Boehm, effigy to Elizabeth Dacre Howard, 1883

...

horizontal

53. William Goscombe John, Leverhulme tombs, 1913–25

54. Memorial to Bishop John Charles Ryle, 1900

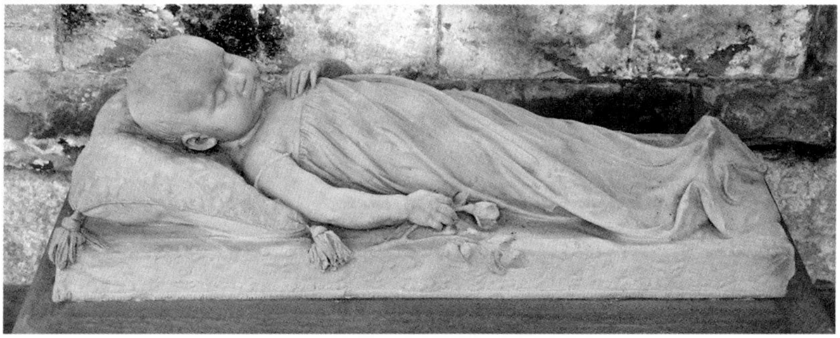

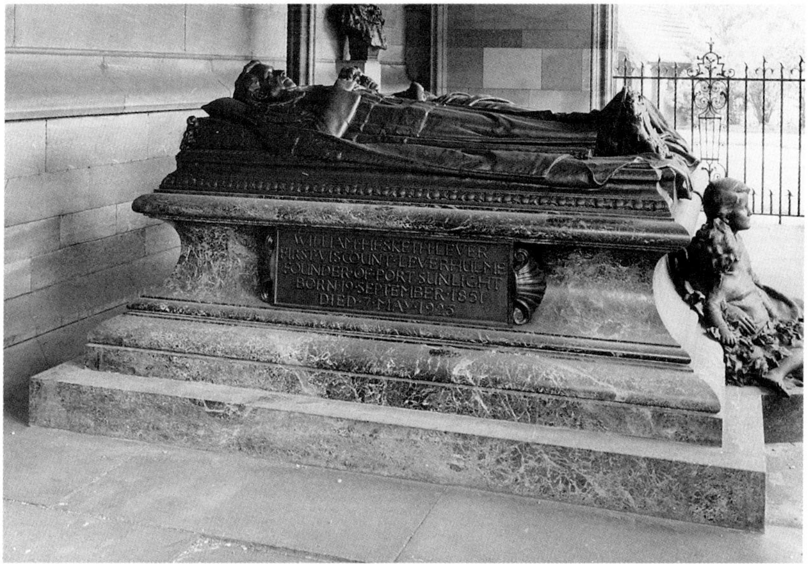
WILLIAM HESKETH LEVER
FIRST VISCOUNT LEVERHULME
FOUNDER OF PORT SUNLIGHT
BORN 19 SEPTEMBER 1851
DIED 7 MAY 1925

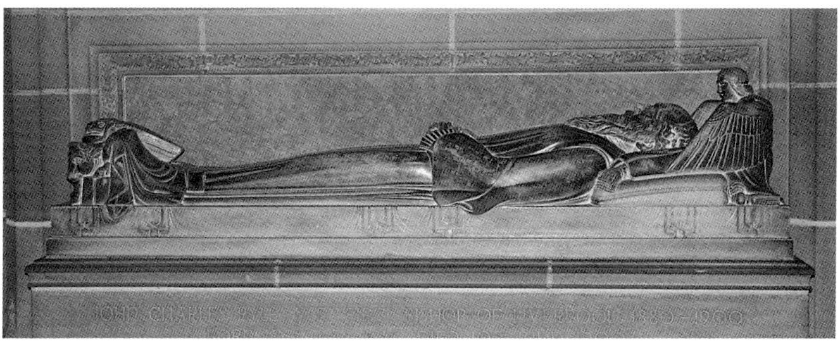
JOHN CHARLES RYLE
BISHOP OF LIVERPOOL 1880 – 1900

These medievalising ecclesiastical effigies are balanced by the revival of the effigy of the knight in armour, notably exemplified by that to the Duke of Clarence, who was known for his attention to dress as a soldier. Alfred Gilbert's **Clarence Memorial**, placed within Henry de Triqueti's earlier Albert Memorial Chapel of St George's Chapel at Windsor, lays out the Duke like an offering on a plinth (or on a mortuary slab), as a 1909 photograph makes plain. Close by lie further effigies: the original one to Prince Albert (by Triqueti, 1874) and to Prince Leopold (by Boehm, 1884).[8]

All these projects, however, are predated by Alfred Stevens's **Wellington Monument**. Stevens's competition model was one of several entries exhibited in 1857 in Westminster Hall. By the time of its eventual completion in St Paul's in 1912, the Duke's great military achievement at Waterloo dated back nearly a century. His effigy lies on the tomb, at rest.

55. Alfred Gilbert, Duke of Clarence Memorial, 1894

The relationship between armour (real or sculpted) and the sculpted figure is resonant. Both are empty, but both represent the figure of the man, in close detail. Gilbert understood this very well. He fashioned both the figure and its accoutrements in metal, speaking at one and the same time of the body, and of its absence.

horizontal

...

56. Alfred Stevens, competition model for the Wellington Monument in St Paul's Cathedral, 1857

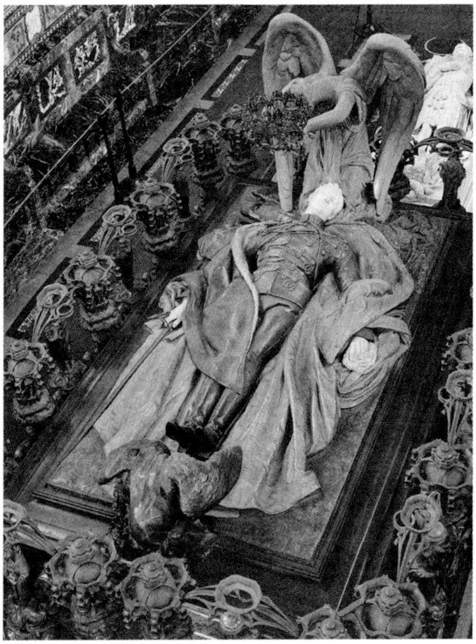

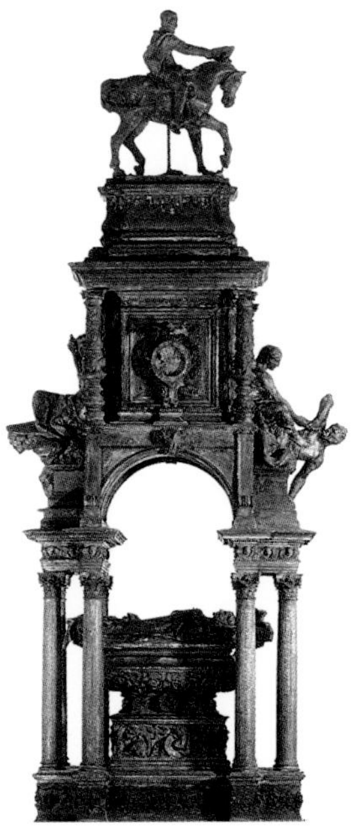

The same effect is wrought in sixteenth-century tombs, even when fashioned in stone or alabaster. We seem to look inside the helmet only to feel the absence of the body itself. An early sixteenth-century example at Exton, the tomb of **John Harington**, shows head on helmet and gauntlets at the side; we might add, a little later in Ashby-de-la-Zouch, the tomb of **Francis Hastings**, and a further striking example from Breedon, where the helmet supports the head of **Francis Shirley**. The empty helmet stands for the man, in life and in death, and this custom is still visible in the far-fetched mores of the Knights of the Garter in the Chapel of St George, with their invented crests and wooden swords hung up in their stead.

...

horizontal

57. Detail of the tomb of John Harington showing his head resting on a helmet, 1524

58. Detail of the tomb of John Harington showing gauntlets by his side, 1524

59. Tomb of Francis Hastings, 2nd Earl of Huntingdon, 1561

60. Tomb of Francis Shirley, c.1571

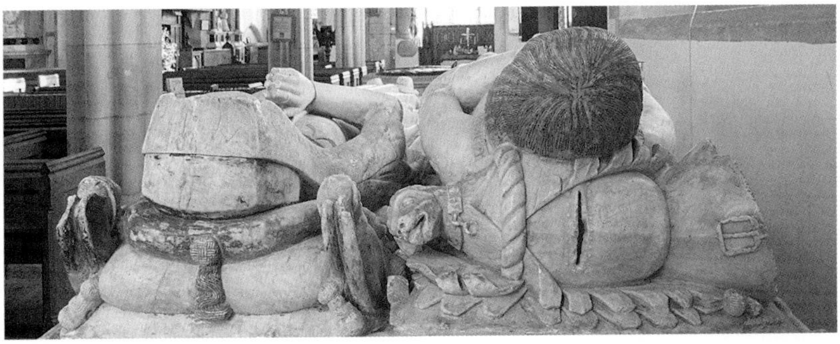

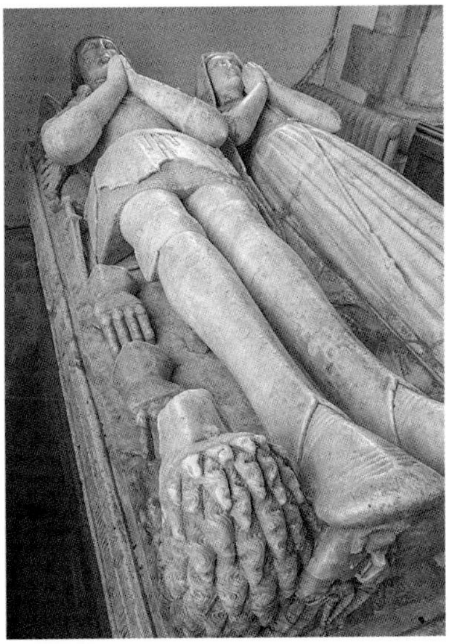

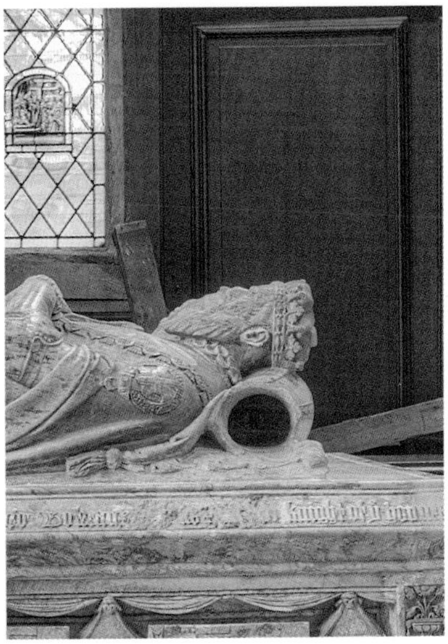

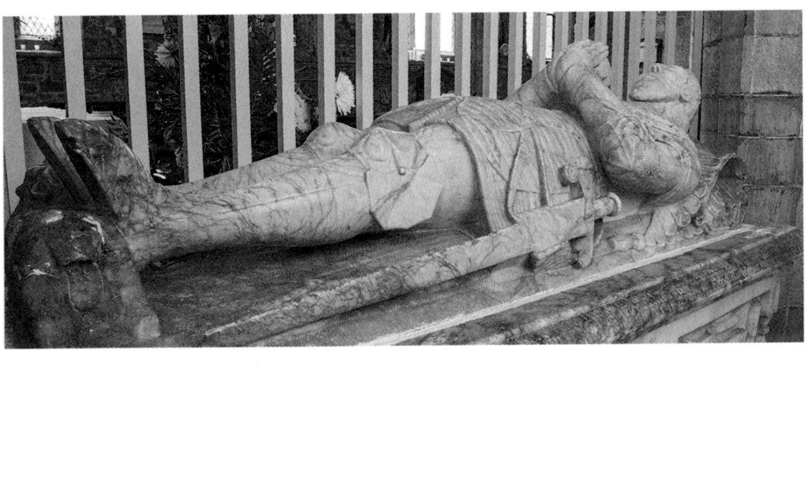

The sword at rest represents the man at rest; its horizontality is abnormal, and marks its definitive shift from the active to the passive state. It is also highly personal, even anthropomorphic, in suggesting the scale and strength of the upright and active figure.[9] The proximity of sword to cross is made clear in tombs such as those at Norton Disney, Bottesford, and Exton (all-mid- to late-fourteenth-century), where the top of the tomb chest to **Nicholas Grene** is marked by a sword that resembles a cross.

Alison Wilding's low black sculptures evoke both the effigy and the grave, as if the knight is at rest, his arms crossed, his armour laid out, waiting for the passage between this world and the next. ***Cold Face*** comes with its own cover, steel seeming to smother black rubber, one emerging, one covering, in sinister equilibrium. ***In Shadow***, made in concrete on the floor of the chapel of Skipton Castle, suggests its own near disappearance.[10] The tomb seeks to merge with the earth itself.

- - -

horizontal

61. Tomb of Nicholas Grene, late 14th century

62. Alison Wilding, *Cold Face*, 1997

63. Alison Wilding, *In Shadow*, 1998

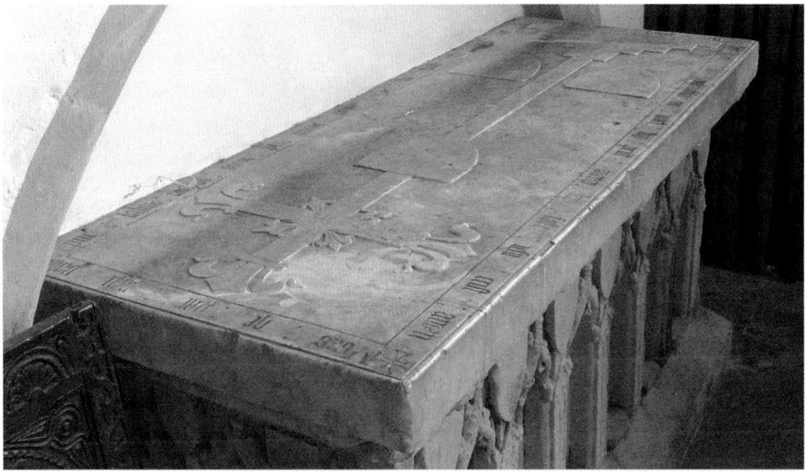

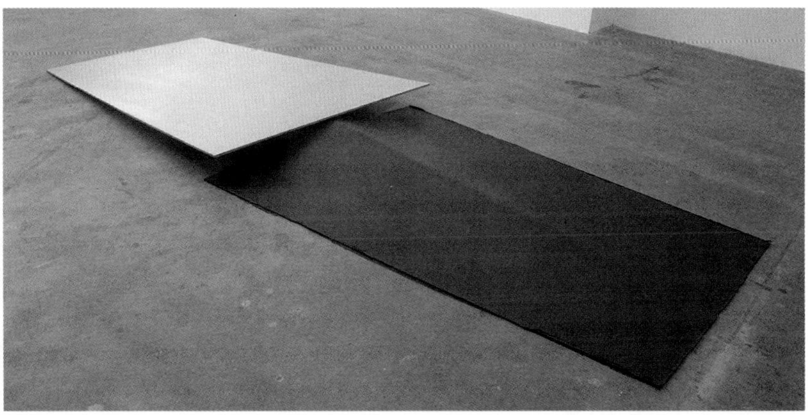

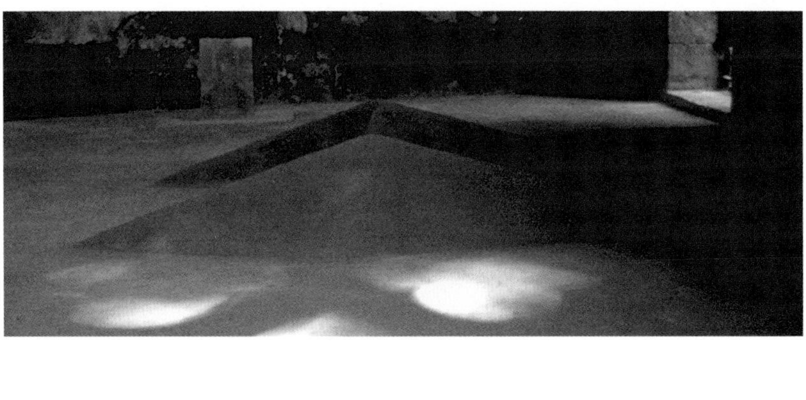

The Duke of Wellington is shown in different states within one monument, alive and dead. Complex tombs allowed for such multiplicity, and indeed conveyed something of the complexity of a religious understanding of what remains. Death is rarely explicitly portrayed, but on occasion the tomb chest is metaphorically opened up to reveal the skeleton beneath, as with **Bishop Fleming** in Lincoln Cathedral.[11] His shroud too is opened, as if he were ready to meet his Maker on Judgement Day. Thus a representation of the living surmounts a representation of the actual dead figure that lies under its image.[12]

The later sixteenth-century example at Breedon on the Hill, to commemorate the Catholic **George Shirley**, places a more generic, if nonetheless realistic, skeleton beneath the larger family that kneels above; this is more conceptual and less actual. The body lies above the sarcophagus, laid out as if on a small bed (and is resoundingly empty).

- - -

horizontal

64. Alfred Stevens and John Tweed, Wellington Monument, 1856–1912

66. Tomb of George Shirley, 1598

65. Tomb of Bishop Fleming, 1431

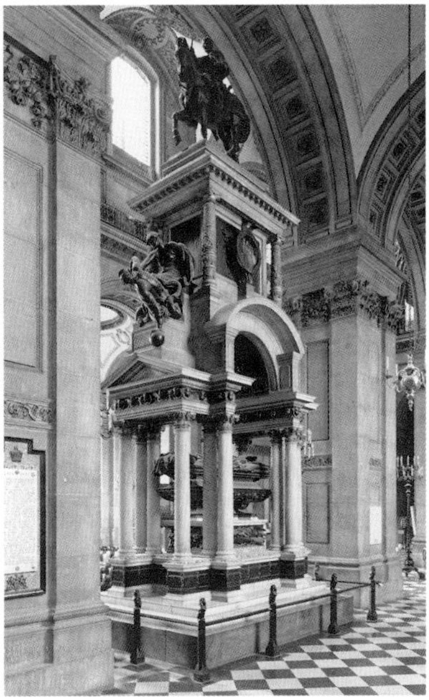

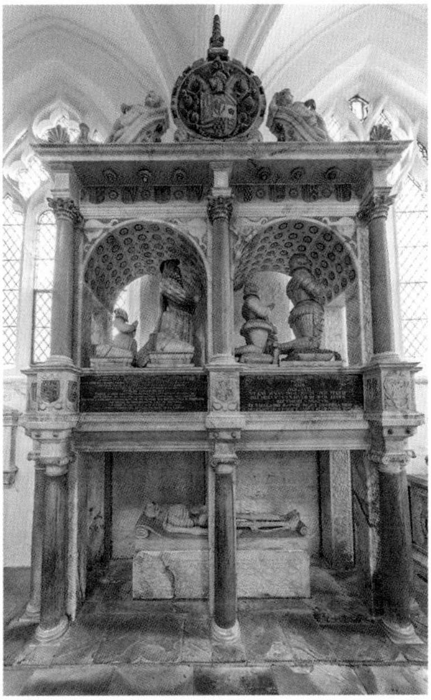

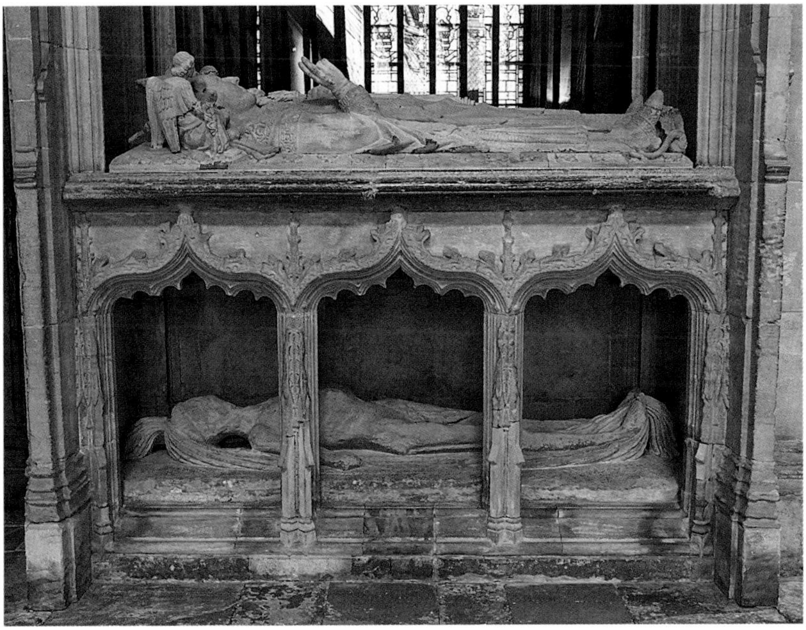

An alternative, and perhaps rarer, nod to reality is when, on occasion, figures, rather than being raised up for display, seem instead almost to sink below ground level, as if they were really in the grave. This is the case with the tomb of **Neville de Stoke** at Stoke Rochford who lies, with a woman who is presumably his wife, under what might be seen as a blanket.

The blanket may also be a shroud, as we have seen, and yet its simplicity here suggests that it is indeed a blanket, perhaps not completely removed from works by British sculptors such as Alison Wilding, Shirazeh Houshiary, Richard Deacon or **Jacqui Poncelet**.[13] These artists became known for works that were described as being between objects and sculpture, and used the floor not so much in the way Anthony Caro had done a generation earlier, but more as a component of the sculpture itself. The blanket lies on the floor as if it were something between a rug and a shroud, a grave blanket for goods of value, a protection.

---

horizontal

67. Tomb of Neville de Stoke, 1320

68. Jacqui Poncelet, *Clay, bronze, wood and fabric*, 1994

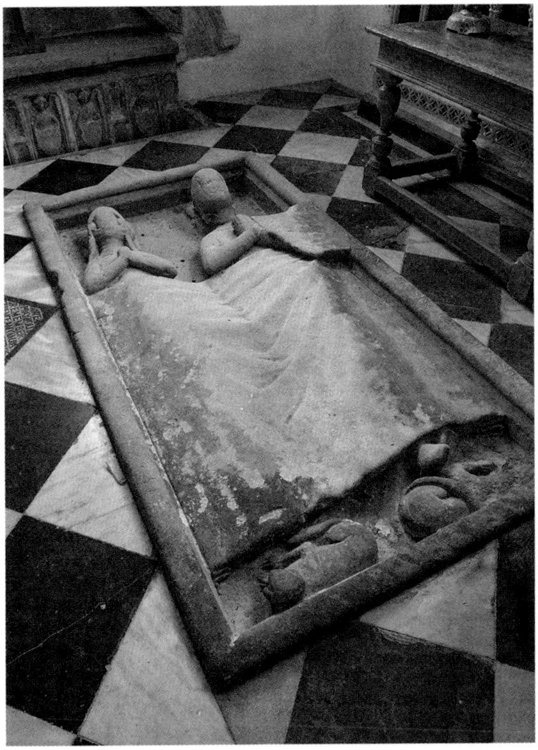

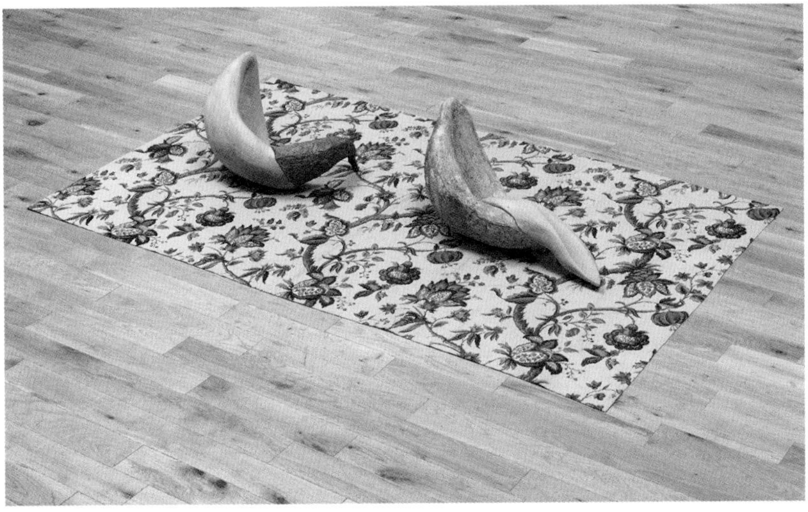

The bed-like quality of the grave is reminiscent of the mattress made by Bernini in 1620 at the request of Cardinal Borghese, who needed a base on which to lay his newly acquired antique ***Hermaphrodite***, and it restores the potential sexuality of the combination. **Rachel Whiteread** might well be said to have played on an analogous conjunction with her many cast mattresses, which began with known mattresses used by those close to her, alive or dead.

...

69. Gian Lorenzo Bernini, mattress base for *Sleeping Hermaphrodite*, 1620

horizontal

70. Rachel Whiteread, *Untitled (Mattress)*, 1991

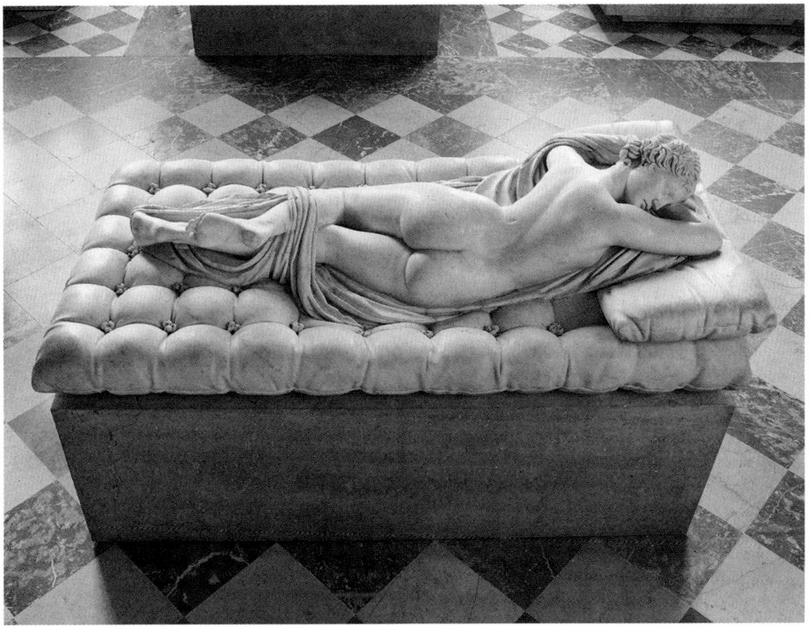

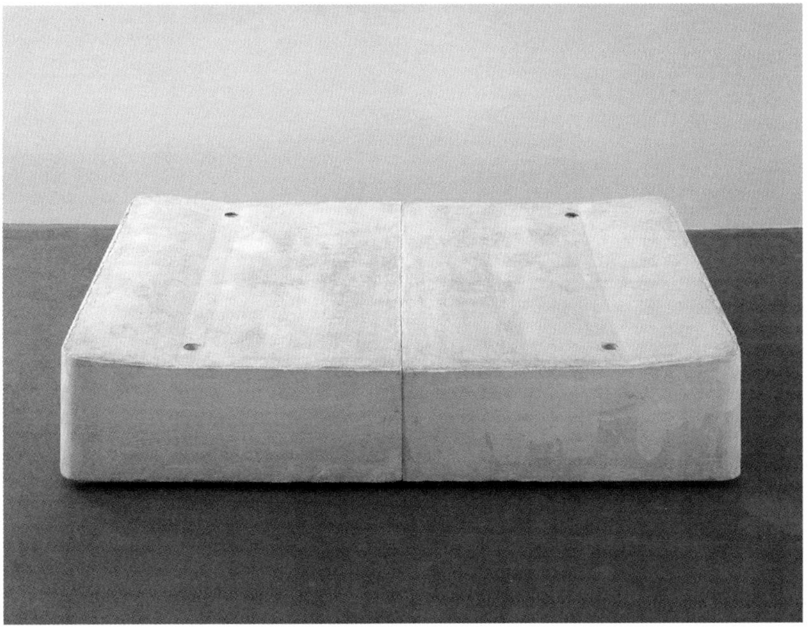

This alternative reading of the reclining figure is perhaps most familiar in the form of the Vatican's ***Sleeping Ariadne***, who was indeed additionally placed on a sarcophagus, reinforcing the nexus between sleep and death. Until the early 1800s her identification as Cleopatra reinforced the deathly connotation of the form.[14]

...

horizontal

71. *Sleeping Ariadne*, 2nd century BC.

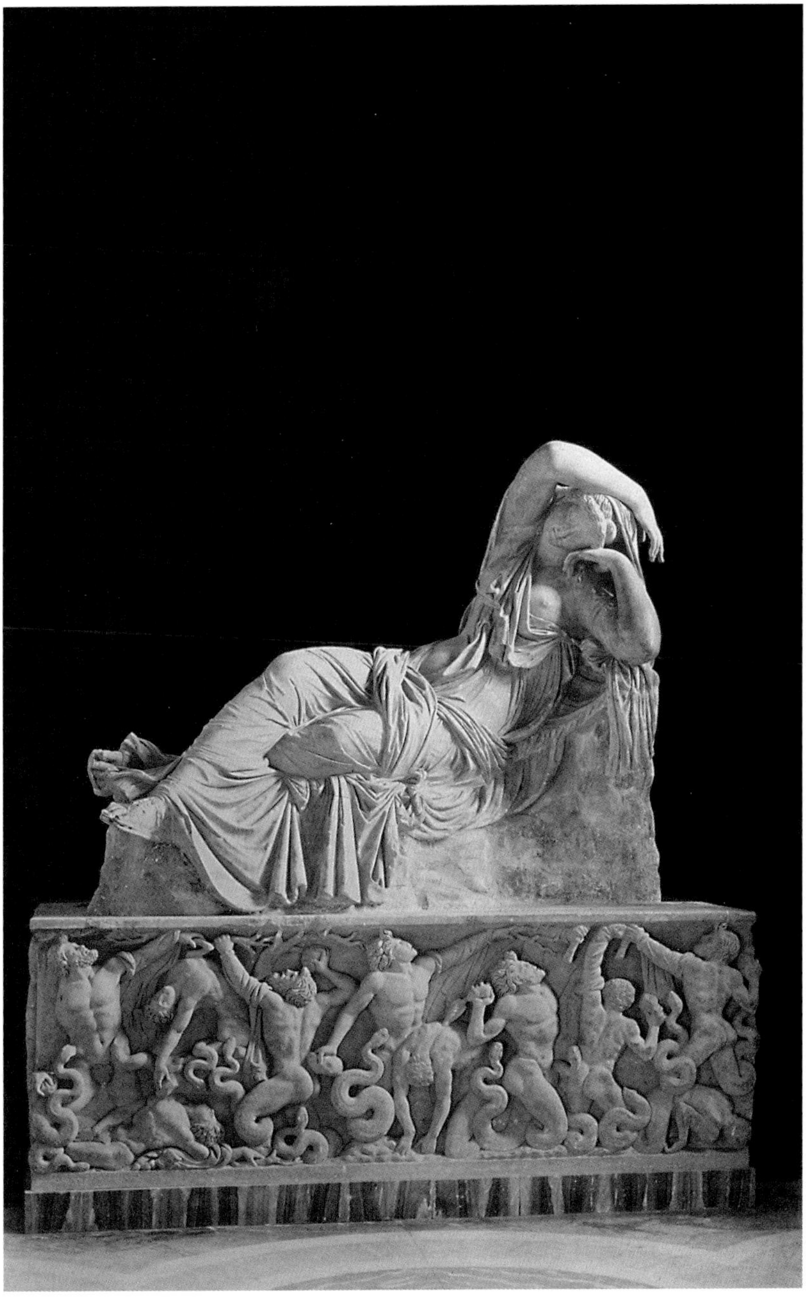

73

This threshold was well demonstrated by **Cornelia Parker** in the piece she constructed with Tilda Swinton, in which the actress lay in a coffin-like vitrine, apparently asleep, surrounded by personal effects of the famous dead. Although Swinton was clothed, there is a similar frisson in the encounter with Edward Onslow Ford's ***Shelley***, which lies naked on its ornamented plinth, effectively set apart from the sculpted artifice beneath by virtue of the apparent reality of its unadorned marble. This makes Ford's sculpture less of an ecclesiastical monument and more of an ideal sculpture – despite its surroundings in Oxford – and closer in mood to his last work, ***Snowdrift***.

...

72. Cornelia Parker and Tilda Swinton,
The Maybe, 4–10 September 1994

horizontal

73. Edward Onslow Ford,
Shelley Memorial, 1892

74. Edward Onslow Ford,
Snowdrift, 1901

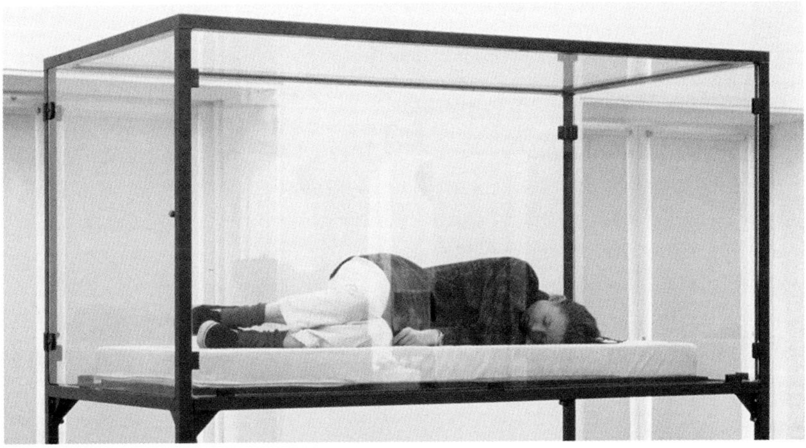

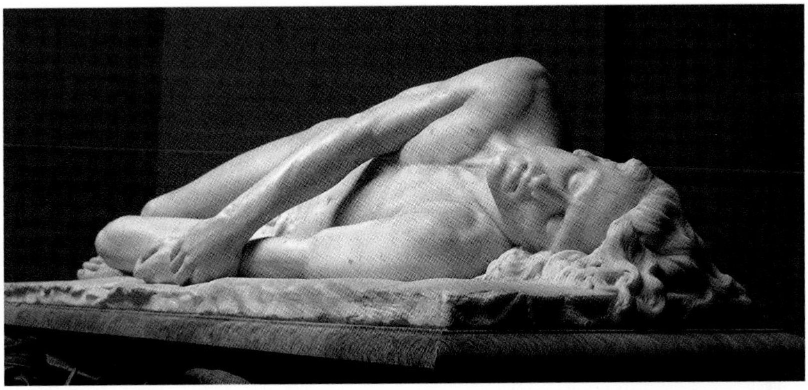

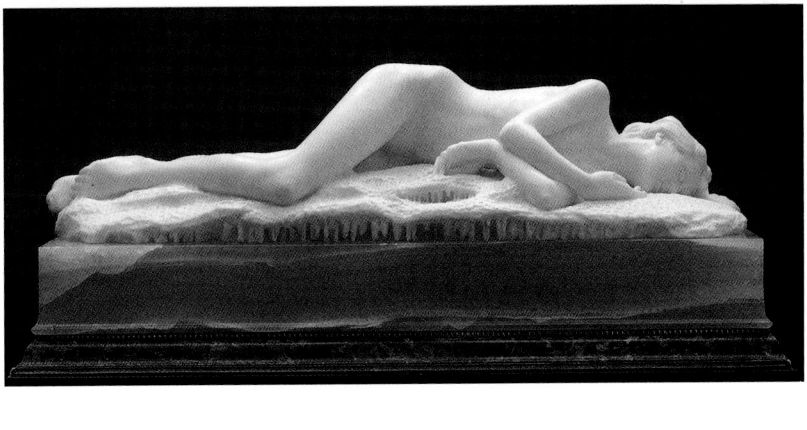

Thomas Banks's monument to the five-year-old **Penelope Boothby** and Francis Chantrey's conscious reprise in his memorial to the **Robinson Children** show children more alive than dead; in the latter they lie on a buttoned mattress, with a pillow supported by a rolled-up blanket. Sculpted babies are a conceit, largely fashioned in the Victorian era, which played upon this ambiguity; hovering between sleep and death, they are charmingly misleading, deliberately perhaps, and may offer perpetual illusion. Again they feature in the homes of aristocratic patrons, very often of women, and it is never hard to imagine that they represent lost children, as they almost certainly do in the case of **Josephine Bowes**, who built the collection at the Bowes Museum.

75. Thomas Banks, tomb of Penelope Boothby, 1791

---

horizontal

76. Francis Legatt Chantrey, monument to the Robinson Children, 1817

77. French school, *Sleeping Baby*, c.1855

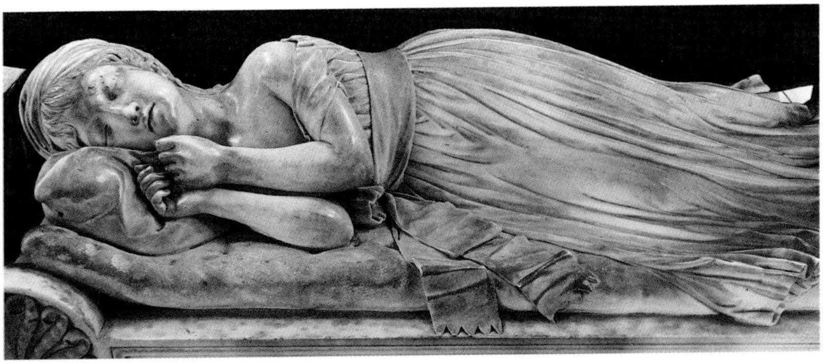

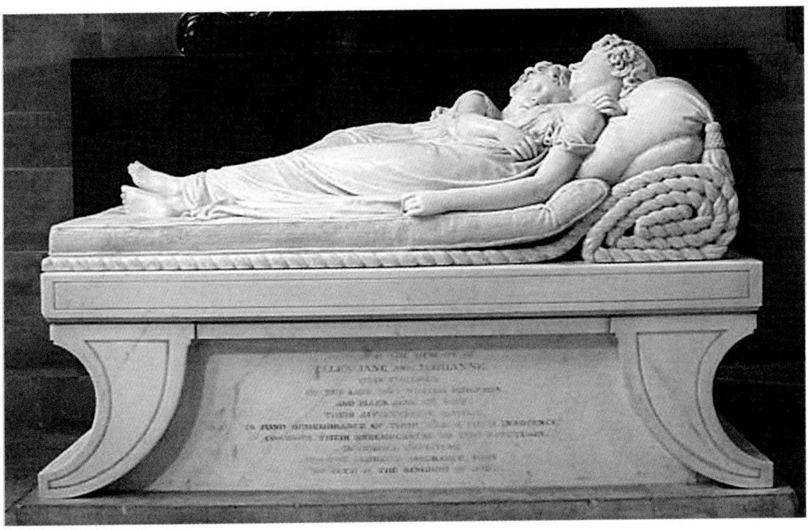

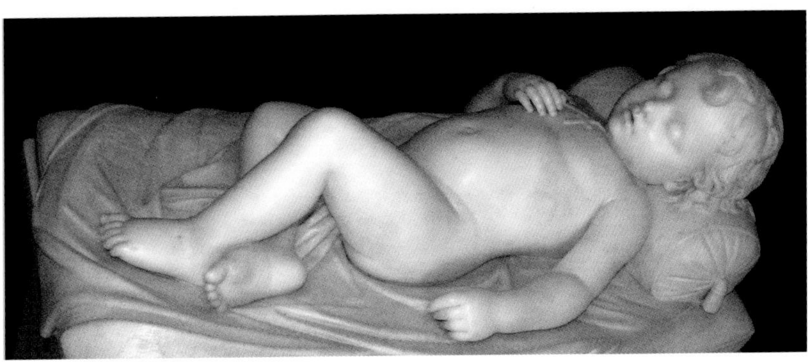

Although the effigy had made a distinct return to the commemorative sculptural vocabulary of the early twentieth century, it was in its most death-like form; prone, enshrouded, clearly a corpse. It was Henry Moore who may be credited with resuscitating the effigy, giving it new currency, taking the form away from the church and into the wider public sphere.

But before turning to Moore I want to cite an exceptional, if anomalous, contemporary example of sculpture that embodies positioning and potentiality: Jacob Epstein's ***Consummatum Est***. This massive carving clearly holds within it the idea of resurrection, represented in the sculpture's potential righting, from the horizontal to the vertical. Its maker was pessimistic about its context, even resigned: 'I imagine a waste world...', he wrote in 1942, where 'no human thing is left alive. The feet are weary from having trod the earth in vain, the hands with their wounds turned to the sky, the face calm... Like the enigmatic stones of a far island that face the sea, my stone will face the sky and give no answer'.[15] Its counterpart might be seen as ***Lazarus***, one of his last carvings, in which the figure, in its shroud, has indeed been raised from the dead.

78. Jacob Epstein, *Consummatum Est*, 1936–7

horizontal ...

79. Jacob Epstein, *Lazarus*, 1947–8

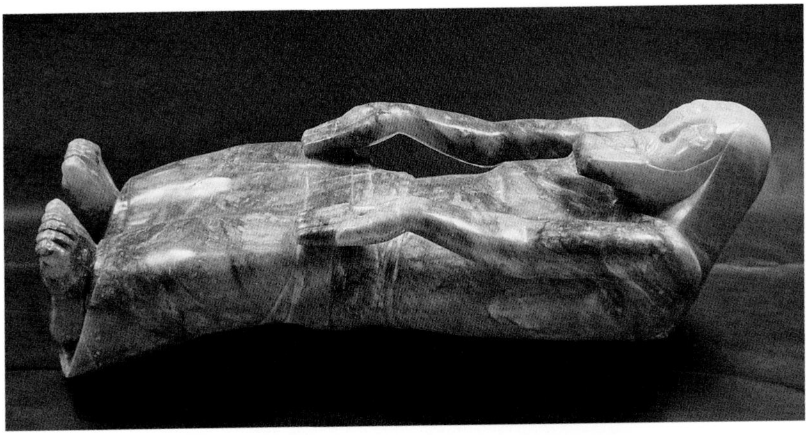

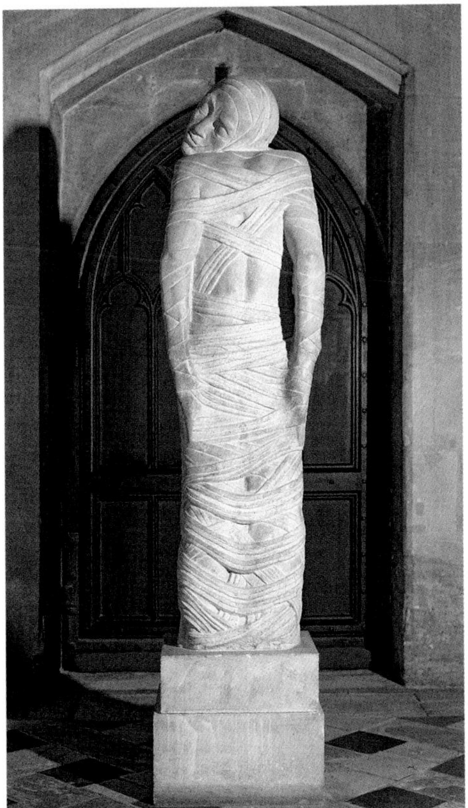

Henry Moore was much more faithful, and more consistent in his use of the effigy, and used its implicit connection with death to give his sculpture a deeper cultural root. Moore's love of the medieval tombs at St Oswald's, **Methley**, is well known, but obscures the fact that his own borrowing was less medieval than modern. Perhaps he had taken note of the **Savile tombs** by Peter Scheemakers and Joseph Wilton in the same church? He certainly took up the conversational recumbent figure, as featured in the tomb monuments of the seventeenth and eighteenth centuries, in his own reworking of the Etruscan form.

...

80. Tomb of Lionel, Lord Welles and his wife Cecilia, 1461

horizontal

81. Joseph Wilton, tomb of John Savile, 1778

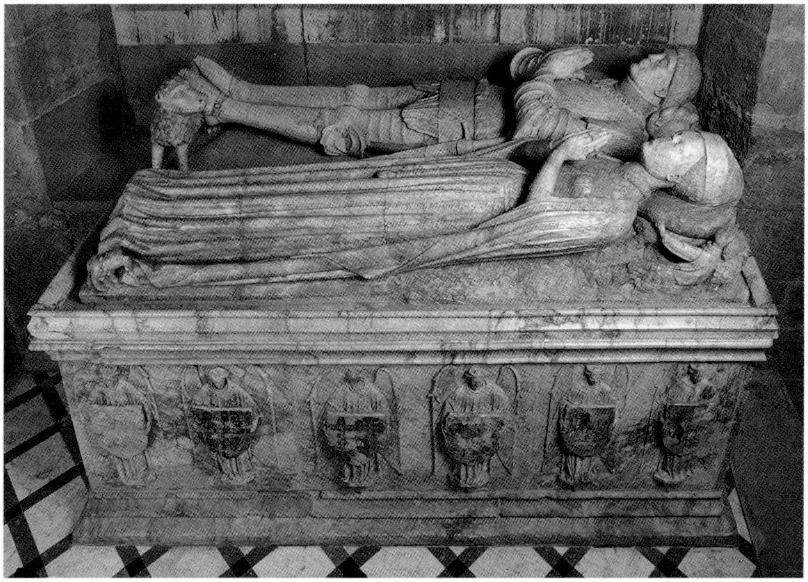

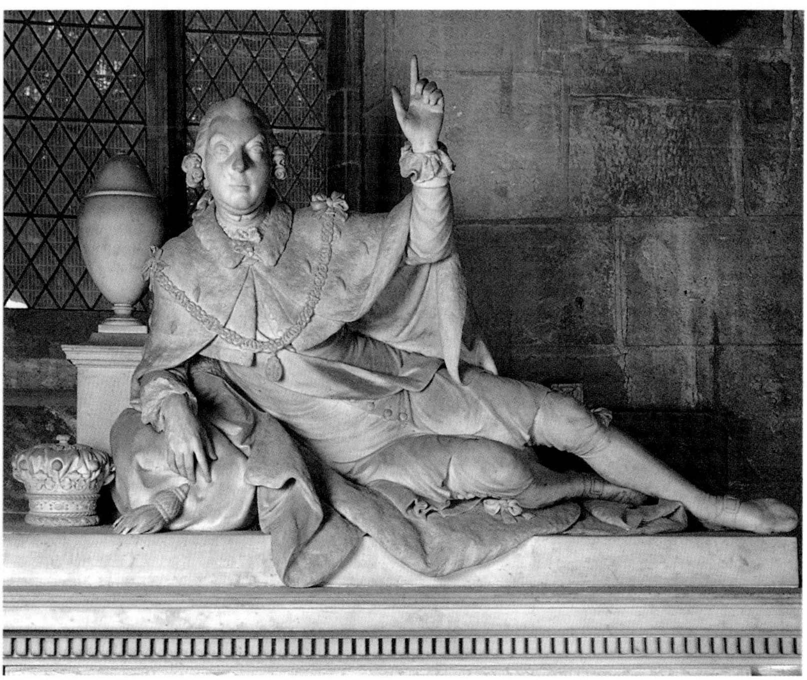

By the end of the seventeenth century the upper body of the effigy had been lifted so as to be merely recumbent, rather than prone. A good example, of 1700, is Pierre-Étienne Monnot's monument to the fifth **Earl of Exeter** in Stamford, which appears to acknowledge death in its semi-recumbency, but also to suggest life, before or after. The slightly later monument at Stapleford by John Michael Rysbrack to **Lord Harborough** similarly lifts up his torso and shows him in conversation.

...

82. Pierre-Étienne Monnot, monument to John Cecil, 5th Earl of Exeter, 1700

horizontal

83. John Michael Rysbrack, monument to the 1st Earl of Harborough, 1732

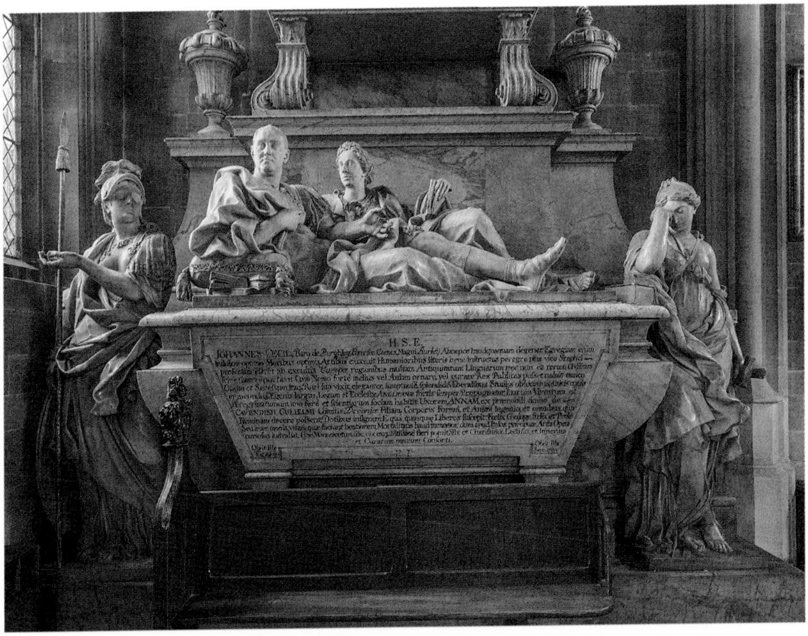
H. S. E.

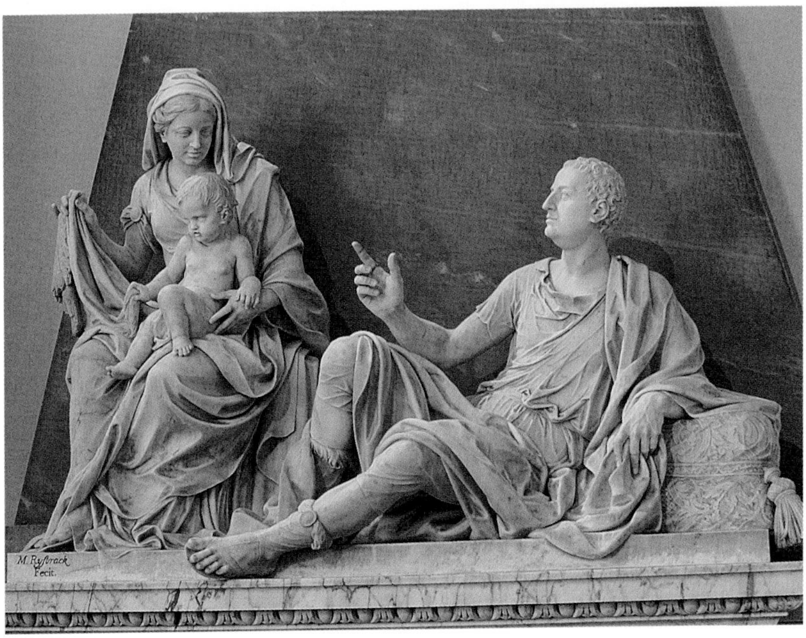
M. Rysbrack
Fecit.

Like Rysbrack, **Moore** brings the figure up from the horizontal to face us; this is a frontal (or civic) address, rather than an aerial (or heavenly) one. Even when Moore's reclining figures are monuments to the departed, they are definitely awake and not asleep. Indeed, Moore's figures are never quiescent, and like many of these English monuments, similarly suggest the unfinished conversation. In this they are more worldly and less spiritual, as John Webster had noted back in 1614, with the Duchess of Malfi receiving as answer to her question: 'Why, do we grow fantastical in our death-bed?/ Do we affect fashion in the grave?':

> Most ambitiously. Princes' images on their tombs
> Do not lie, as they were wont, seeming to pray
> Up to heaven, but with their hands under their cheeks,
> As if they died of the tooth-ache: they are not carved
> With their eyes fixed upon the stars; but
> As their minds were wholly bent upon the world,
> The self-same way they seem to turn their faces.[16]

horizontal

A century later, John Dart, in his account of Westminster Abbey, described the evolution of the **reclining figure** to the point at which the deceased now appeared to be 'On Cushions lolling, stretch'd with careless pride'.[17]

- - -

84. Henry Moore, *Memorial Figure*, 1945–6

85. Monument to Sir Edmund Uvedale, 1606

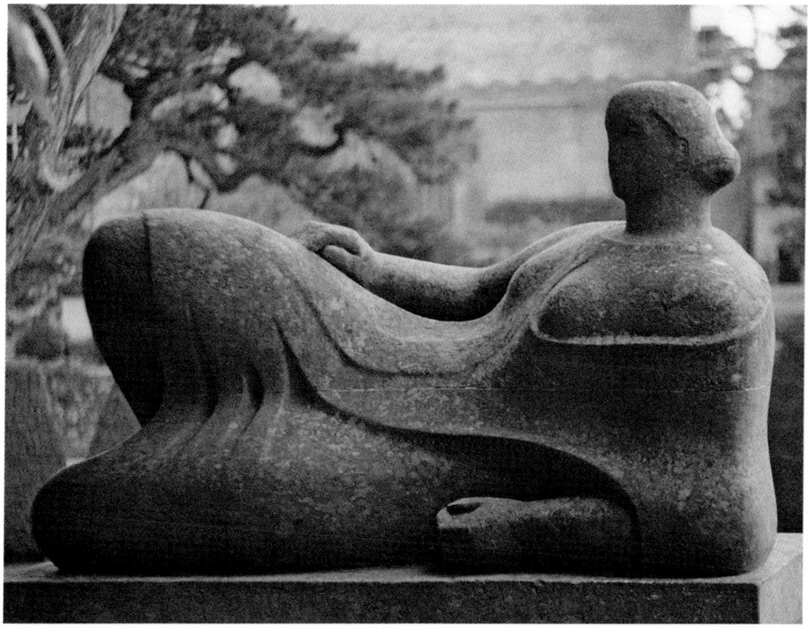

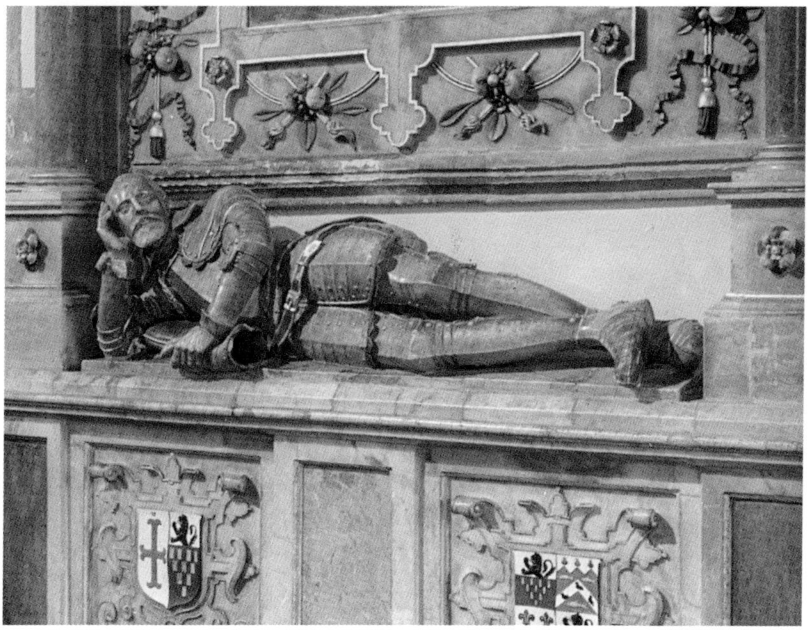

An exception in Moore's oeuvre is his ***Falling Warrior***, in which the just recumbent form is falling rather than rising. The wounded warrior had little currency in British imagery, and this work is perhaps very particular to its time, even if its use of the shield takes it almost instantly back to the classical warrior and to the medieval knight and his accoutrements.[18]

The technical link here between the casting of armour and the casting of the body seems material, and on occasion the armour, even if translated into stone, comes to stand for the art of the metal-smith, which, in life, had fashioned the casing for the living figure. Laura Ford's ***Armour Boys*** use a similar combination of historic and technical associations to create their effect, and use bronze to make that simple and effective elision between living body and fallen corpse; the clothing of the upright figure and its representation in death.

...

horizontal

Casts can be uncannily life-like, even if they betoken or indeed cause the death of the small creatures that were the subject of a renewal of this technique in the early Italian Renaissance, when the bronze that was to preserve their features burnt them alive. Modern life casts were accompanied by a smaller but significant subset of casts from death, normally focusing exclusively on the head.[19]

...

86. Henry Moore, *Falling Warrior*, 1956–7

87. Laura Ford, *Armour Boys* (detail), 2006

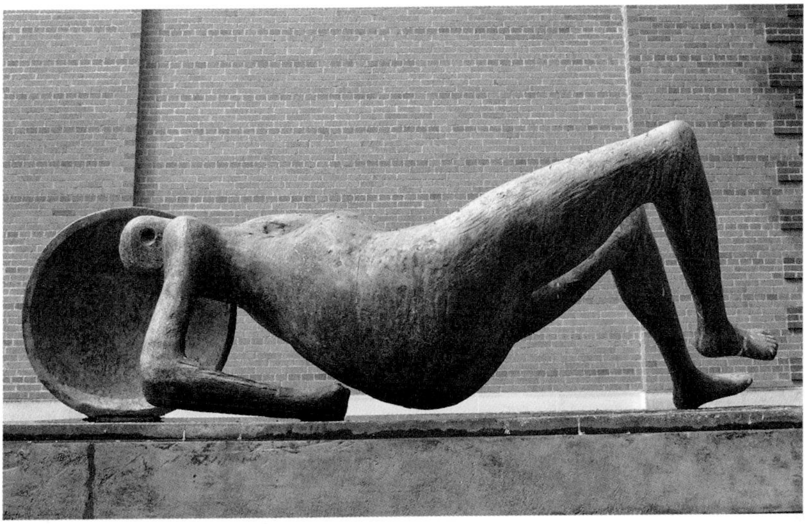

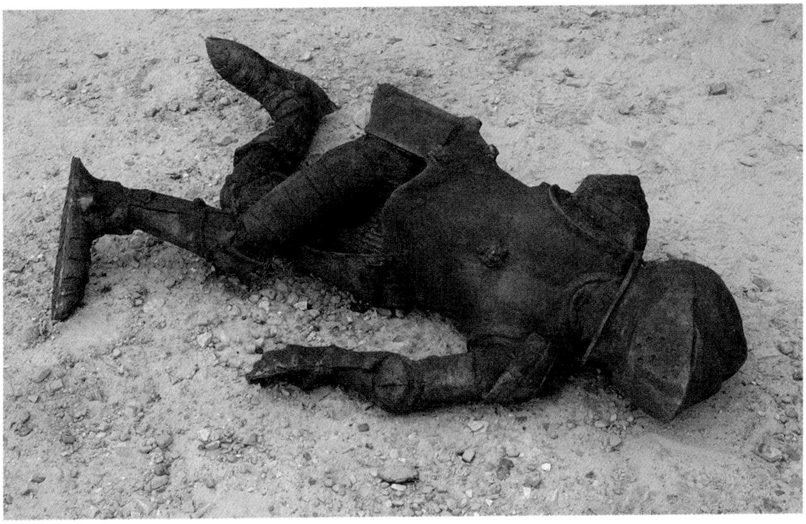

In the nineteenth century the urge to document allowed the cast's fidelity to detail (in a wide range of materials) briefly to rival photography as a form of scientific documentation for flora, fauna and anthropological specimens. The concurrent fashion to cast the great monuments of an earlier age means that plaster casting is perhaps indissolubly associated with architectural sculpture and especially with the tomb, as is evident in museum complexes of the period, notably the **Cast Court** of the South Kensington Museum (now the Victoria and Albert Museum) and the Musée de la Sculpture Comparée (created in Paris in 1882).

The space between life and death is hinted at by Moore in his sculpture, and even more so in his drawing, which seems especially suited to conjuring up a hinterland propitious for revival and resurrection. His miners and his **underground sleepers** have an Arthurian or Dante-like air of semi-wakeful sleep.

...

horizontal

88. Cast Court of South Kensington Museum, 1873

89. Henry Moore, *Shelter Scene: Bunks and Sleepers*, 1941

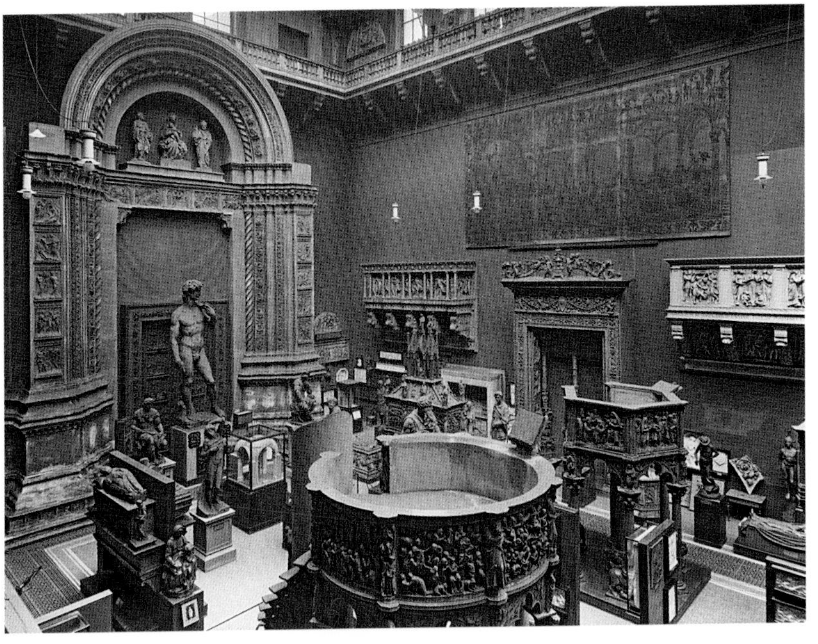

89

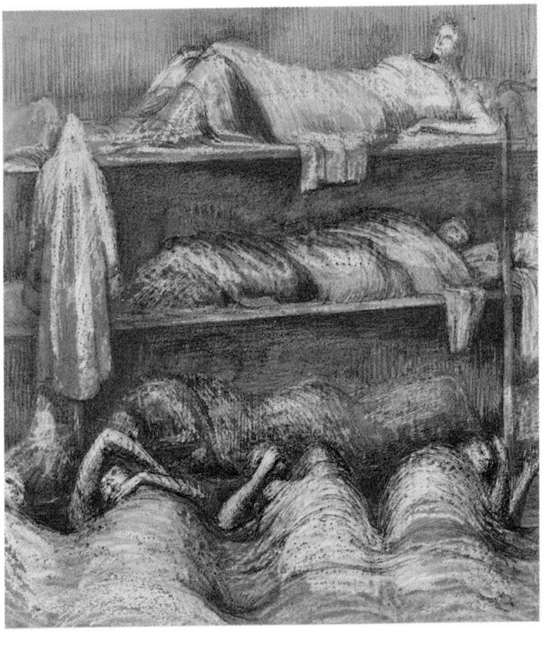

Technical innovation seemed oddly to restore to life the victims of historic disaster, as with **Giuseppe Fiorelli**'s casts of those whose bodies had been surrounded by lava and ash from the eruption of Mount Vesuvius in Pompeii, nearly two millennia earlier. These graphic human forms inspired some memorable sculpture. This kind of material translation, from void to solid, or from bandaged effigy to shroud, is more implicit than explicit, working almost subliminally in the viewer, as in the transition from Fiorelli's plaster cast to **Arturo Martini**'s parched drinker, carved in volcanic tufa.

Martini's sculpture is founded upon his understanding of the threshold between life and death, conceptually and formally, and between material and meaning.[20] Tufa absorbs water, like a sponge, and is thus cruelly apposite for a sculpture about thirst or drought. The need for refreshment, physical and spiritual, is embodied in this work.

---

90. Giuseppe Fiorelli, one of twenty plaster casts of preserved victims of the eruption of Mount Vesuvius in 79 AD, 1863

horizontal

91. Arturo Martini, *La Sete*, 1934

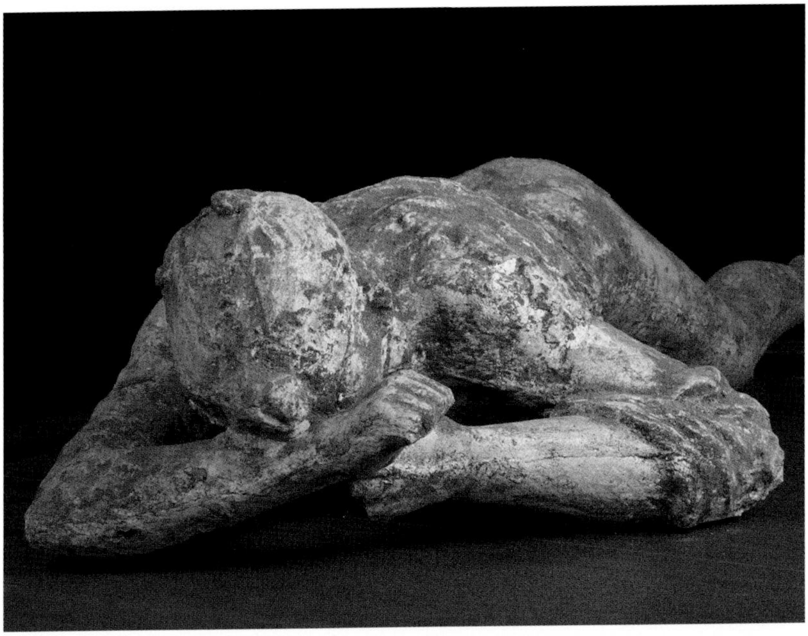

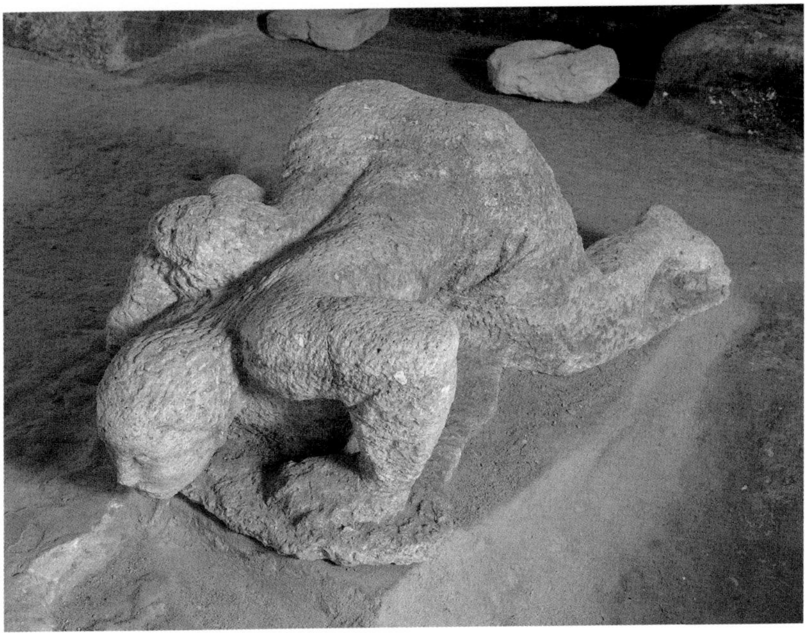

The positioning of ***Ariadne*** near a fountain in the Vatican gallery may have influenced the placing of John Cheere's copy for Stourhead, where its site within a grotto reinforced the association of the nubile waiting woman with a secret, watery resting place. The statue of Cleopatra/Ariadne was often ascribed a voice, and in Alexander Pope's translation from Castiglione, 'On the Statue of Cleopatra, made into a Fountain by Leo the Tenth', she makes clear that even if the Romans had imprisoned her within a rock, Leo could 'give [her] back [her] tears/ Release [her] eyes, and let them freely flow', 'lull'd' as she now was by the surrounding fountains.[21] Water animates, restores, brings back to life.

The voice of Cleopatra echoes that of other more plebeian 'living' or speaking statues of Rome, such as ***Marforio***, and the Fontana del Babuino, both of which were again associated with water. Such figures, poised between activity and passivity, suggest a more equal relation to the viewer than much classical statuary. This is partly, I suggest, because their horizontality means they are more clearly sculpture, or more clearly stone. They have not been upended, made to balance on a plinth, but take their ease, as if part of the natural sedimentary fabric that lies between earth and sky. The speaking sculptures of Rome operate on a material threshold between art and life, hosting the comments of the citizenry in a kind of unattributed limbo.[22]

horizontal

...

92. John Cheere, *Sleeping Nymph (Ariadne)*, 1766

93. *Marforio* (River God Fountain), 1st–2nd century

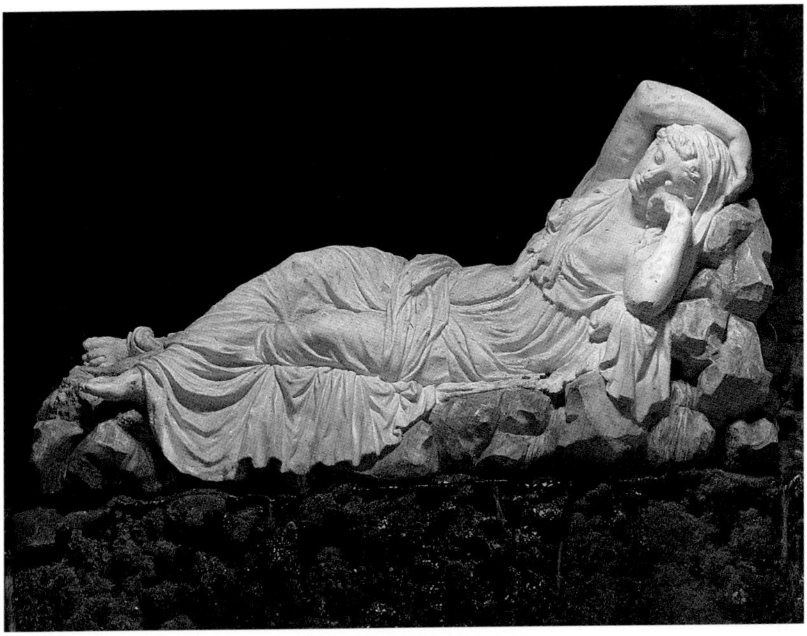

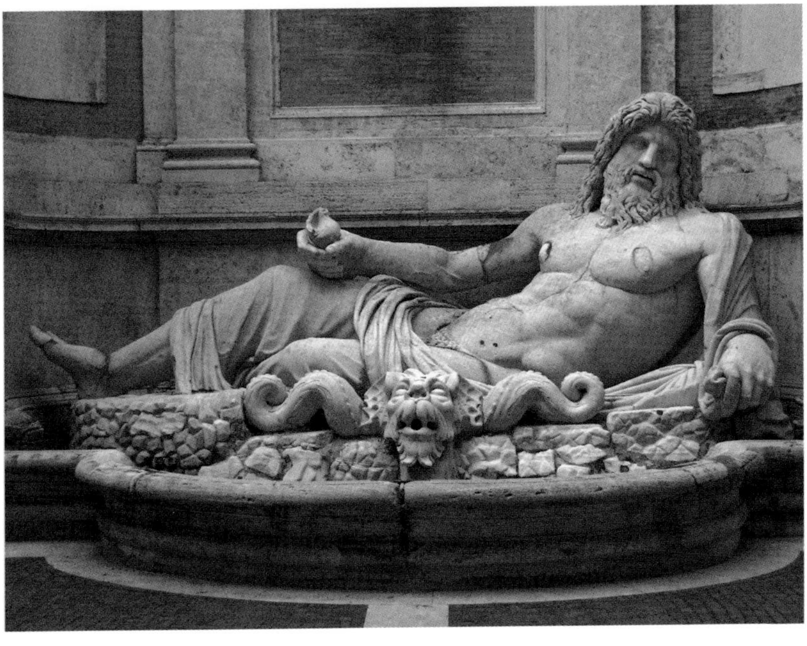

Their representation of a natural element (water, or air) aligns these sculptures with the horizontal, and here the conventional classical nymph might be compared to modern allegorical figures like the Four Winds on the London Underground Headquarters. **Henry Moore**, who was one of the four young sculptors commissioned by the older Eric Gill, went on in his work in a way quite unlike any of his peers (other than Aristide Maillol) to exploit the horizontal format, covertly restoring it to its early associations with water, and thus with life.

...

horizontal

94. Henry Moore, *West Wind* (in progress), 1928–9

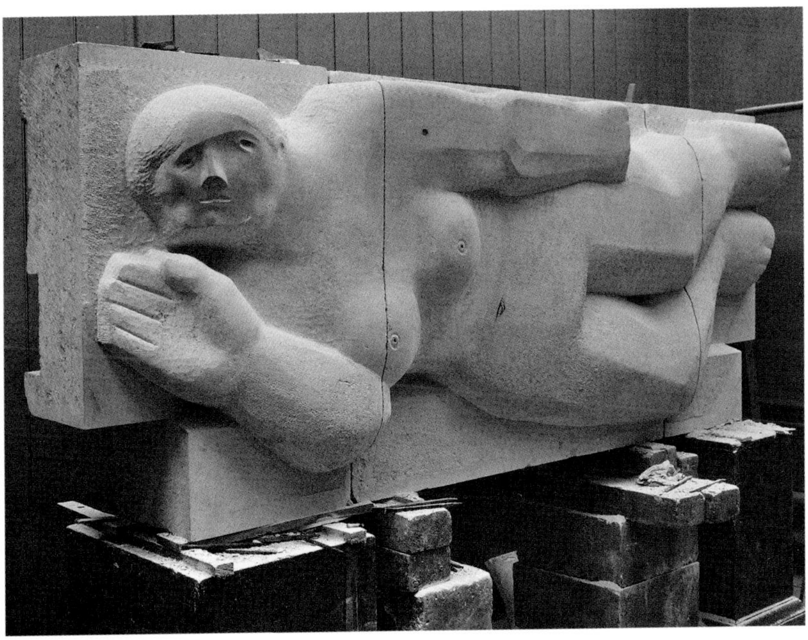

The level of water, and indeed of the water table, has been played out in more recent sculpture, without recourse to figuration, in the work, for example, of Garth Evans, Craig Wood, Keith Wilson and, most literally, in Richard Wilson's ***Watertable***, which takes us to ground level and below. Water, as they say, finds its level.[23]

The **Boyle Family**'s self-styled Institute for Contemporary Archaeology was set up in the mid-1960s by Mark Boyle and Joan Hills during the height of the Westway excavations in London. The 'sections' of ground they found first in Shepherds Bush, and then all over the world, were transformed only in being hoisted onto the wall, shifting from the horizontal to the vertical, or one might argue, from the sculptural to the pictorial.

...

95. Richard Wilson, *Watertable*, 1994

96. Mark Boyle and Joan Hills, *Institute for Contemporary Archaeology: Holland Park Avenue Study*, 1967

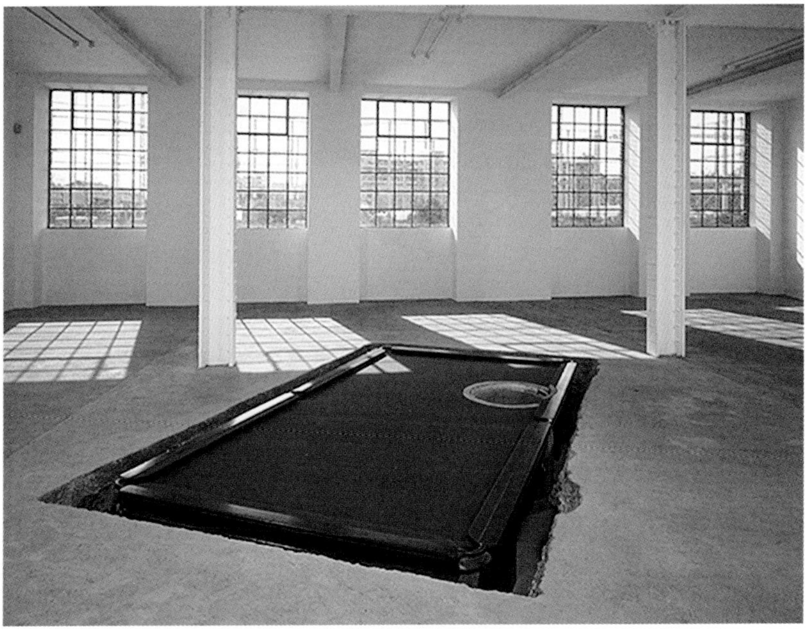

97

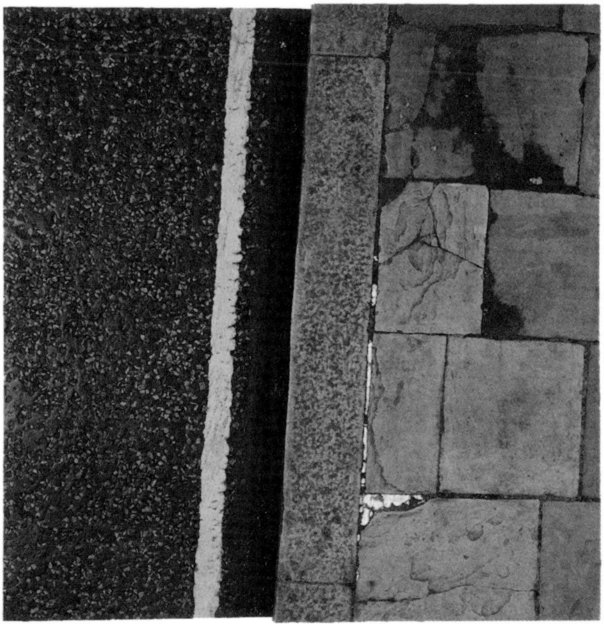

Somehow on the margin between the two, Roger Hiorns's **dust works** suggest both sculpture and painting, poured out like flotsam or jetsam, a tidemark or slick of particulate that, we are told, derives from sources ranging from military weaponry to an altar stone. Hiorns's particles are absolutely dry, crying out, perhaps, for water.

In his ***Puddle***, Keith Wilson had in a sense made a work that was exactly the opposite, and Wilson went on to combine earth and water in his project at Whitby Abbey (2000), where he played on the archaeological fieldwork going on around him to fill in the gaps within the cycle of excavation, using plastic cloches to create an above ground to mirror what was going on below, and suggesting a possible rebirth or renewal.[24]

In her work ***Field***, Judith Dean comes closest to making a sculpture out of earth, combining the physical alchemy of bronze with the form of the earth from which it was extracted. There is in these works a sense of the Promethean life force that both lies in the ground and that is given back to the earth by the artist.

horizontal

...

97. Roger Hiorns, *Untitled*, 2008

98. Keith Wilson, *Puddle*, 1999

99. Judith Dean, *Field*, 2005

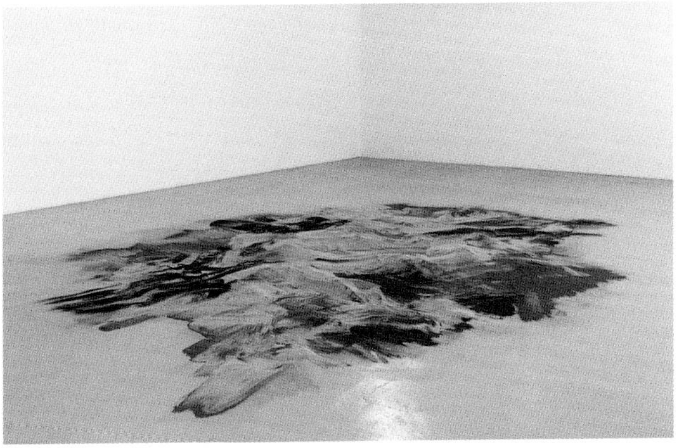

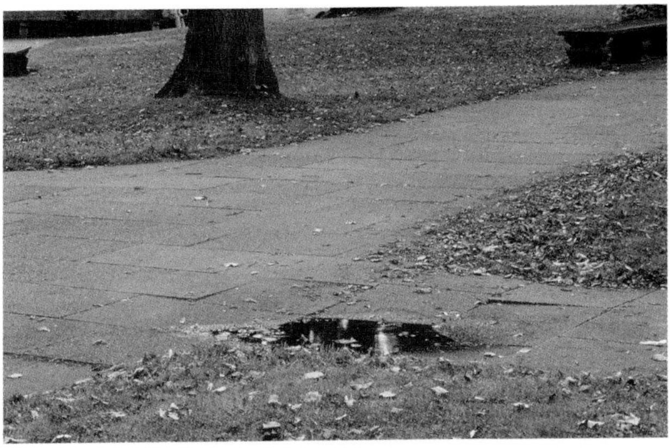

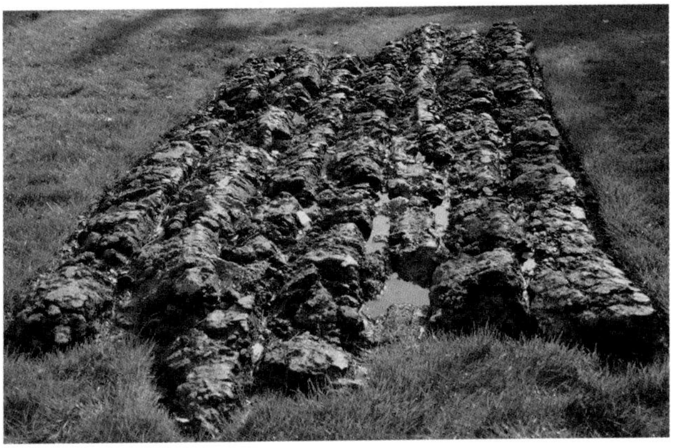

The ground as ceremonial site, as a site of origins and of ends, is especially clearly signalled by the **coronation stone** at Dunadd, in the Kilmartin Valley in Scotland, the capital of the ancient Gaelic kingdom of Dal Riata. This is more properly styled the inauguration footprint, with its ogham inscription in Old Gaelic, and is believed to have been the site where new kings were instated. Another coronation stone - the stone that would become known as the **Stone of Scone** - was taken from Argyllshire to Perthshire, possibly by one of the Dalriadan kings. It stayed in Scone for four centuries until Edward I took it to Westminster in 1296, whence it was only recently repatriated.

...

100. Coronation stone and footmark, c.500 AD

horizontal

101. Stone of Scone, pre-840 AD

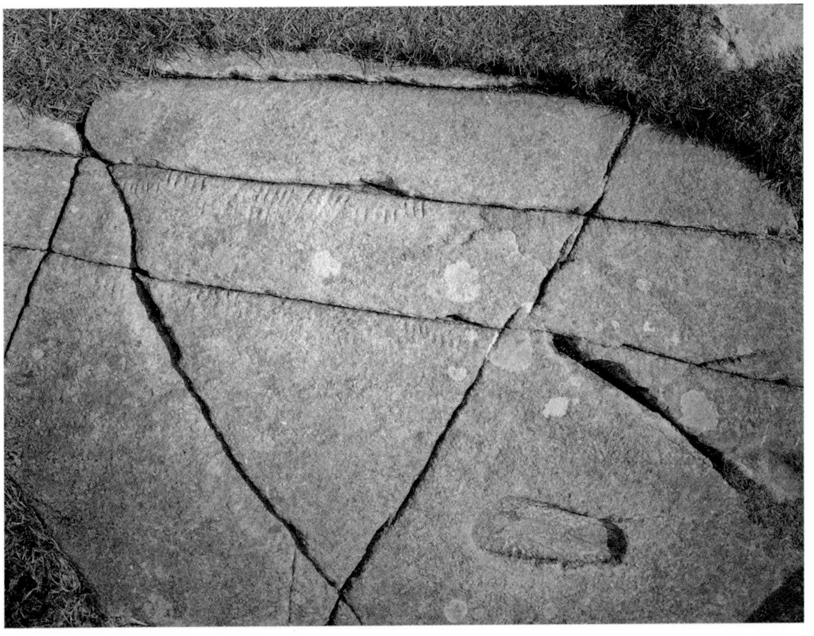

101

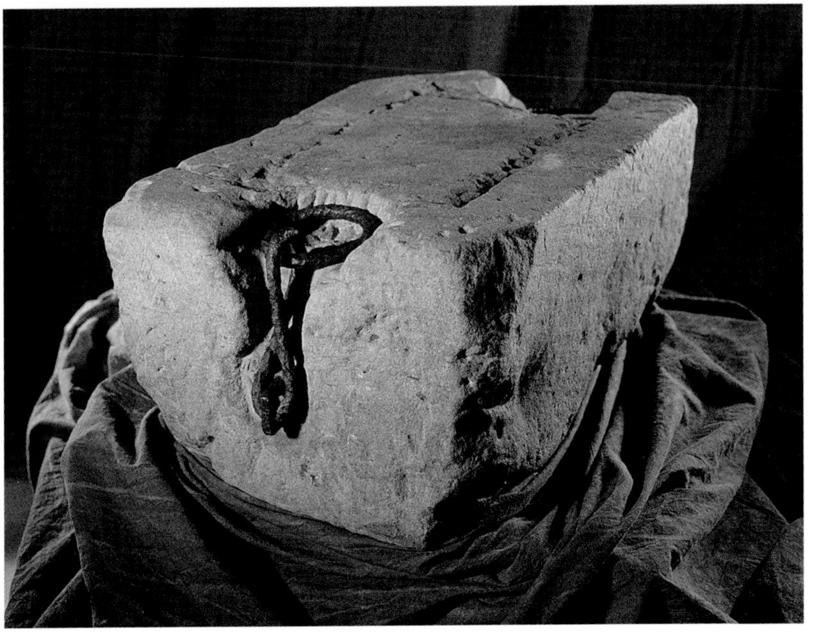

The fascination with the ground, and the space beneath us, might be seen to have reached its apogee in the late 1960s and early 1970s, most familiarly in American Land Art, but also in Britain, with the work not just of Richard Long and Hamish Fulton, and Barry Flanagan and Roelof Louw, but also of Keith Arnatt. Their work coincided with the first moon-walk, in the summer of 1969. Three months later came Arnatt's ***Self-Burial (Television Interference Project)***, shown (like the moon-landing) on television. Such works seem, firstly, to suggest the artist's own grave but, secondly, and more fundamentally, the essentially sculptural nature of the ways in which we mark our end. Other pieces by Arnatt conflate shadow with death, as in *Portrait of the Artist as a Shadow of his Former Self* and, more particularly, the shadow and the grave: as in ***Invisible Hole Revealed by the Shadow of the Artist***.

- - -

horizontal

102. Keith Arnatt, *Self-Burial (Television Interference Project)*, 1969

103. Keith Arnatt, *Invisible Hole Revealed by the Shadow of the Artist*, 1968 (photograph, exhibition copy for *Seven Exhibitions*, Tate Gallery, 1972)

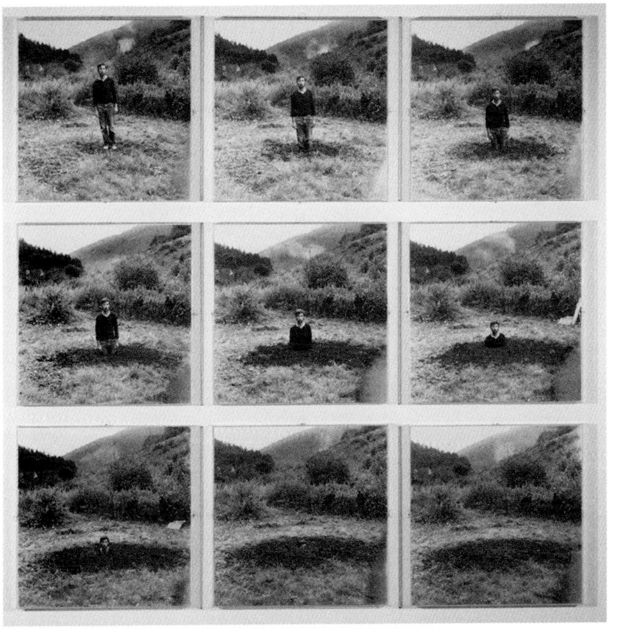

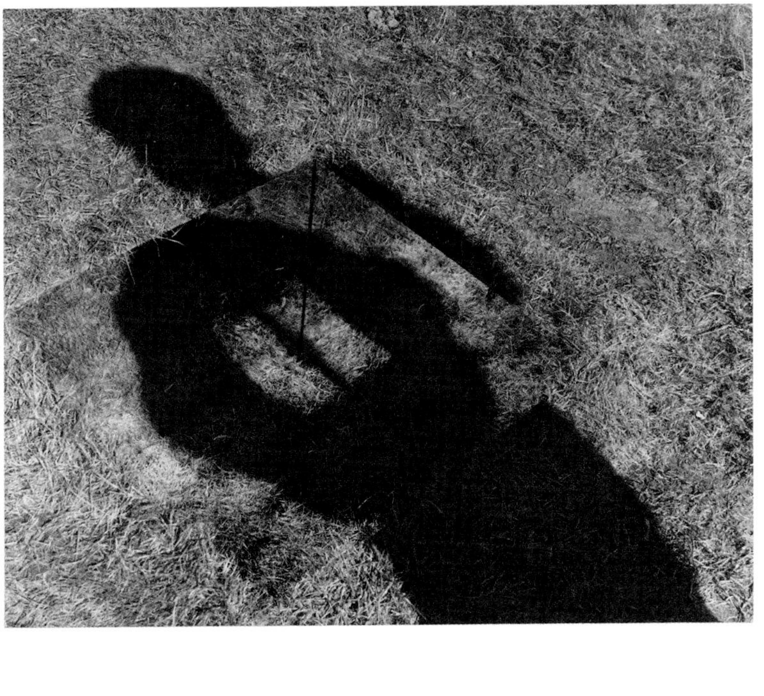

The shift from the three-dimensional imprint of the defunct to the two-dimensional icon may also be effected in metal, as we know from the common practice of fixing memorial brasses to the floor of the church. They emerged in the thirteenth century, with their origins in the altar tomb, which shifted first into the relief on the coffin lid, and then the incised slab, known in the twelfth century. Their material (copper and zinc) came chiefly from Cologne, until the late sixteenth century, and some were indeed re-used continental brasses, turned over.

English brasses, which are found chiefly in the eastern counties, are cut round the figure, unlike the continental, which were closer to the slab in their plate form. Brasses both inform us about armour and are informed by its inventory, representing armour as they mostly do, and its changing fashions: from chain mail, to banded mail, cuir bouilli, complete plate suit and so on, each marking a lapse of only one or two generations. Very often, if not necessarily, life size, they seem almost to carry the idea of the suit of armour, cast in metal, down to the ground. The soft mimicry of armourer's metal takes its final resting place.

104. Brass commemorating Geoffrey Sherard and his wife, 1490

horizontal

Fewer brasses show civil, ecclesiastical or academic costume, and there are later and smaller examples, principally from the sixteenth century, that represent children, and show the deceased in their shrouds. The brass of **John Claymond** in the chapel at Corpus Christi, Oxford, is one of these shrouded figures. It lies, as requested by Claymond himself, at the place where the choral rectors chant 'venite exultemus'. There is here a processional link between place and event which the brass plaque marks and even activates. As we walk over these figures as part of the ritual act we might sense their further embrace of the earth, and access to the heavens.

...

105. Rubbing of brass commemorating John Claymond, 1537

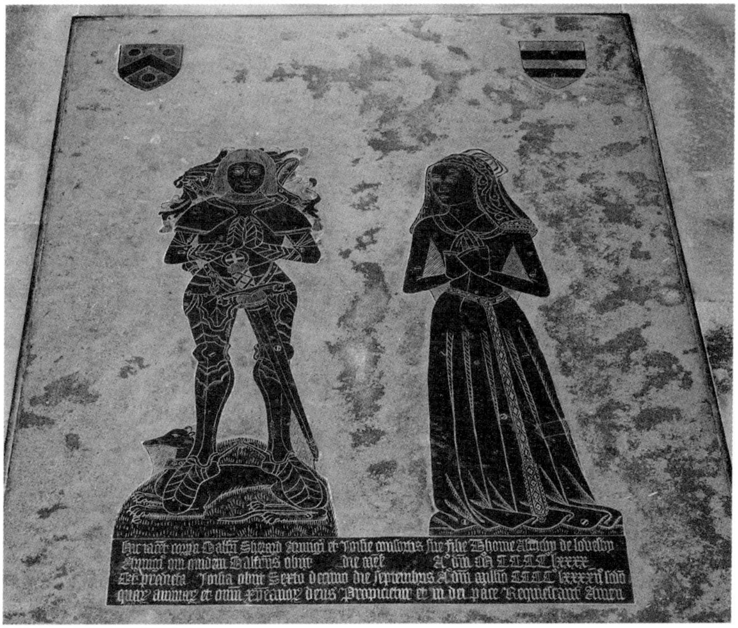

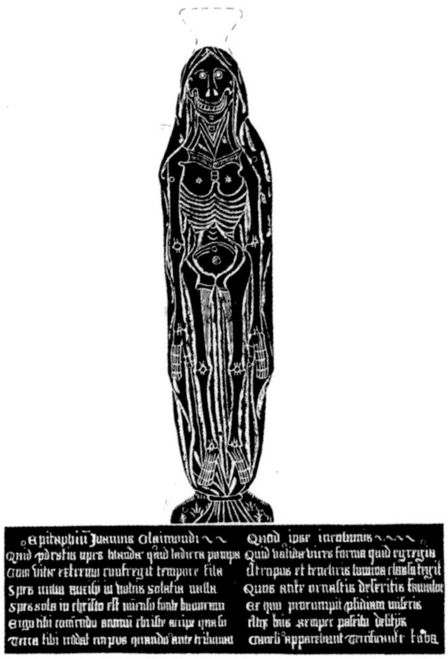

Such pavement inscriptions may mark the place where a man fell, his execution or condemnation to death, but also the more peaceful lying-in-state of the body, as on the floor of **Westminster Hall**. These are the final events, but they are relived and activated, either through the liturgy or by acts of pilgrimage and faith, which bring us to this place and to walk upon it.

The stone as a tomb marker, as we have seen, tends toward the head rather than the foot. Nonetheless, the tomb itself is inevitably horizontal, and many simple gravestones lie on the ground, marking both head and foot. In Leeds the **General Cemetery** has seen the creation of something of a perverse combination, with a path made of headstones. After the University acquired the cemetery in 1965 it was largely cleared, but the paupers' graves, with their multiple names, were used by the architects Chamberlin, Powell and Bon for paving, and the architects added further slabs with invented hieroglyphs to continue the conceit. Here we walk incongruously on a horizontal designed to be vertical, somehow in contravention.

...

106. Floor plaques marking the lying-in-state of King George V and Queen Mary. Westminster Hall, London

horizontal

107. Path made of headstones. Leeds General Cemetery

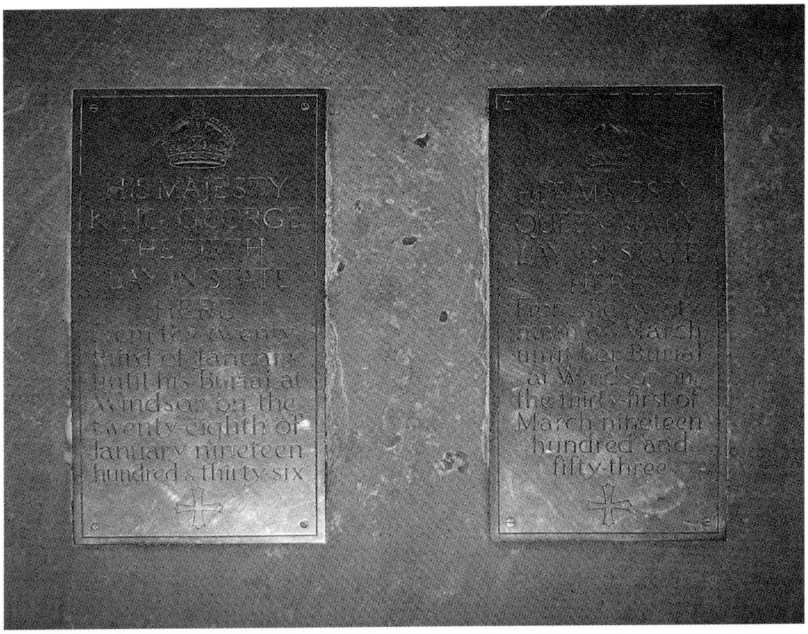
HIS MAJESTY
KING GEORGE
LAY IN STATE
HERE
From the twenty-
third of January
until his Burial at
Windsor on the
twenty-eighth of
January nineteen
hundred & thirty-six
LAY IN STATE
HERE
at Windsor on
the thirty-first of
March nineteen
hundred and
fifty-three

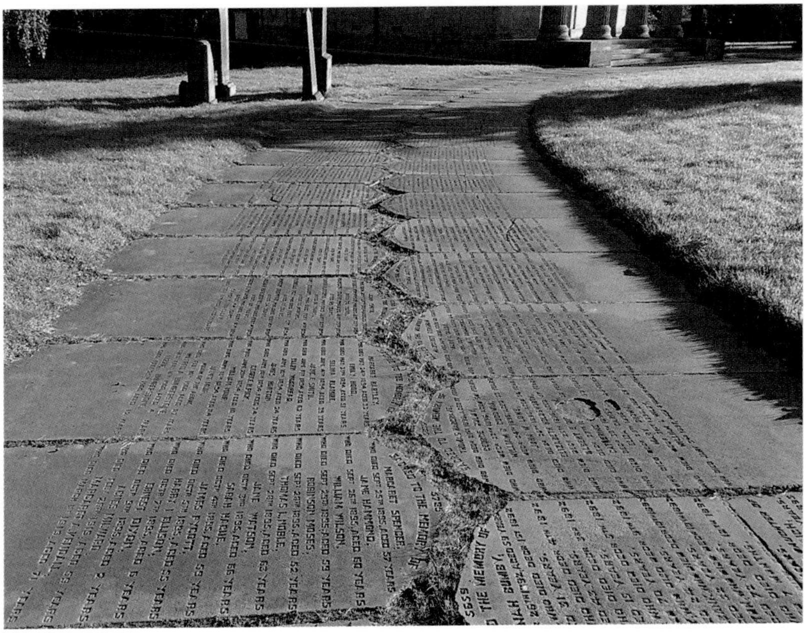

Nearby in Leeds is Eric Gill's controversial First World War memorial, which embodies a type emphasising the horizontal over the vertical, to be seen also in some of Charles Sargent Jagger's friezes and in the work of **Tyson Smith** at Liverpool. All three sought ways in which to commemorate the Great War. In Liverpool the great length of the monument allows for a commonality of address; it is notionally democratic, and the apparent endlessness of the two friezes (each thirty-one feet across) connotes the impossibility of describing the awful narrative of that which is commemorated, which has no clear beginning or end. This also reflects wider official thinking, which tended away from the outdoor monument and towards a Hall of Remembrance, with mural panels appropriate to the massed detail of warfare. This is a non-hierarchical monument in which the address is almost filmic, certainly walked out rather than stationary, as much haptic as visual. This graphic approach to the modern memorial was most famously to be developed by Maya Lin in her monument to commemorate the dead of the Vietnam War, where the shallow inscriptions are traced out by individual mourners.

108. Design by Lionel Budden with bronze reliefs by Tyson Smith, Liverpool Cenotaph, 1926–30

horizontal

The notion of a ceremonial walkway in stone goes back to the Cyclopean wall of the pre-classical period, a concept reprised in the mid-twentieth century by architects in search of an alternative to classicising monumentality, as with Gunnar Asplund in Sweden and José Luis Sert around the Mediterranean. Something of that random ceremonial is harnessed by Richard Long in his stone walkways, and indeed in his simple walks over the land.

However, in Long's earliest works, such as the **stick piece** made in his first show at the Konrad Fischer Gallery in 1968, the focus is more fundamentally on the floor than on the walk. Such loose configurations of an image held together by its inaccessibility were pushed further by William Turnbull, Garth Evans, Daryl Viner and Tony Cragg in their work between the 1960s and the 1980s, pushing sculpture to its shallowest, hugging the floor.

109. Richard Long, *Untitled*, 1968

...

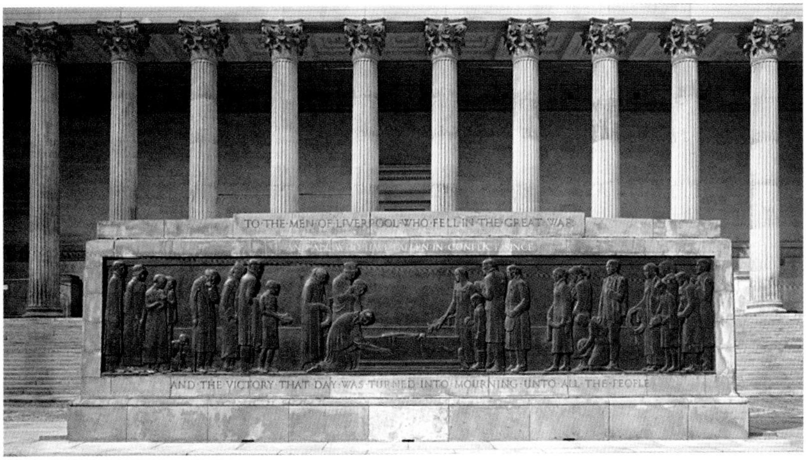
TO THE MEN OF LIVERPOOL WHO FELL IN THE GREAT WAR
AND THE VICTORY THAT DAY WAS TURNED INTO MOURNING UNTO ALL THE PEOPLE

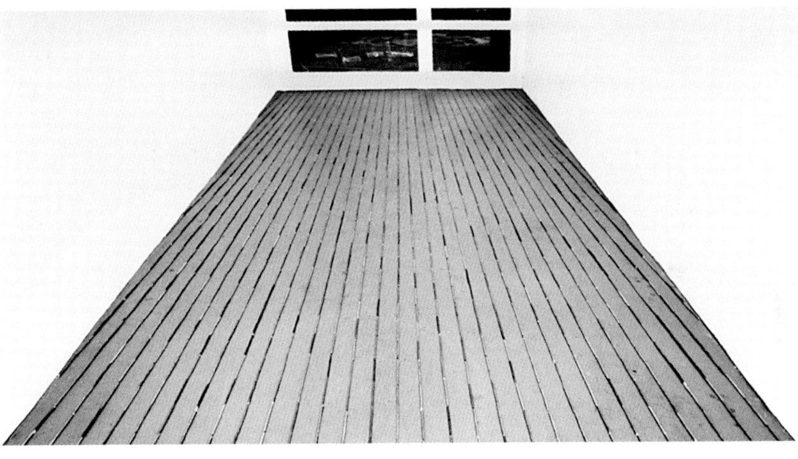

Around 1990 **Bethan Huws** made three floor pieces, each for a different gallery in London, Bern and Frankfurt. Each was made in oak or beech parquet, and was seventeen centimetres high, the height of an average step. They were made to fit snugly into the rooms as found, and to blend with or complement the existing flooring. They presented a floor as a special place.

The vertical and the horizontal, the marker and the marked, both congregate around the subject of death. But these horizontal forms, typified by **Richard Long**'s *Line Made by Walking*, mark the body and the land, and tend towards depression, so that the body seems to seek the ground.[25] Far from the upright marker standing out against the sky, these forms are closer to the fabric of their environment, and claim a kind of absorption, and even a right of return.

110. Bethan Huws, *Riverside Piece*, 1989

horizontal

111. Richard Long, *A Line Made by Walking*, 1967

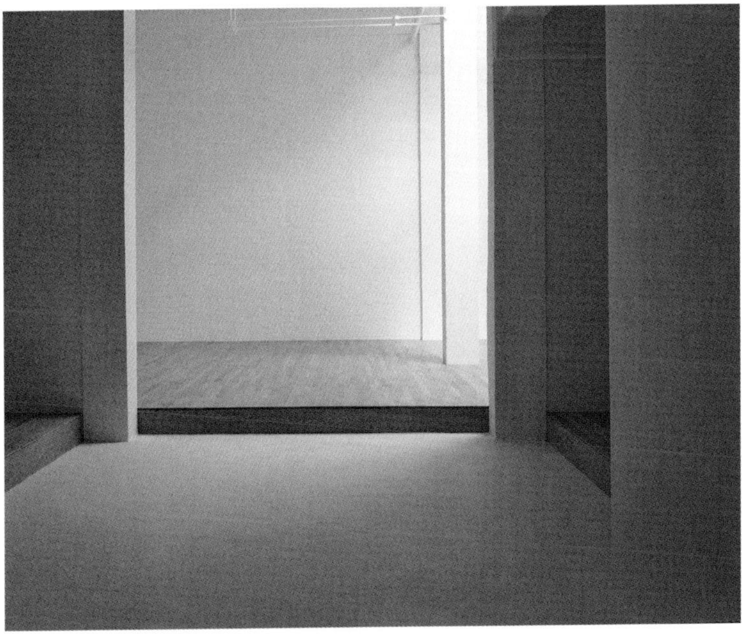

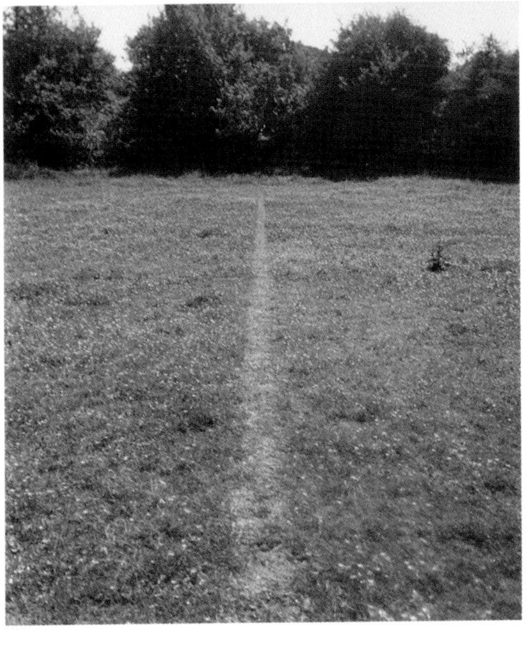

closed

iii

closed

Looking at sculpture that is closed necessarily juxtaposes exterior with interior, entailing the idea of content, or that which is enclosed. Proposing that something is inside a sculpture usually suggests that it is protecting something precious. Being made of hard and durable materials, sculpture lends itself to the container form, and the contained brings with it its own vocabulary of meaning and association.

- - -

In Harry Bates's ***Pandora***, the kneeling girl holds an ivory casket, which remains closed. (The fact that the story of Pandora is normally focused on the opening of the box makes its closedness here more significant.) The contrast between the materials – the marble figure with an ivory box – makes that box more box-like. On its **lid** is a reclining figure, supported by a charioteer holding the reins of a leaping horse; a **frieze** works its way around the sides, and upright bronze figures of Mercury guard the corners. Bronze also demarcates the lock. The frieze shows the fashioning of the statue of Pandora herself; the lid her transit from Olympus.[1]

...

112. Harry Bates, *Pandora*, 1890

113. Harry Bates, lid of the ivory casket from *Pandora*, 1890

114. Harry Bates, frieze on the ivory casket from *Pandora*, 1890

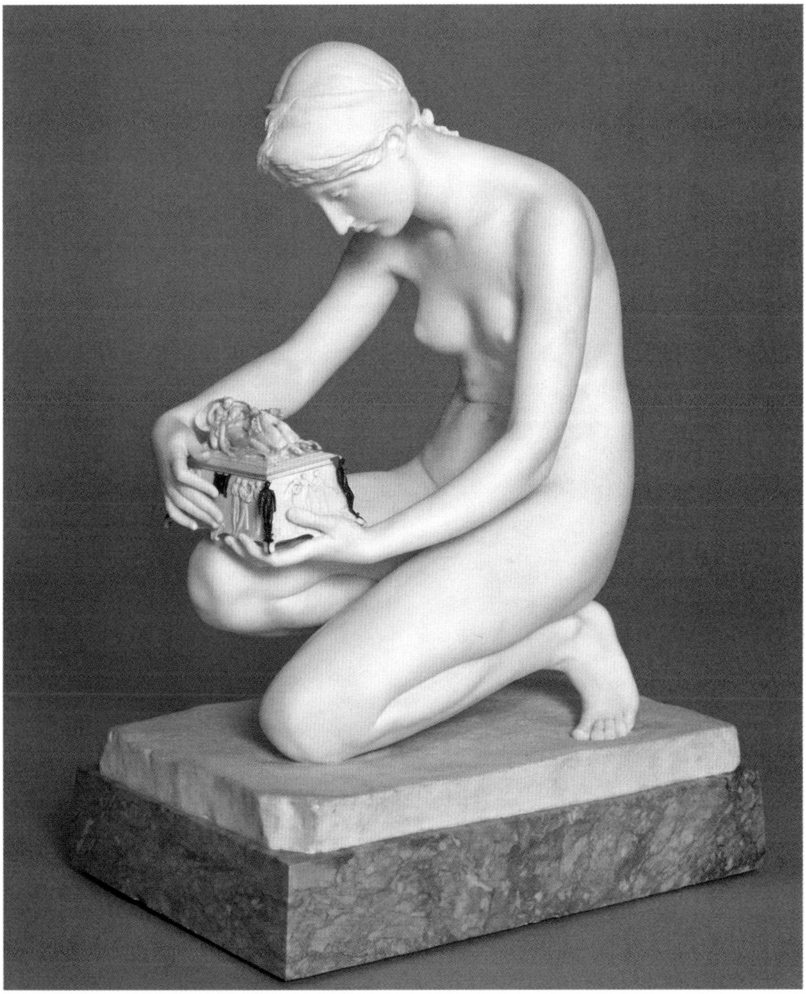

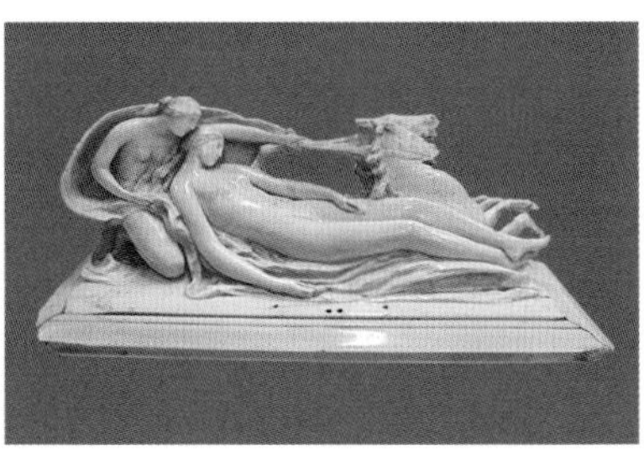

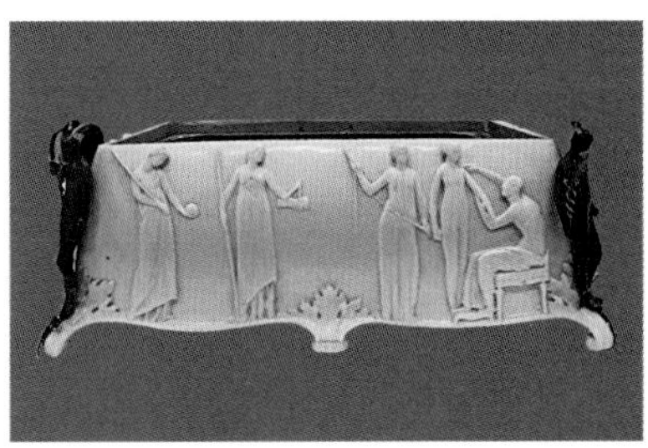

The common story of Pandora inevitably tells us that the casket must contain the ills of the world, even if its decorative surface simply depicts the story of the statue. If we saw the casket instead as akin to a reliquary, the form of which it does indeed resemble, we might understand in a slightly different way the relationship between interior and exterior: the mourner (pleurant) who supports or watches over the tomb, and the tomb chest with its figurative representation. (The casket might even be seen to contain ashes.) The marble girl kneels, absorbed in her care for the box, unlike her ivory representation, in which she is merely an object.

The underlying form of the casket is perhaps more obvious in **John Gibson**'s version, which contrasts clothed woman with plain box. Reliquaries themselves are similar in form to the tomb and exchange signification with it; they are often covered with scenes from the lives of the saints whose relics they contain. This is not unlike Bates's or Gibson's *Pandora*, and would suggest that we see her box in a different way, as if containing the relics of the statue turned woman, now turned statue again.

...

115. John Gibson, *Pandora*, 1856

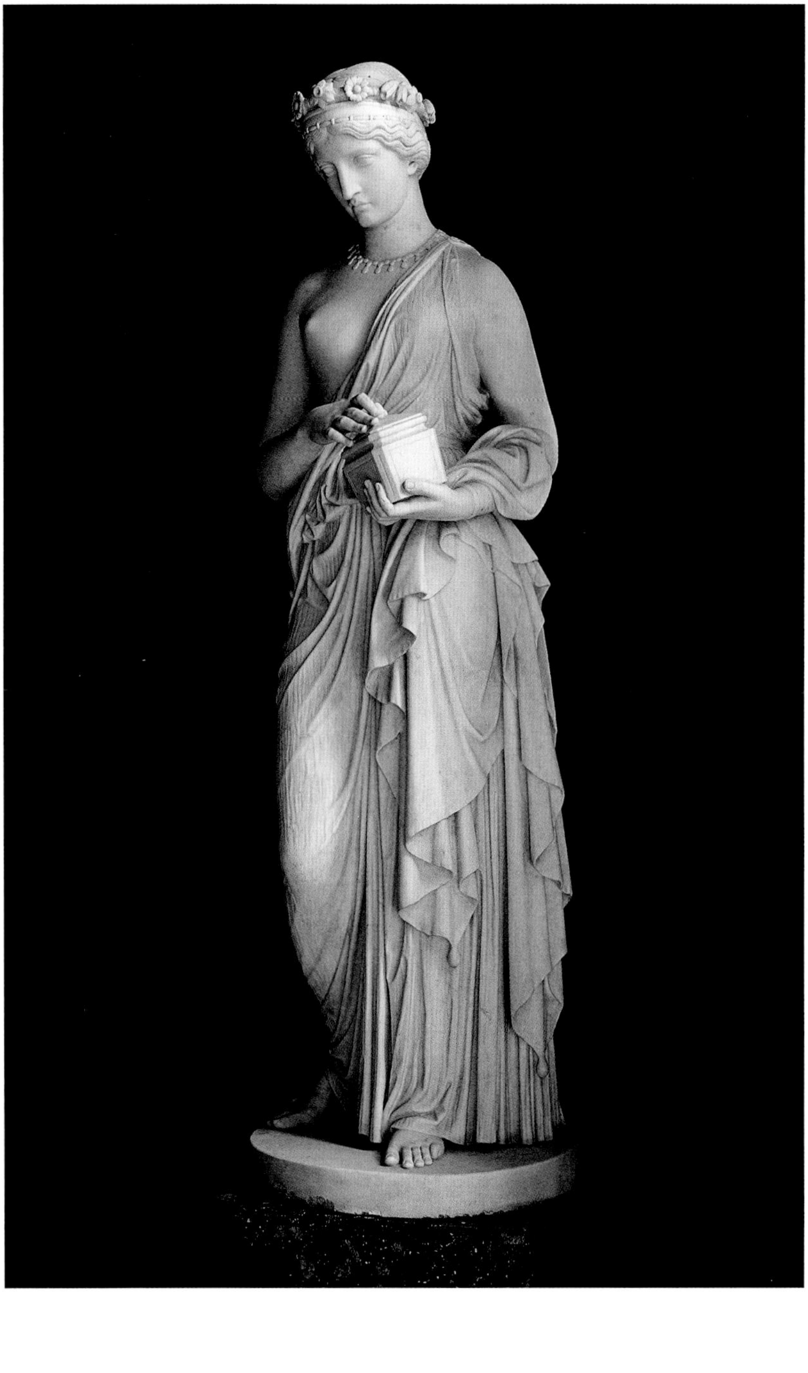

Until the late Middle Ages it was customary for relics to be hidden from sight within the closed box. A remarkable eighth-century reliquary, associated with **Monymusk** House in Aberdeenshire, in silver and bronze-plated wood, has lost all its narrative iconography (believed to have denoted St Columba) but the form is clear. A probably English example is the reliquary casket with scenes from the martyrdom of **Thomas Becket** at the Metropolitan Museum in New York, and a French example is the **Becket Casket** in the Victoria and Albert Museum, both made within a generation of his murder in 1170. The life of the saint is depicted around the box like a frieze (like *Pandora*).[2] The shrine to Thomas Becket was one of the first to be targeted in the Dissolution of the Monasteries, and its actual form is only recorded in various souvenirs, an important one being the Metropolitan Museum's pewter **pilgrim badge**, with the gable shrine above the tomb and the effigy.[3] The doubling or tripling that is so common in funerary furniture is clearly demonstrated here, with the figurative image, its actual resting place and its representative resting place in reciprocal relation.

...

116. Monymusk reliquary, c.8th century

117. Reliquary casket with scenes from the Martyrdom of Saint Thomas Becket, c.1173–80

118. Becket Casket, c.1180–90

119. Pilgrim's badge of the shrine of Saint Thomas Becket at Canterbury, 1350–1400

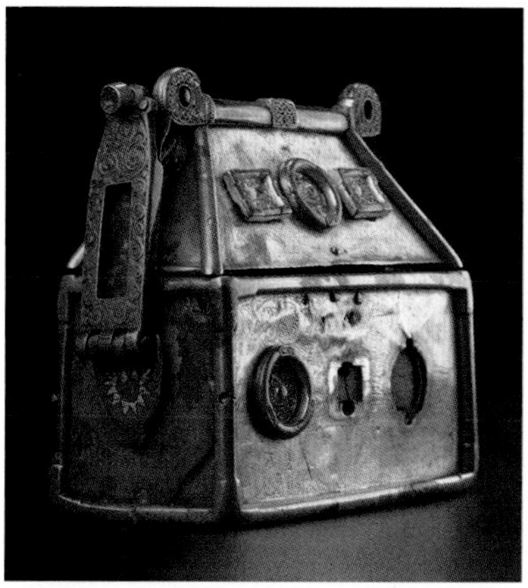

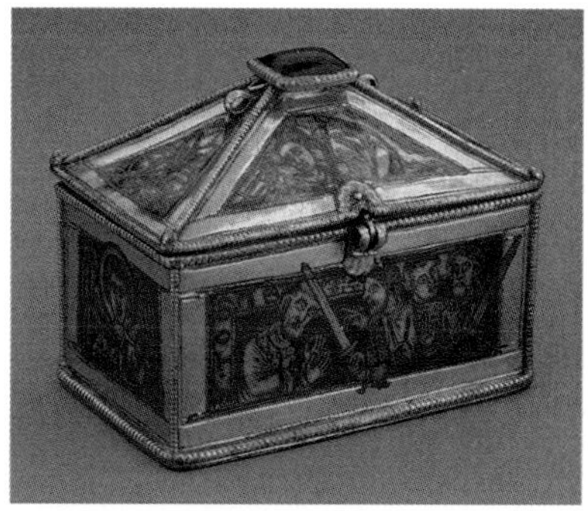

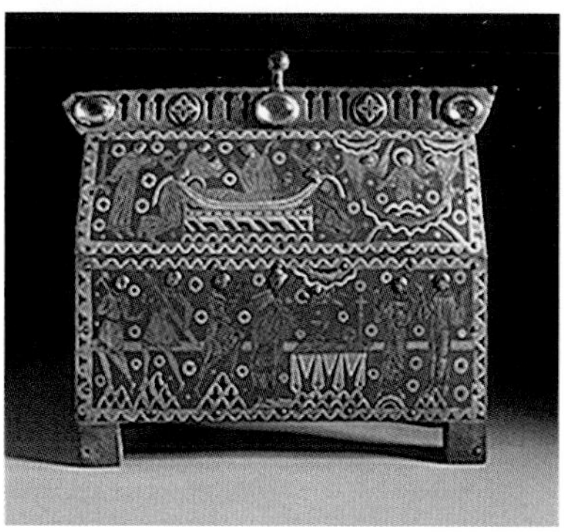

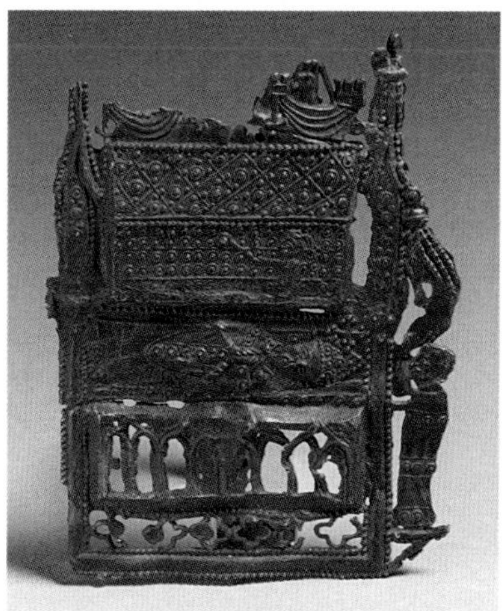

The late sixteenth-century tomb to the lawyer **Robert Kelway** shows both the defunct and, in front of him, a reprise in the form of his grandchild, lying on a little box; an admixture of coffin, coffer, bed and plinth. A similar profile is evident, three hundred years later, in Alfred Gilbert's tomb for the **Duke of Clarence**. His model for the royal tomb, dating from the outset of his commission in 1892, is reminiscent of the *Pandora* casket (which was made only two years earlier).

...

120. Detail of monument to Robert Kelway and the Harrington Family, 16th century

121. Alfred Gilbert, model for tomb of Prince Albert Victor, Duke of Clarence and Avondale, 1892

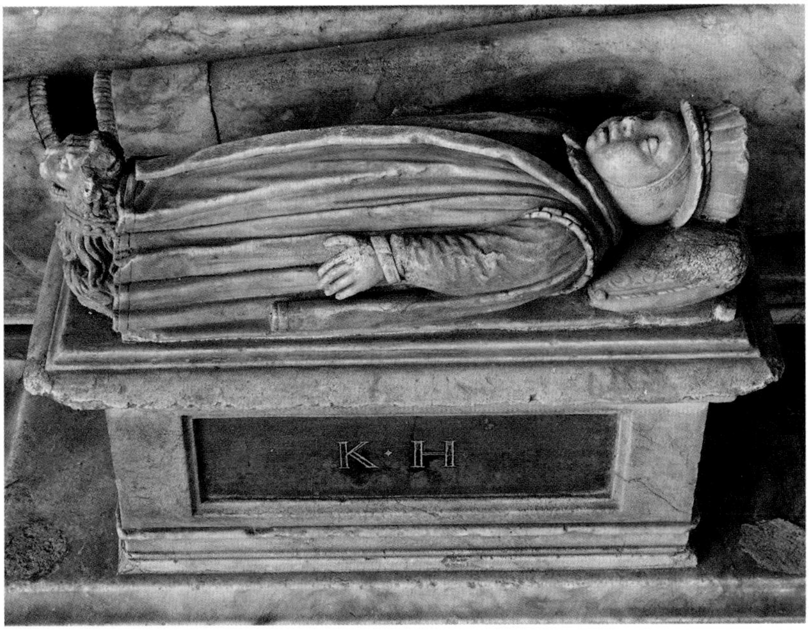
K·H

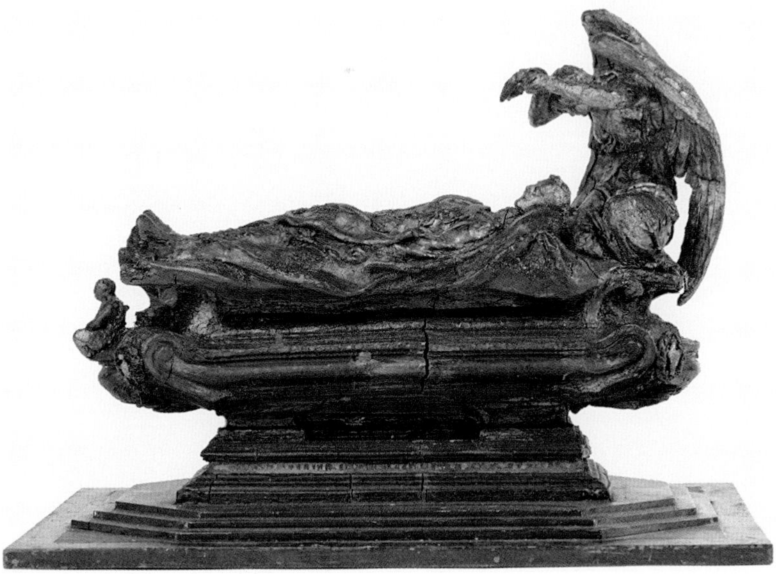

The notion of the box and its content has been a rich one in twentieth-century sculpture. Marcel Duchamp is perhaps the most obvious example of an artist who helped to make a cult object out of the box, but we might cite also John Latham, whose ***Art & Culture*** touches very closely on the reliquary. In this case the relics of Clement Greenberg's eponymous text are preserved but no longer accessible. A similar approach was taken in the 1970s by Clive Barker when he asked twelve artists to burn their paintings so that he could put the ashes into wooden caskets. Richard Hamilton, David Hockney and Joe Tilson agreed.

- - -

closed

122. John Latham, *Art & Culture*, 1966

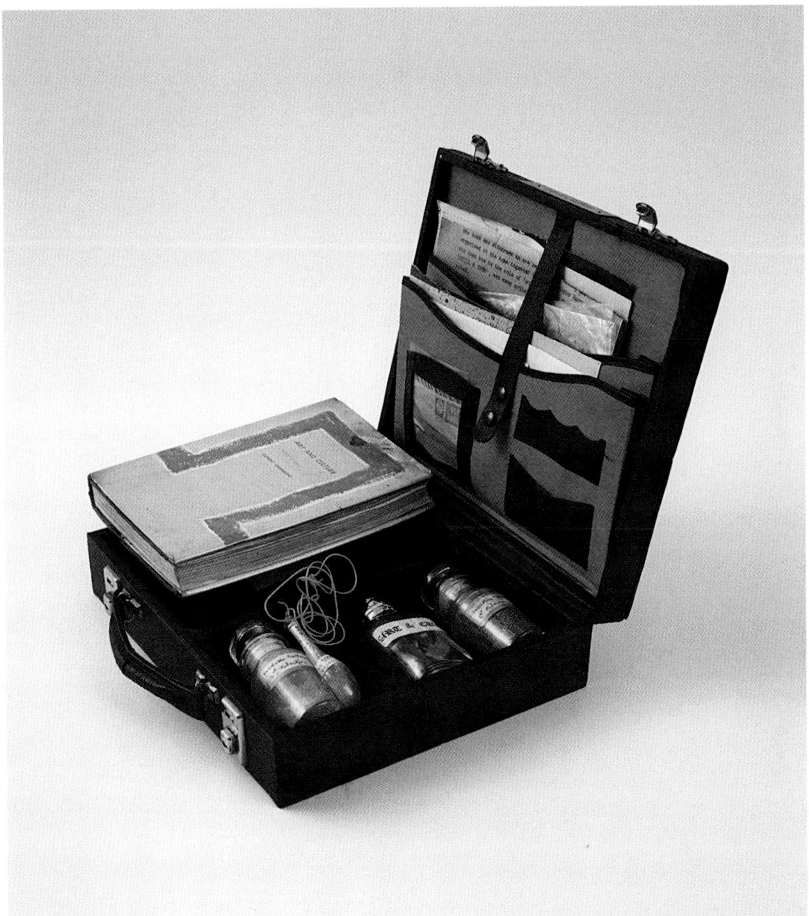

From the twelfth century reliquaries increasingly came to mimic the body parts that they carried (even if there was a mixture of parts and from different sources), and might combine, as in the case of the **Saint Eustace Head reliquary**, both reliquary box and head, in which metal sheets are beaten over a wooden head-shaped core. There is a sense of the medieval reliquary in George Frampton's ***Lamia***, in which bronze and opals encase the bodily core, set apart in ivory. The fact that the Victoria and Albert Museum holds a plaster mask that seems to be a preparatory piece for *Lamia* heightens the interiority that we sense in this work, as if the body might really be inside.[4]

...

123. Saint Eustace Head reliquary, 1180–1200

124. George Frampton, *Lamia*, 1900

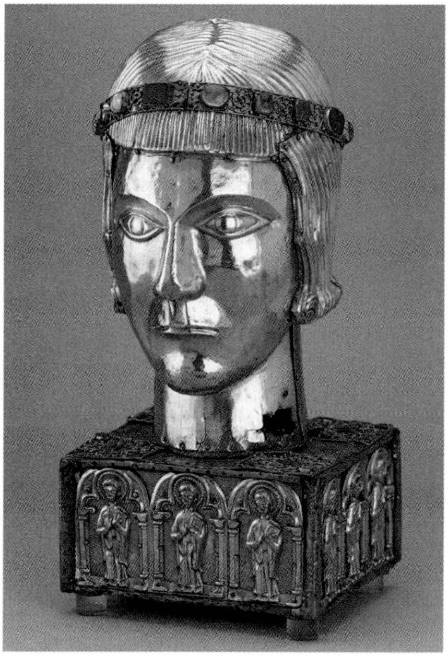

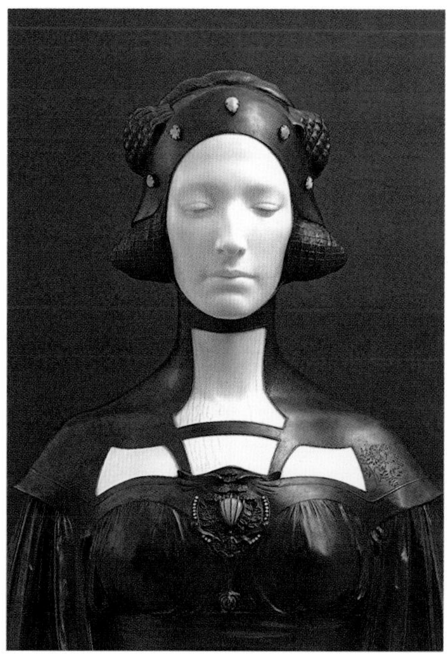

A similarly medieval wrapping of metal, in this instance simply lead, and around twenty-four everyday objects of little value, is the key to the appeal of Antony Gormley's ***Natural Selection***, in which the inner cores are conserved in an inert and timeless state. Gormley may have started with inanimate objects, but made his name with the wrappings of his own body, in which he continued to foster connections with an earlier tradition.

...

125. Antony Gormley, *Natural Selection*, 1981

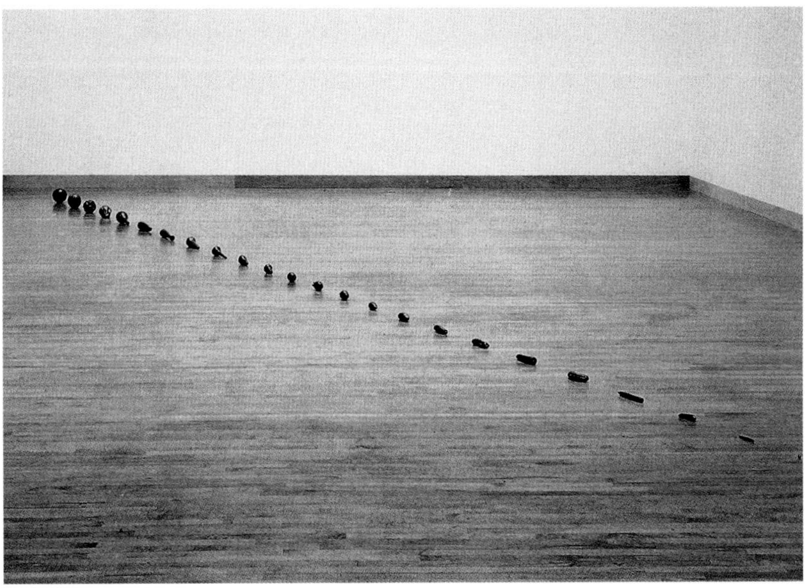

The wrapping of the physical features of the human body is clearly at play in the death masks made from the sixteenth century onwards. **Henry VII**'s effigy at Westminster Abbey has plural sources: the bust in the Victoria and Albert Museum and the face of the effigy being so similar that both must derive from the same cast, and were probably made by the same sculptor, Pietro Torrigiano.[5] Death masks were at first limited to the exceptionally powerful, notably monarchs. Oliver Cromwell's effigy (1658) was exhibited,[6] and marks a shift from sacred to secular viewing. Thereafter they were more often made of the talented (such as John Keats and William Blake), and ultimately of victims and criminals. Oddly enough artists often made the masks of other artists, even though one might think this was a merely technical job. John Michael Rysbrack may have done Newton, Benjamin Robert Haydon did **Keats**, Samuel Joseph, Constable, and Thomas Woolner, Turner.

...

126. Henry VII's death mask, 1509

127. Benjamin Robert Haydon, plaster cast of the life mask of John Keats, 1816

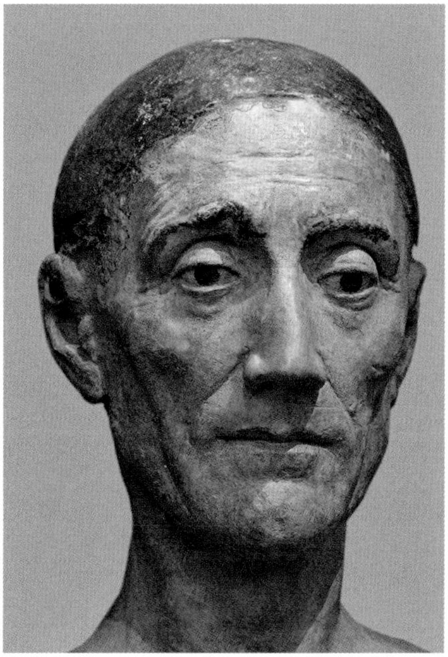

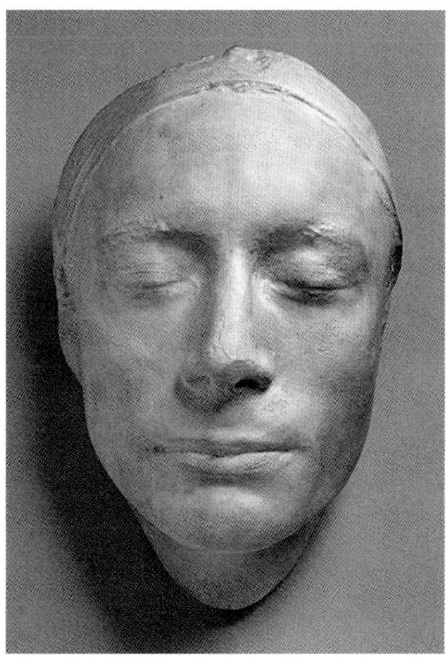

Even odder is the transformation of mask to bust, as is the case with **Samuel Johnson**. More common, as with Cromwell, Newton and Constable, is that the mask remains clearly a mask, but there was also a habit of making medallions or other compositions out of them, as with George Frampton's mask of Herbert Beerbohm Tree (1918), the remarkable mask of **Thomas Lawrence** and Reuben Townroe's mask of Alfred Stevens (1875). Such artfulness seems almost to deny the plain evidence; to make art out of science, something living out of something dead, and indeed there is here an odd area of crossover between factual documentation and creative artifice.

...

128. William Cumberland Cruikshank and James Hoskins, plaster cast of a bust incorporating the death mask of Samuel Johnson, 1784

129. Death mask cast in plaster of Thomas Lawrence, 1830

closed

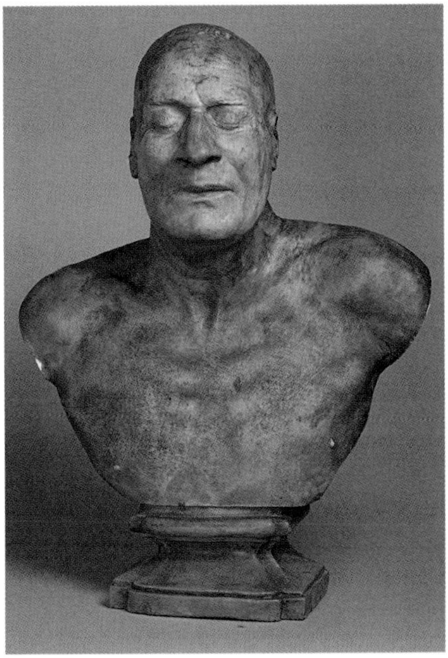

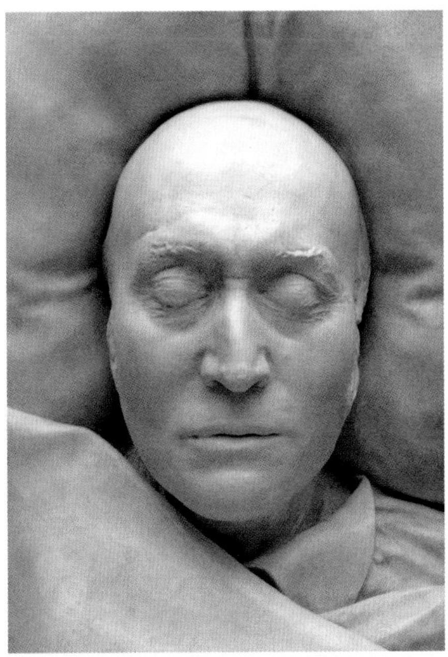

The box, casket or urn contains, or may rather serve to remind us of what is not contained. The word 'cabinet' is used in seventeenth-century inscriptions, and links to the 'jewel' or 'gem' which is variously present or absent. The tomb of Anne Littleton, who died in 1623 and is buried in London's Temple, reads:

> Keep well this pawne, thou marble chest
> Till it be call'd for, let it rest:
> For while this Jewell here is set,
> The grave is but a Cabinet.[7]

The ***Inner Eye*** maquette by Lynn Chadwick holds a glass nugget, as if it too were a cross between a physical and a human treasury. In the 1980s Eric Bainbridge enlarged and covered a number of everyday forms in fake fur; ***Sugar***, a box for an engagement ring, suggests its sentimental heart has been somehow frozen deep within its monumental casing.

Medieval reliquaries were designed to protect and carry the relics of the saints. Later reliquaries increasingly made visible the relics, and these too used the human body as support, as with a fifteenth-century figure of a **monk** found in London. The container is no longer so much a container as a support for the 'content'.

...

130. Lynn Chadwick, *Inner Eye (Maquette III)*, 1952

131. Eric Bainbridge, *Sugar*, 1989

132. Reliquary figure of a Benedictine monk with a heart-shaped orifice in its breast for a relic, 15th century

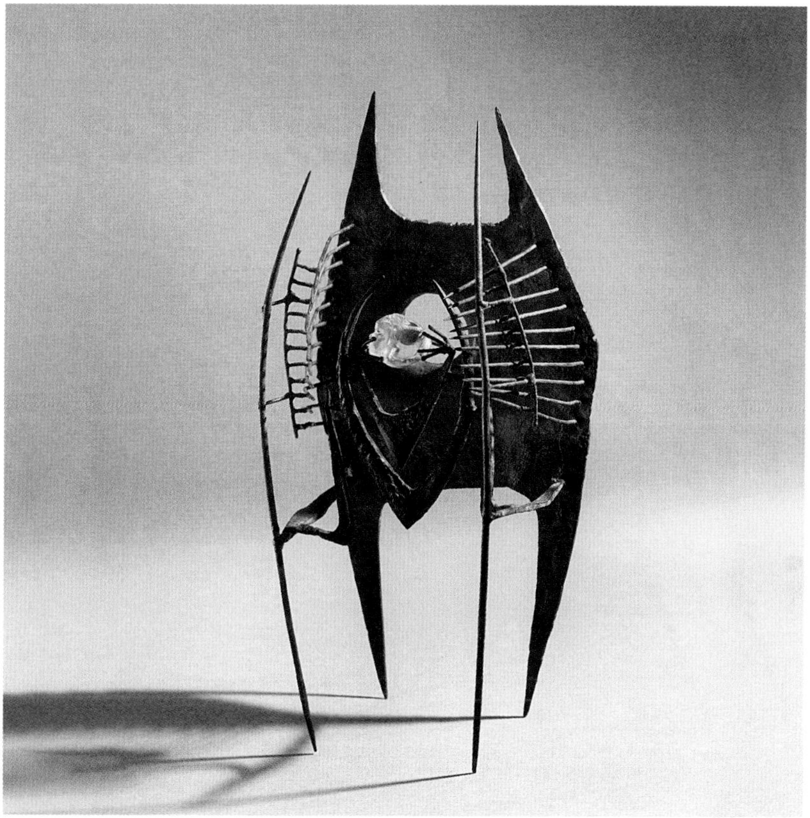

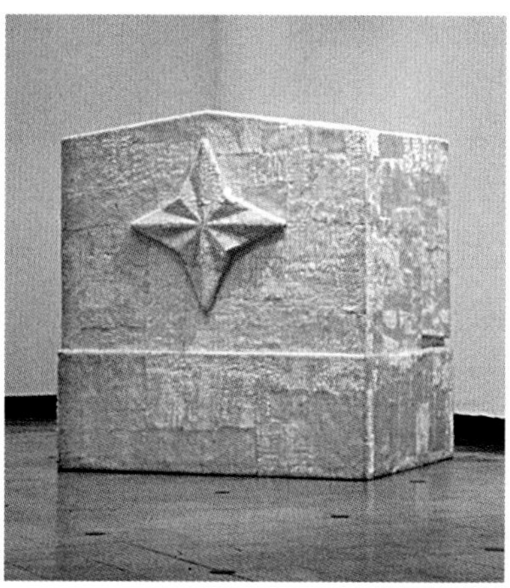

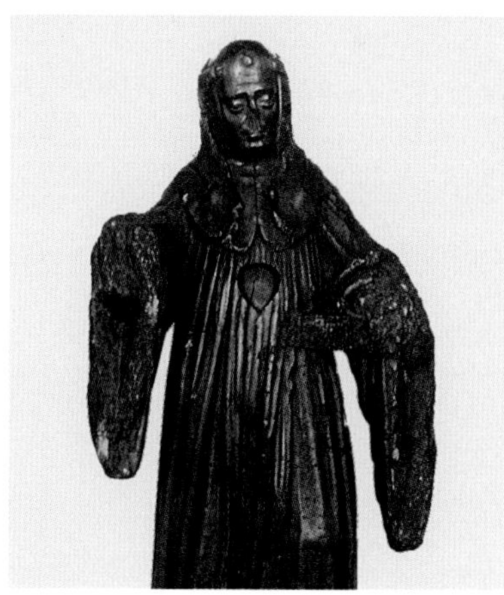

The reliquary or sarcophagus form persists in the rare examples of Easter Sepulchres to survive the Reformation, especially in the free-standing wooden chests as found, apparently, at **Coity**, Glamorgan, and at Copthorpe, Yorkshire, both of which date from c.1500. During the Good Friday ceremony, a crucifix was wrapped and laid in such a sepulchre (normally made of wood), and then on a tomb to the north of the altar (very often expressly positioned there by its patron). The door was shut, or the curtain drawn, until Easter Sunday.[8] In this sense these containers were only briefly 'reliquaries', and might more accurately be seen as places of transformation.

---

closed

133. Easter Sepulchre at Coity, c.1500

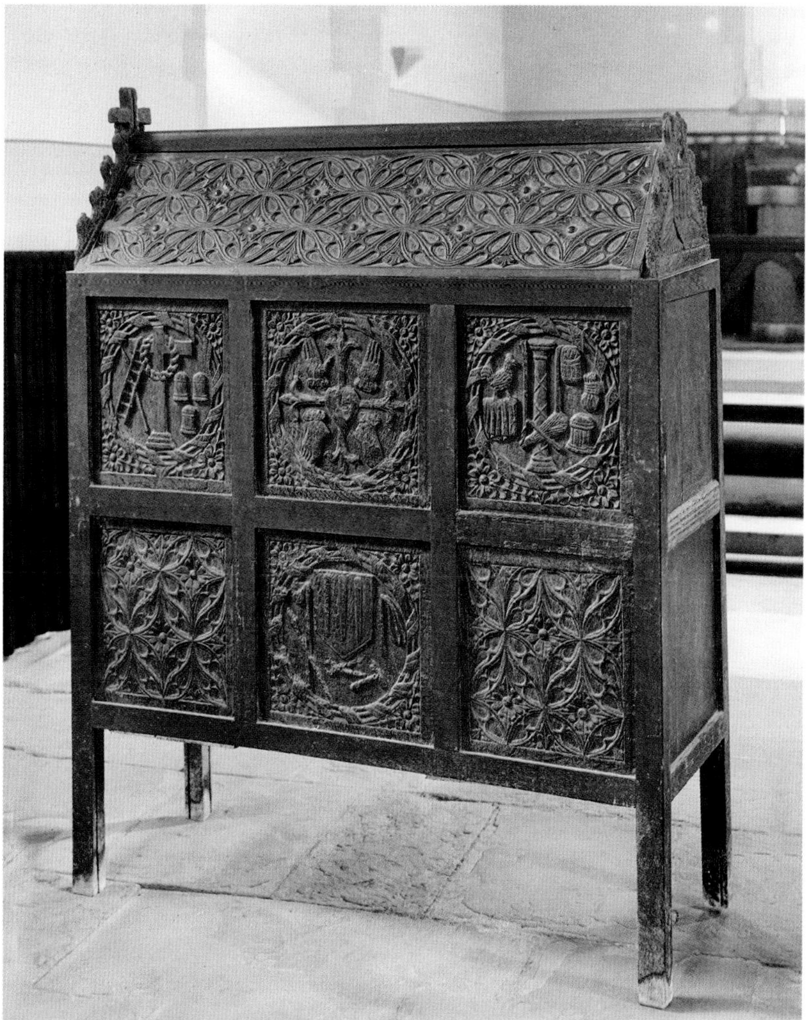

Later examples of funerary furniture often use the profile of the reliquary, whether or not they house the relic. Nonetheless, though they have largely become empty boxes, they are still representative of the body, and return us of course to their origins, in the **sarcophagus** form found most famously in Ancient Egypt, Japan and the Mediterranean basin, but also in much simpler versions such as this late third- or fourth-century example from London.

Tomb chests in this form are known to exist from the medieval period, but are very few in number; they only become common in the 1600s. The hollowness of the tomb chest is an obvious testimony to what is lost, and the altar is a clear echo. The inscription, the words, speak of the absent body. The chest, purporting to contain some kind of treasure, is empty.

The tomb chest to **Sir Thomas and Katherine Moyle** shows the shields of arms of the defunct. The representative scale of the chest suggests the bodies of the departed, and signs indicate their status. Their actual bodies, we presume, were once below the chest, but they are not represented on its exterior. The shields, as in life, might be read as defending or protecting the mortal body within, but rather defend its status than its material being.

...

134. Sarcophagus, early 4th century

135. Tomb chest monument to Sir Thomas Moyle and his wife Katherine, 1560

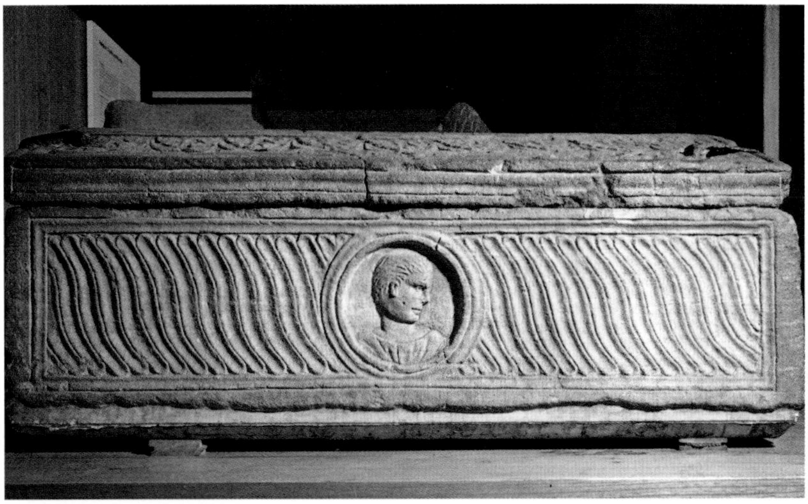

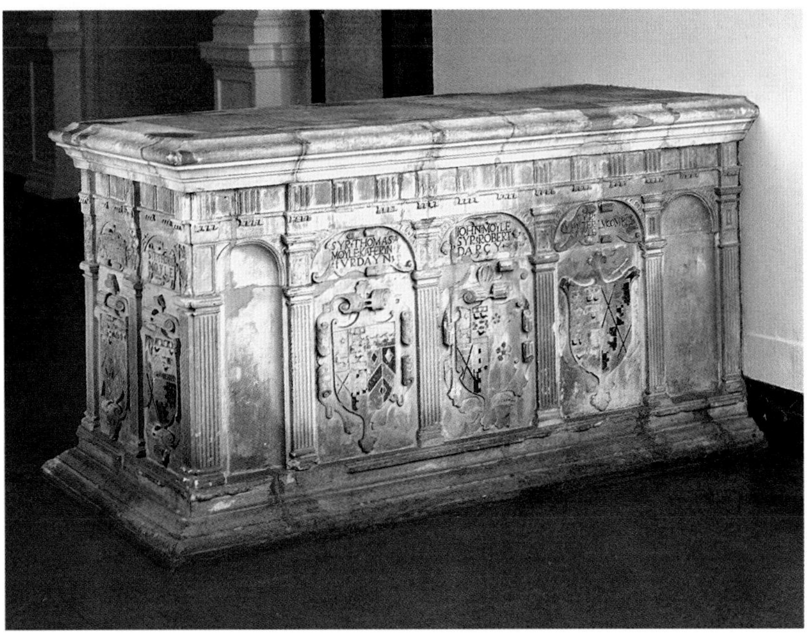
SYR·THOMAS MOYLE·KATERIN CVRDAYN
JOHN·MOYLE SYR·ROBERT DARCY

Very close in date is the monument to the second **Earl of Huntingdon**, with a similar but more beautiful use of the shield along the sides of the chest, which effectively supports the effigies that now lie above. Being housed within the church, such tomb chests have an elaboration uncommon in the churchyard, where the emptiness of the chest itself can be more strikingly apparent.

...

136. Tomb of Francis Hastings, 2nd Earl of Huntingdon, 1561

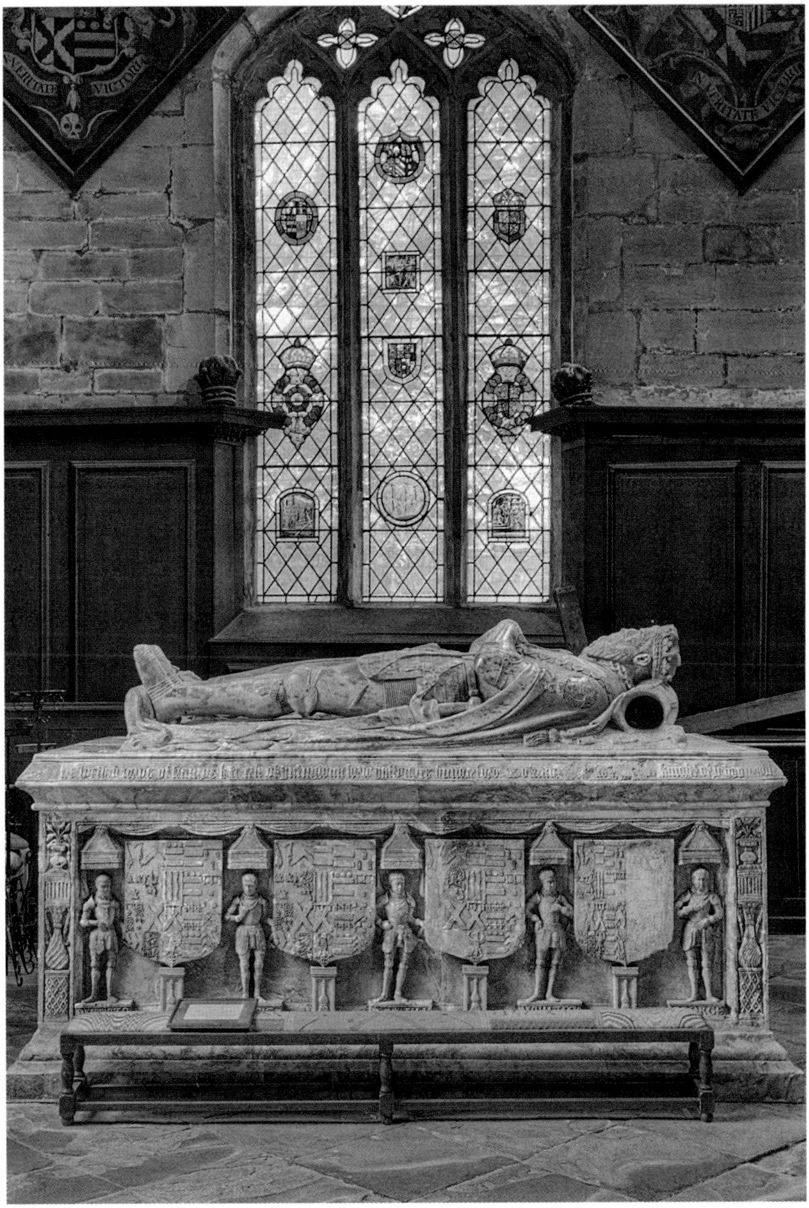

As we move into the eighteenth century, with its increasing reliance on Roman prototypes and accounts (notably Pliny and Polybius), we find a type of tomb that both refers to the boxes in which Roman families kept their family likenesses, medals and accessories, and to the habit of the female representative bringing them out. Wax effigies were also kept in wooden boxes by distinguished Roman families, and brought out for relevant family funerals.[9] The monument to **Robert Lord Willoughby**, which lifts the sarcophagus onto the altar-like plinth, but allows it to suggest a commemorative pantheon grouped above it and around the urn, is very much like a family shrine.

- - -

137. Monument to Robert Lord Willoughby, 1738

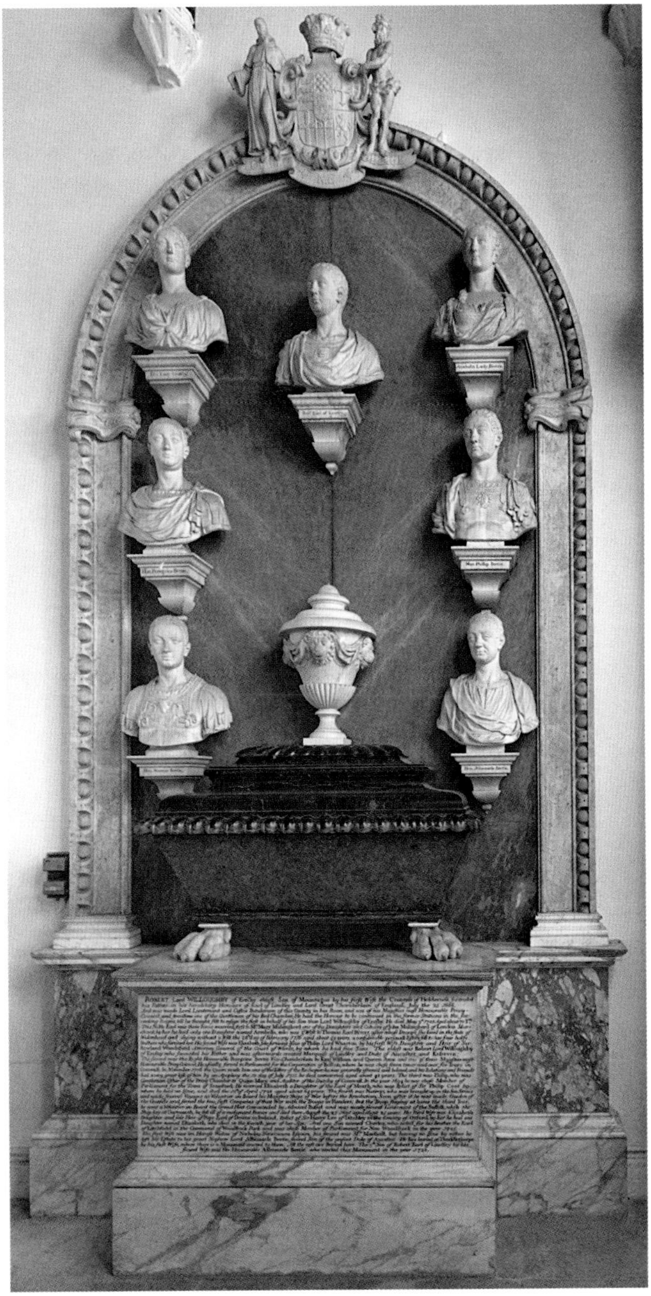

The tomb chest is operationally plausible, whereas the representation of the sarcophagus that begins to appear in British tomb furniture in the eighteenth century is essentially a sign. It is normally figured alone, and well above the earth, acting more like a plinth or altar.[10] A print by **C. F. Greville** celebrates the splendid classical language that collectors such as William Hamilton were able to bring to Britain. A famous example is the monument to the 'English spy' Major John Andre in Westminster Abbey by **Robert Adam**.[11] **John Sell Cotman**'s great and probably invented drawing of a sarcophagus echoes some of the more elaborate designs being produced by his contemporaries. Collectors, architects and artists began thoroughly to reinvent the symbolic potential of the sarcophagus, while retaining, nonetheless, some kind of at least vestigial reference to the deceased body itself, and to its container.

...

138. Charles Francis Greville, frontispiece to accompany a set of five engravings commemorating Sir William Hamilton bringing the Portland Vase to England, 1786

139. Robert Adam, monument to Major John Andre, 1780

140. John Sell Cotman, *Sarcophagus in a Pleasure Garden*, c.1806

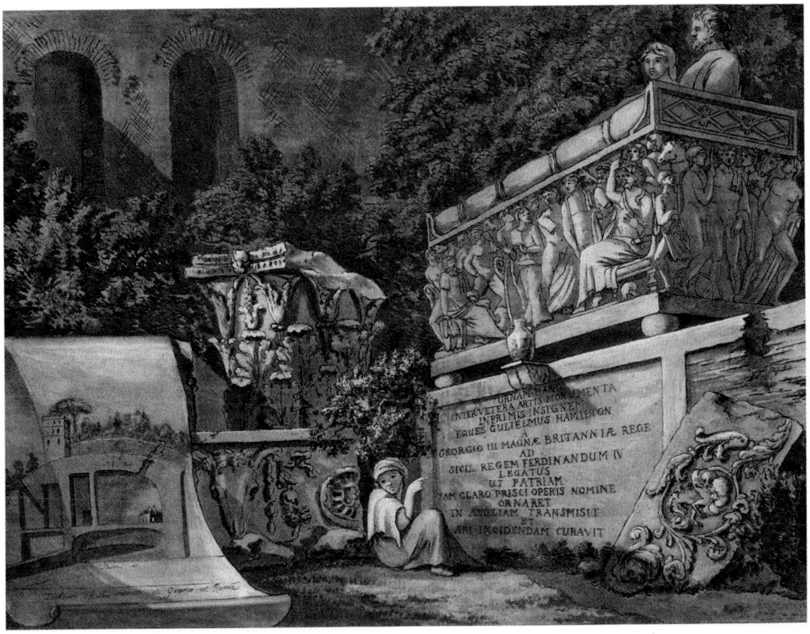
URNAM HANC
INTER VETERA ARTIS MONUMENTA
INPRIMIS INSIGNEM
EQUES GULIELMUS HAMILTON
A
GEORGIO III MAGNÆ BRITANNIÆ REGE
AD
SICIL. REGEM FERDINANDUM IV
LEGATUS
UT PATRIAM
TAM CLARO PRISCI OPERIS NOMINE
ORNARET
IN ANGLIAM TRANSMISIT
ET
AERI INCIDENDAM CURAVIT

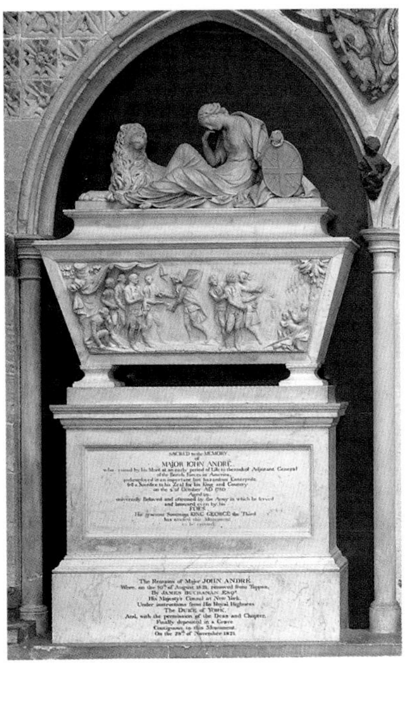
SACRED to the MEMORY
of
MAJOR JOHN ANDRÉ
FOES
The Remains of Major JOHN ANDRÉ
Were, on the 10th of August 1821, removed from Tappan,
By JAMES BUCHANAN Esq.
His Majesty's Consul at New York.
Under instructions from His Royal Highness
The DUKE of YORK.
And, with the permission of the Dean and Chapter,
Finally deposited in a Grave
Contiguous to this Monument
On the 28th of November 1821.

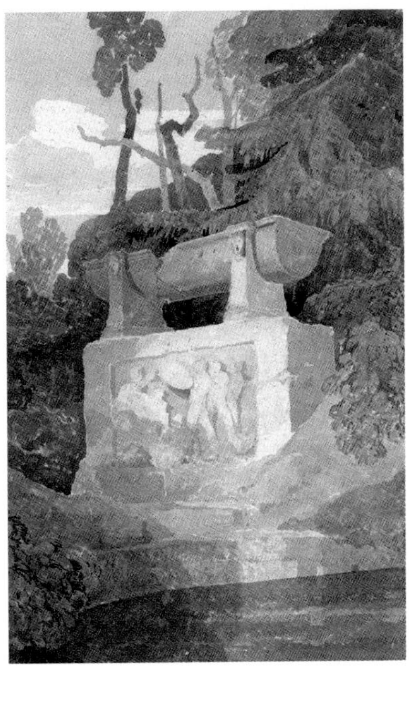

More plainly chest-like is the tomb to **J. M. Whistler**, in Chiswick Churchyard. At the same time Jacob Epstein extends and even caricatures the concept of the tomb chest, firstly in his monument to Oscar Wilde (see p. 177), and more clearly in his monument to **W. H. Hudson**, where he seems to pick up the notion of the tomb chest while recognising the absence of the body; using instead the sides of the chest to represent the Rima figure of Hudson's creation, with echoes also of the *Aphrodite* bas-relief on the Ludovisi Throne (c.460 BC) in its iconography.

...

closed

141. Edward Godwin, monument to James McNeill Whistler, 1912

142. Jacob Epstein, W. H. Hudson Memorial (Rima), 1923–5

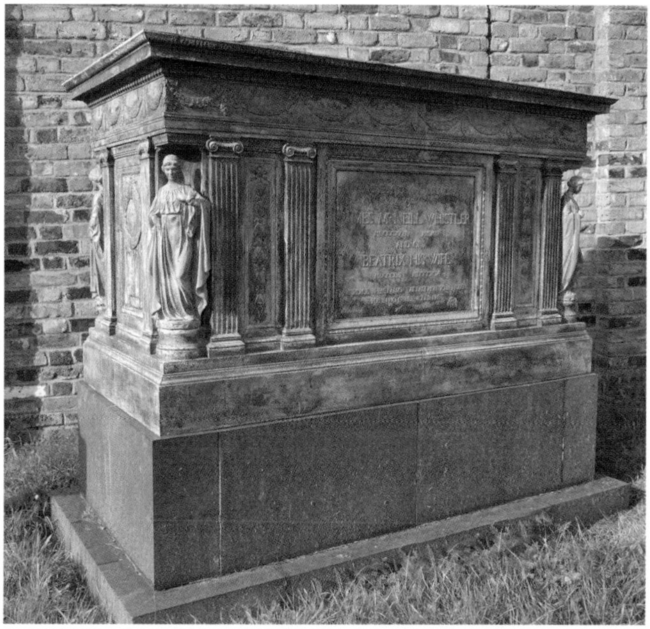

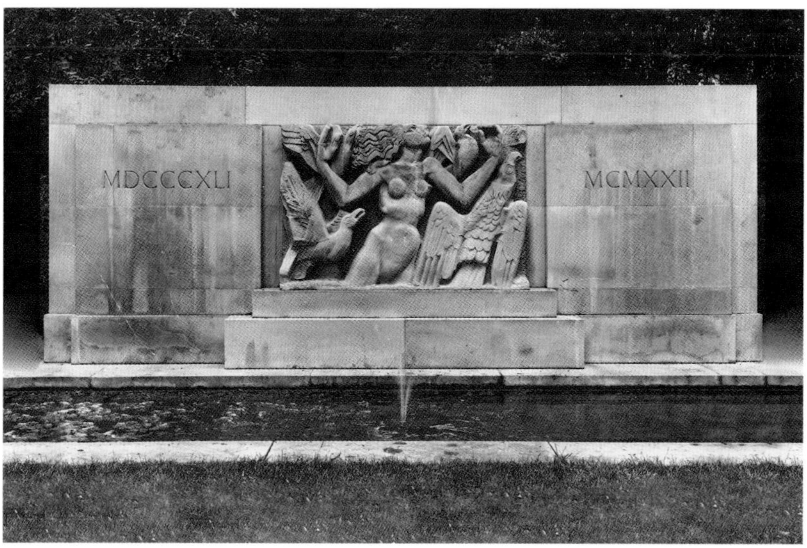
MDCCCXLI
MCMXXII

The rectilinear tomb chest is, I would argue, clearly present as an archetypal sculptural form. This may account for some of the power of post-war works, notably in America, which rely on the massive but hollow form, as with Tony Smith, Donald Judd and Richard Serra.[12] Among Minimalist artists, Robert Morris moves most overtly towards the figure, and even the coffin, in works he made for himself to perform in, such as ***Box for Standing*** of 1961. This enigmatic prop has recently been brought to life by Gerard Byrne in his film *A Thing is a Hole in a Thing it is Not*. Byrne also re-made Morris's *Column*, and the performance too, in which a box falls over on stage at a closely monitored signal. In the film's loop, the box falls over again and again.

Rachel Whiteread's ***Monument*** played cleverly on these combined traditions. Reliquary, tomb and chest, conveyed within the form of the plinth itself, a new monument to an unknown warrior or, indeed, another empty cenotaph, it has an auratic quality not unlike Cotman's imaginary sketch.

- - -

143. Robert Morris, *Untitled (Box for Standing)*, 1961

144. Rachel Whiteread, *Monument*, 2001

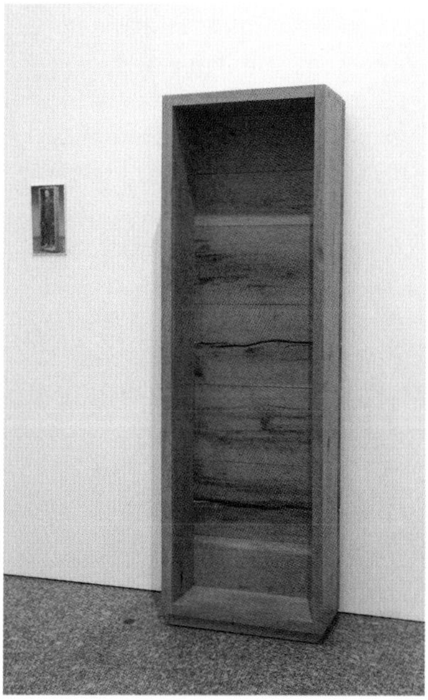

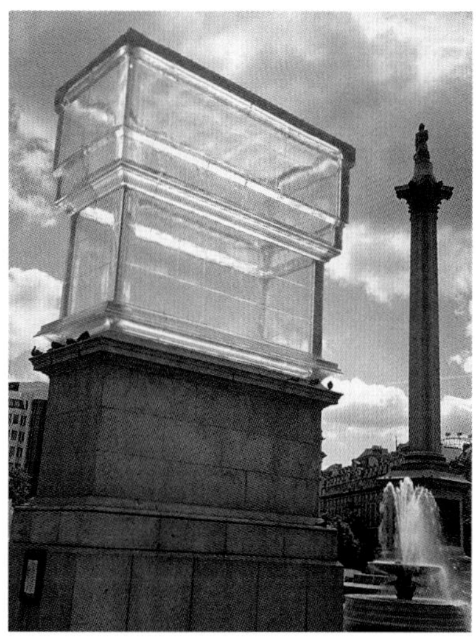

In Germany Joseph Beuys regularly used the box, but also allowed the vitrine to suggest the coffin, as in ***Das Paar*** in which two plaster figures, male and female, lie in the base of the box, apparently preserved indefinitely. They remind us again of Giuseppe Fiorelli's casts in the museum in Pompeii, where single figures are shown in glass boxes, as if, perhaps, awaiting their resurrection. The transition of the reliquary box from church to museum is achieved. A similar transition is effected at Westminster Abbey, where the wax effigies of certain families, once placed by their tombs, now reside in the museum. Though Charles II had not been represented by a funeral effigy, his **wax memorial figure** was kept in a vitrine or press, and the Duchess of Richmond expressed her wish that her wax effigy be 'put in a presse by itself distincte from the other with cleare crowne glasse before it'.[13]

...

145. Joseph Beuys, *Das Paar*, 1952/53

146. Wax memorial figure of Charles II, 1685

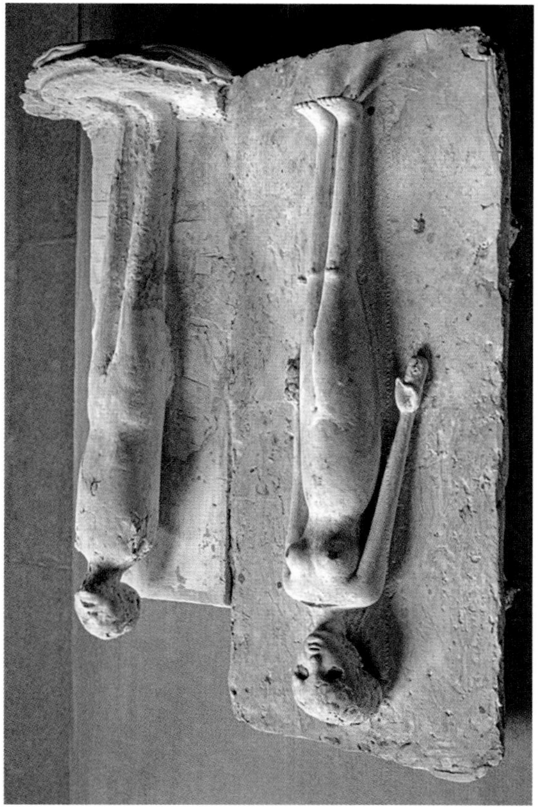

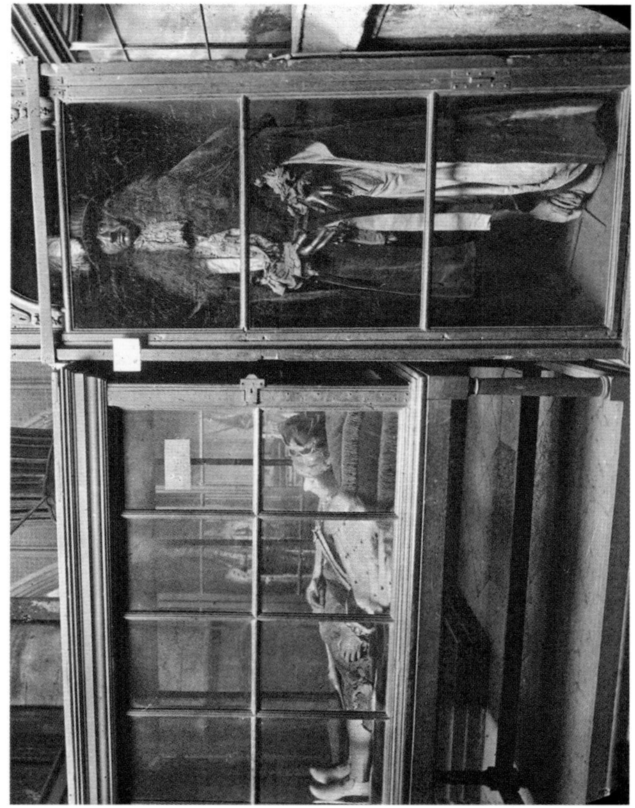

Damien Hirst too has always suggested the traces of human activity and exposed them to view. Works such as ***A Thousand Years*** introduced the duality for which he has become famous, but which goes back, arguably, to join a long tradition of commemoration, in which certain human artefacts are selected, sealed and indefinitely protected. Other artists, such as Julian Opie and Liam Gillick, have used transparent walls to suggest the vitrine or shelter, but usually without Hirst's overt references to life and death. An exception might be Darren Almond's two opposing bus shelters, ***Terminus***, which makes reference at one and the same time to the vitreous shelter and to their departure or alighting point: Auschwitz.

...

147. Damien Hirst, *A Thousand Years*, 1990

148. Darren Almond, *Terminus*, 1999

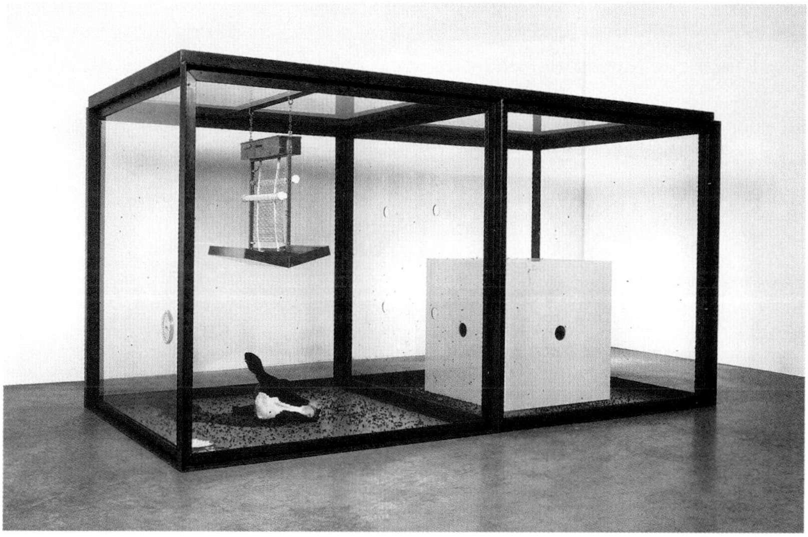

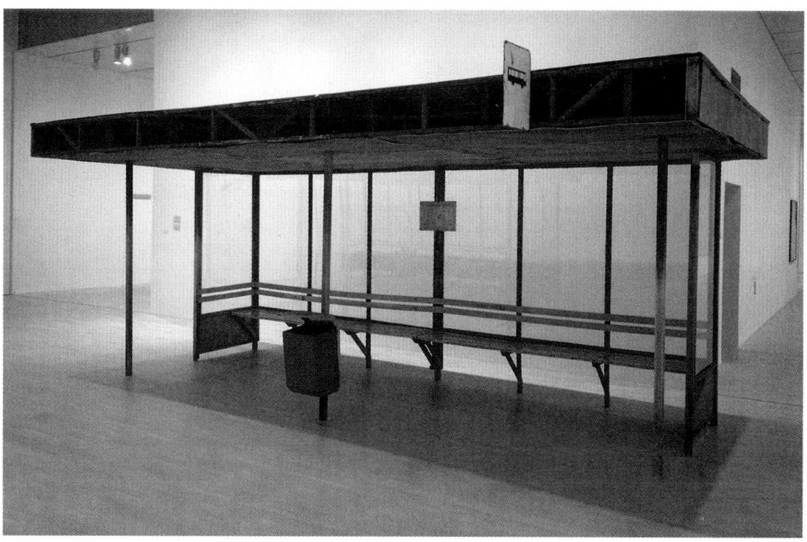

Something of the silence of Beuys, very often using wooden boxes or containers visibly marked by human history, was developed by artists such as Reinhard Mucha in Germany, Doris Salcedo in America, and Tony Cragg, first in Britain and then in Germany. Later works by **Beuys** no longer had recourse to the figurative form, but by using insulating materials such as copper and felt still suggested an animate presence, dead or alive. Works by **Cragg** from the 1980s, such as *Axehead* and *Mineral Vein* (1986) deploy the language of the box; the container and the contained.[14] In choosing to use everyday brown furniture these works speak of their Beuysian lineage, and in doing so make wider international connections.

...

closed

149. Joseph Beuys, *Dumb Box*, 1982

150. Tony Cragg, *Axehead*, 1982

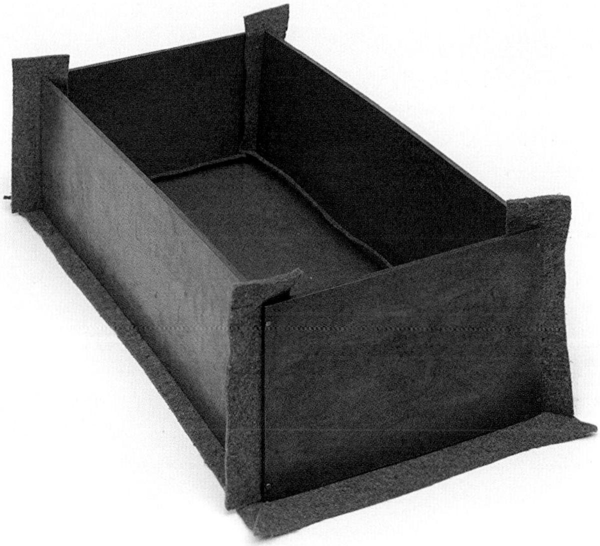

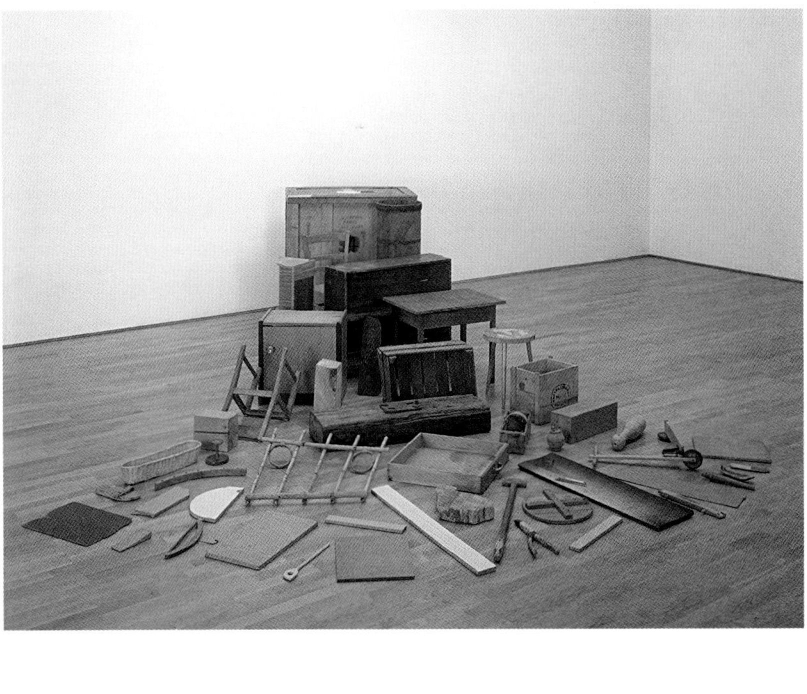

Bill Woodrow's early works (***Untitled***, for example) also unpack forms as if to reveal the contents, original or imagined, in doing so making reference not only to the notion of the 'inner form' inherent in direct carving, but also to the reliquary we are considering here. Woodrow became famous for disassembling box-like forms and inventing new inhabitants for them, but earlier pieces, such as *TV Blind* (1979), and other box-works, in which he lays out the innards of machines, such as ***Tape Recorder***, remind us of his links not only to Cragg, and their shared debt to Richard Long, but also to Nam June Paik (and Susan Hiller) in the recognition of technology's place in the foyer of the home. The interior content of the box is repeatedly on display but ultimately unattainable.[15]

The play of container to contained, and notably the human contained, has met a sustained interpreter in the person of Rachel Whiteread, whose simple casts of furniture rely on human scale for their essential premise. The ***Bath*** works from the mid-1990s operate around the absence of the body to shift the container from connoting the everyday to connoting the im/mortal, but they also rely on the implicit presence of the body, as if it were indeed embalmed within their waxy mass. Adam Colton was already doing something with similar associations in his Promethean carvings of the mid-1980s, as was Daphne Wright only a little later with plaster works including *The Tombs* (1995).

- - -

151. Bill Woodrow, *Untitled (Telephone)*, 1979

152. Bill Woodrow, *Tape Recorder*, 1979

← 153. Rachel Whiteread, *Untitled (Orange Bath)*, 1996

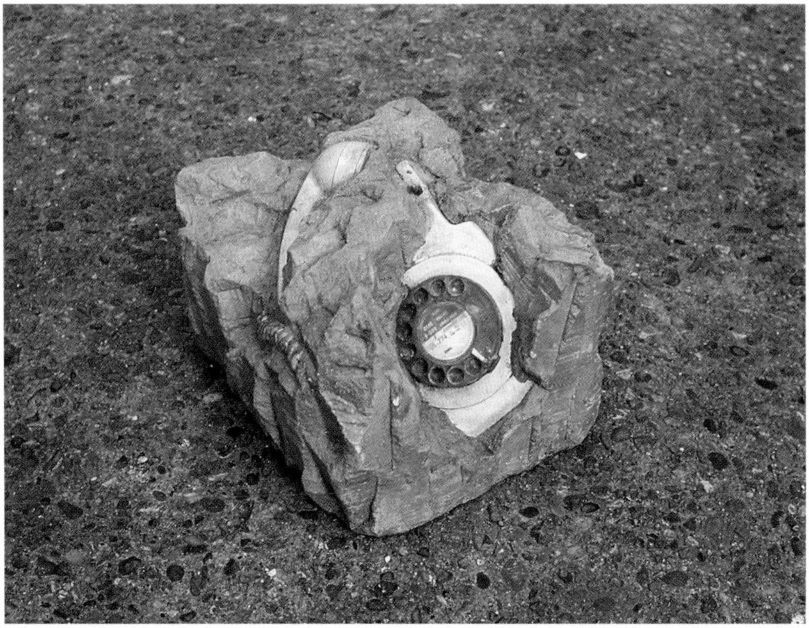

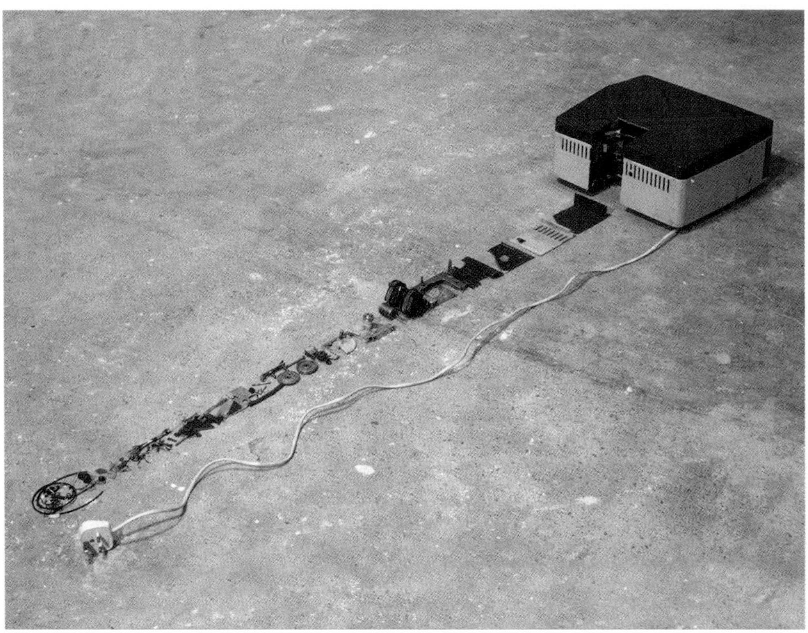

closed

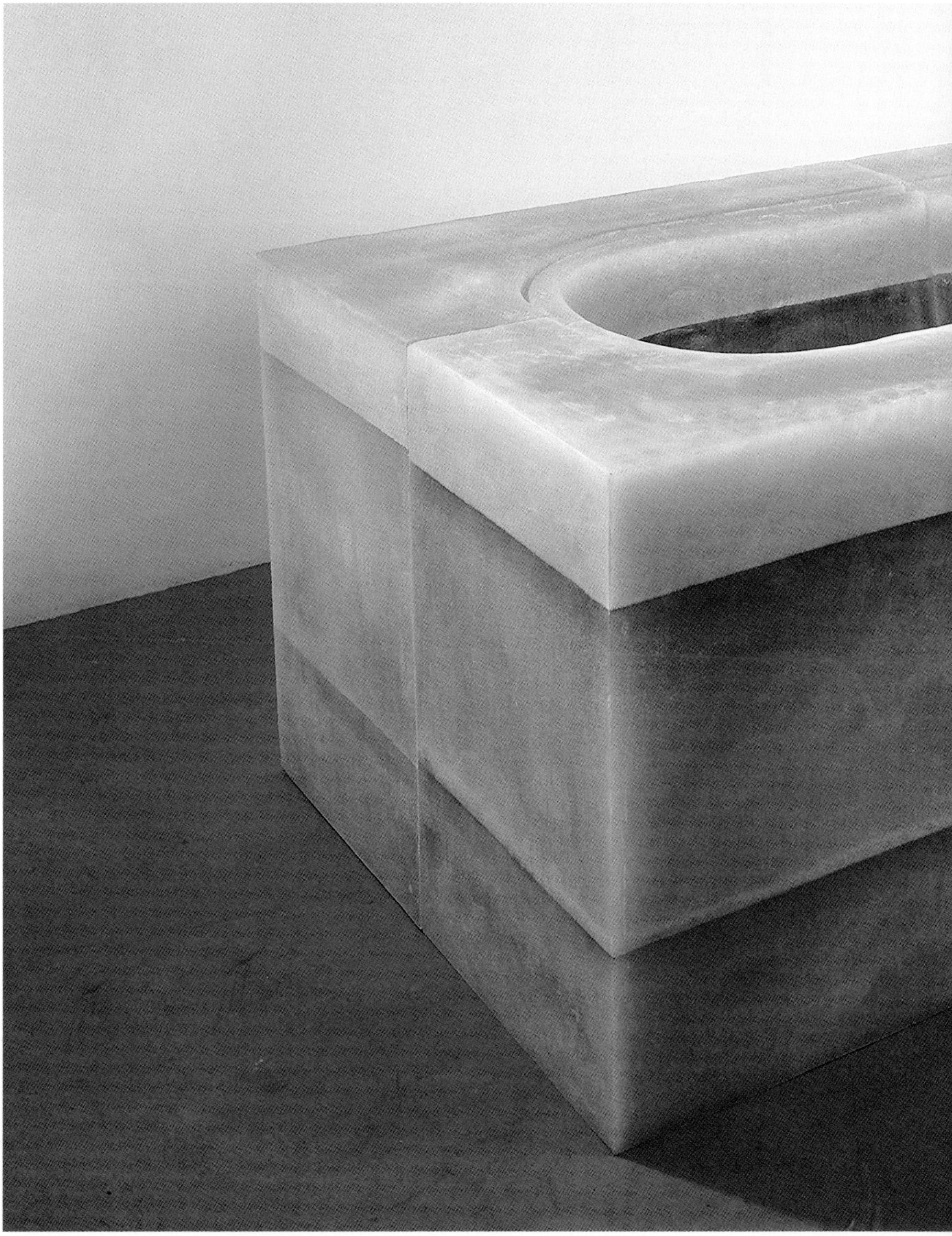

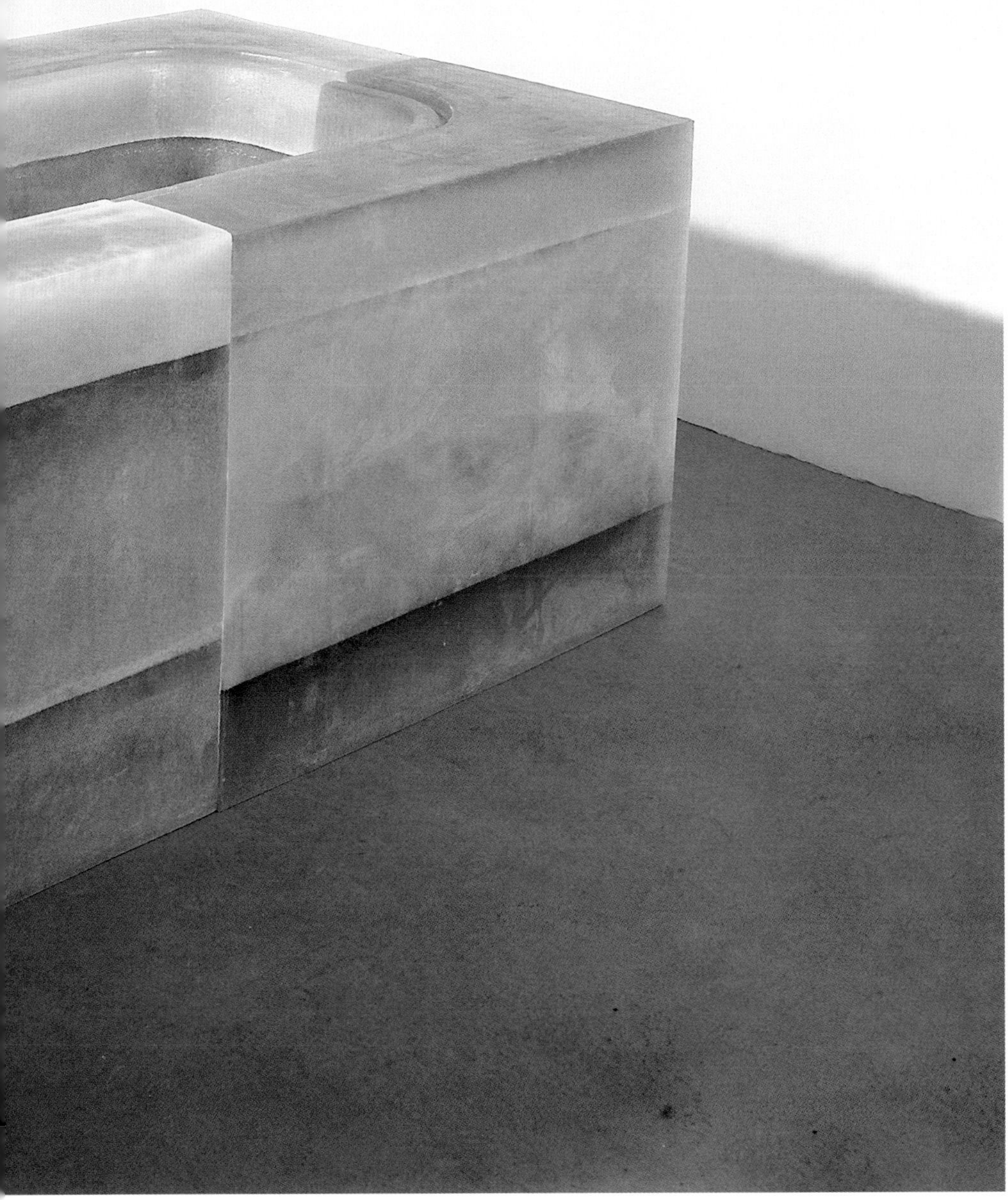

Whiteread has continued with the theme of the interment, going beyond the tomb to the mausoleum, first with *House* (1993), then with the Judenplatz memorial in Vienna (1995–2000) and also with her concrete casts of **garden sheds**, which are solid rather than empty. Mausolea are known in Britain from the mid-seventeenth century,[16] taking over from the chantry chapel, and were formally inspired by the tombs on the Via Appia, as with **Nicholas Hawksmoor**'s mausoleum at Castle Howard, based on the Tomb of Gallienus, which inspired many more.[17] The basement, with its seventy niches for coffins, was plainly visible. There are a number of mausolea by the Adam brothers from the late eighteenth century, principally in Scotland, but notably at Bowood (1761–4). The Pelham Mausoleum at Brocklesby Park, designed by James Wyatt, was modelled on the Temples of Vesta at Rome and Tivoli, which were equally formative.[18] The artist **Thomas Espin** was inspired by the Brocklesby Park example to design a summerhouse in his garden in Louth, which was intended from the outset to become his mausoleum. Whiteread's jump from garden shed to mausoleum is perhaps not so new: the **Johnson Mausoleum** in Spalding Cemetery is even now used as a toolshed.

...

154. Nicholas Hawksmoor, mausoleum, 1729

155. Thomas Espin, summerhouse, 1819

156. Theophilus Fairfax Johnson, Johnson Mausoleum, 1843

← 157. Rachel Whiteread, *Detached 1*, 2012

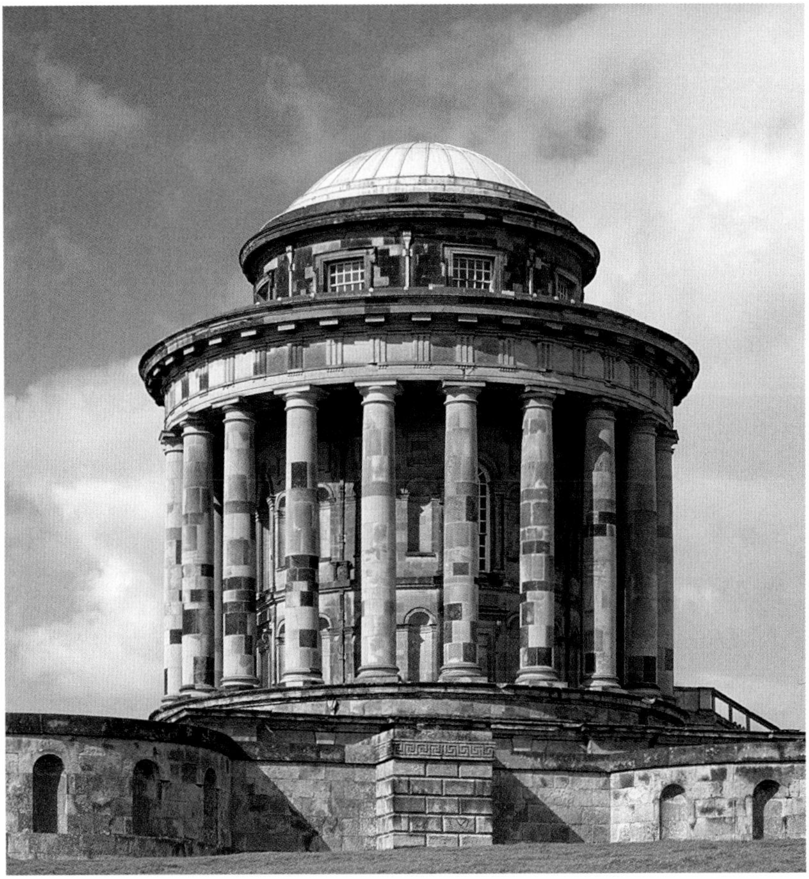

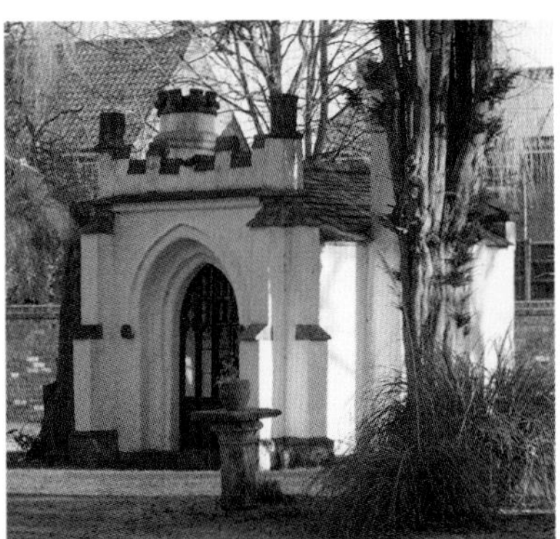

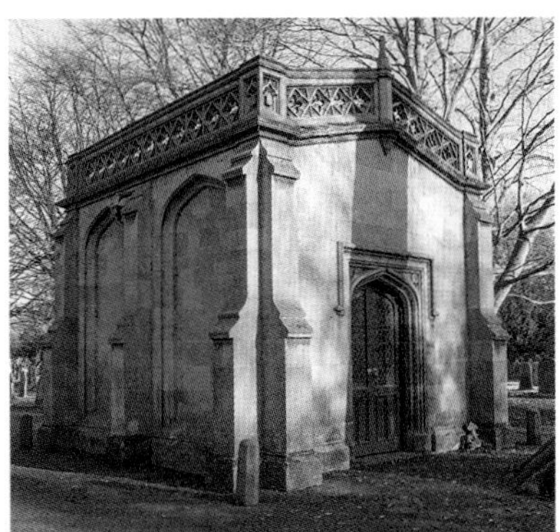

closed

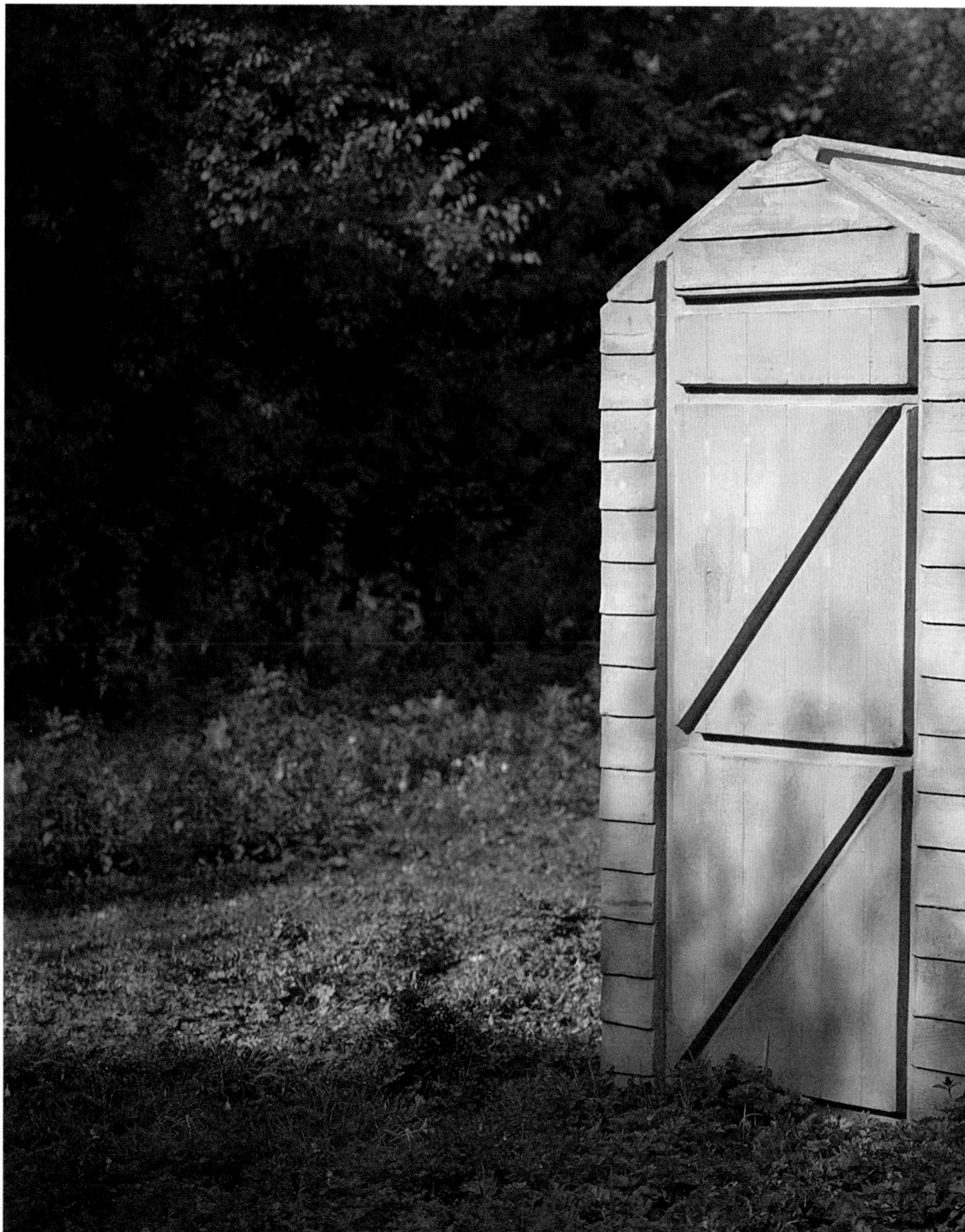

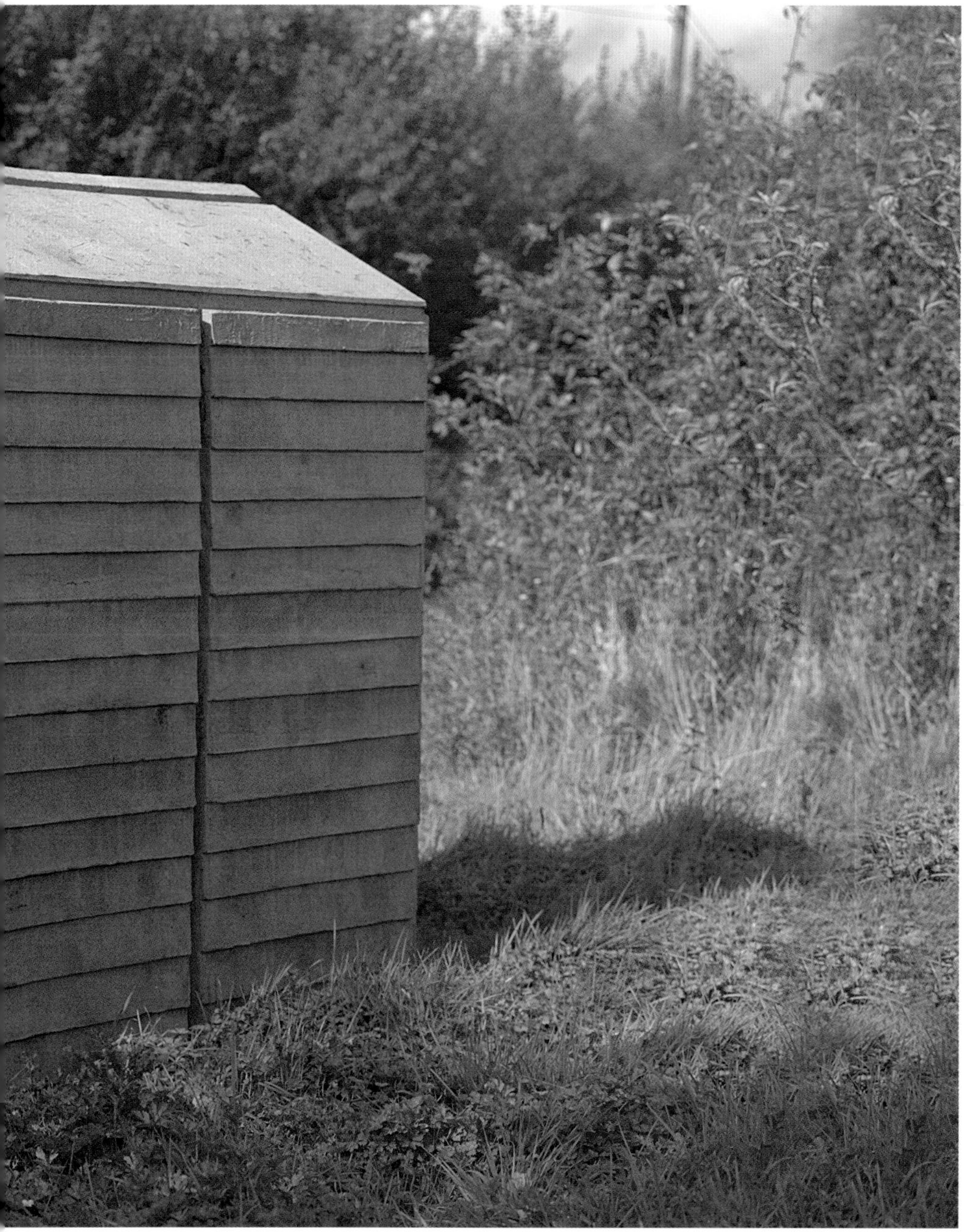

The tendency towards the hut in recent sculpture - one might cite especially Mark Manders and Mike Nelson, but many other artists too[19] – speaks of this same inner world, the mausoleum-like environment in which personal effects are gathered around the defunct. In 'grands projets' such as ***Coral Reef***, Nelson has insisted upon the interiority of his work, so that its outer form is effectively invisible; all precedence is given to what is inside. (In Germany and Switzerland Gregor Schneider and Christoph Büchel work in an analogous way.)

Others however, as with John Frankland, Roger Hiorns and Rose Finn-Kelcey (not to mention Dan Graham) make of the 'hut' something more ethereal, and decidedly less quotidian, as if it had already transported the body to a higher realm. They focus on its exterior form, making its walls more luminous. Its contents are gone; it merely houses the spirit. Finn-Kelcey's work ***God Kennel***, for the 1993 Kassel documenta, if humorous, relies on this lineage for its effect. Upside down, is God/Dog above us or below us? More serious, despite its title, is her contemporaneous ***Royal Box***, a nine-foot square refrigeration unit into which viewers were invited to step.

---

158. Mike Nelson, *Coral Reef*, 2000

159. Rose Finn-Kelcey, *God Kennel – A Tabernacle*, 1992

160. Rose Finn-Kelcey, *The Royal Box*, 1993

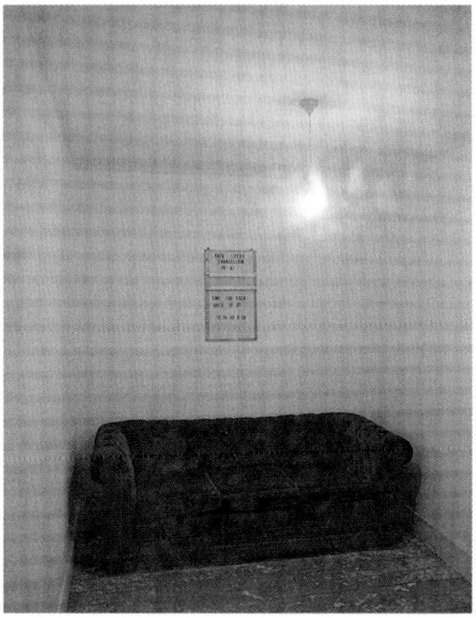

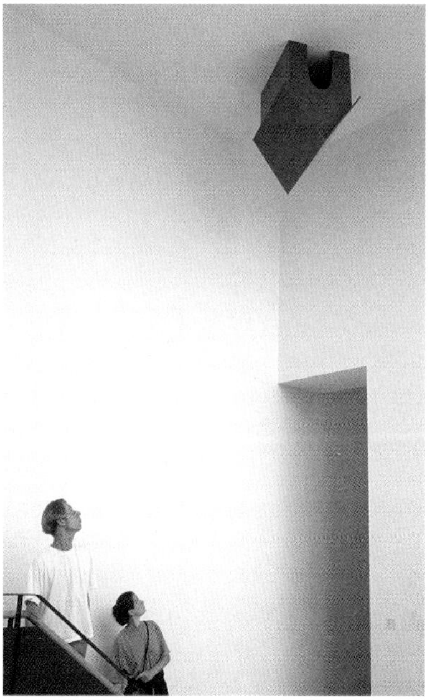

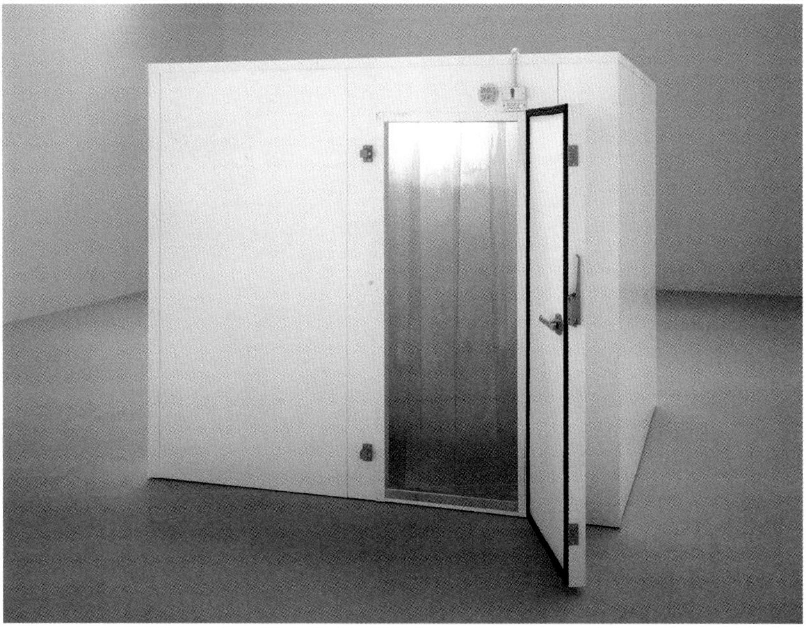

Although the first British crematoria were built as late as the 1880s and only became common in the twentieth century, with the necessary enactment in law, the cinerary urn was used as a device in British monuments well before this date. The monument to **John Donne** at St Paul's, by Nicholas Stone, is unusual in the way in which the urn features as something that is operational, rather than a cipher for what is lost. It shows Donne rising from an urn, which is in a way also like a plinth. In his *Life of Donne* (1640) Izaak Walton wrote a famous account of how the monument came about:

> A monument being resolved upon, Dr Donne sent for a carver to make for him in wood the figure of an urn, giving him directions for the compass and height of it, and to bring with it a board of the just height of his body. These being got, then, without delay, a choice painter was got to be in readiness to draw his picture, which was taken as followeth – Several charcoal fires being first made in his large study, he brought with him into that place his winding-sheet in his hand; and having put off all his clothes, had this sheet put on him, and so tied with knots at his head and feet, and his hands so placed as dead bodies are usually fitted to be shrowded and put into their coffin or grave. Upon this urn he thus stood, with his eyes shut, and with so much of the sheet turned aside, as might shew his lean, pale and death-like face, which was purposefully turned toward the east, from whence he expected the second coming of his and our Saviour Jesus.[21]

...

164. Nicholas Stone, monument to John Donne, 1631

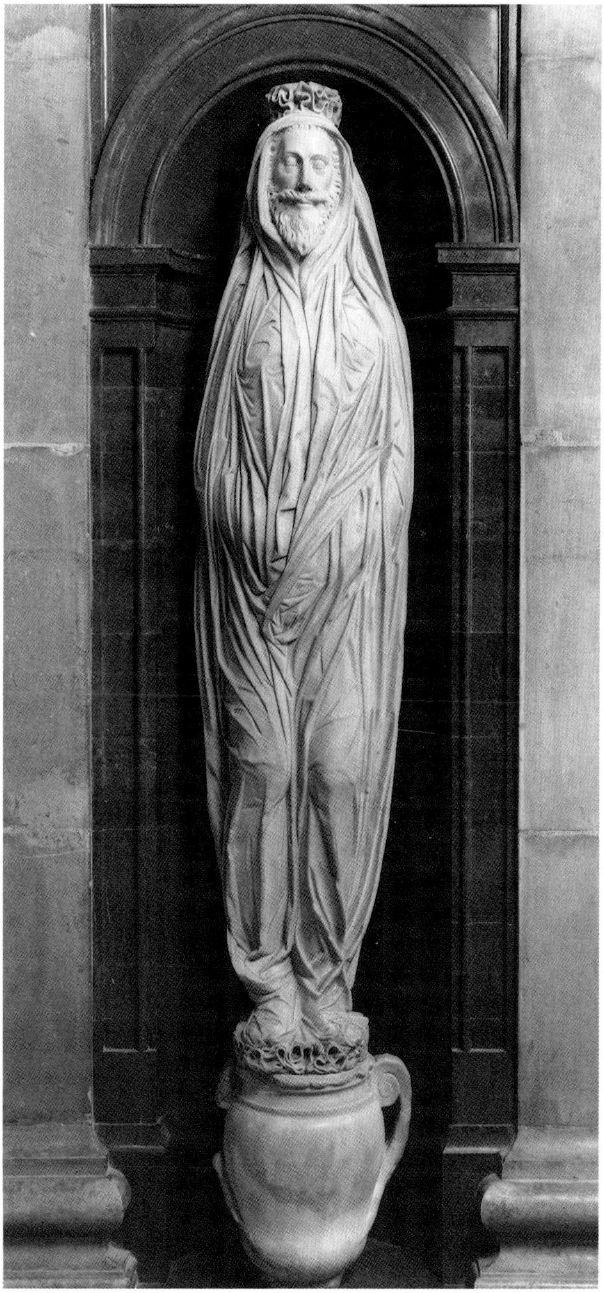

Donne's monument reflects the gradual loss of faith in purgatory and a concomitant focus on the resurrected body.[22] Sir Henry Wotton believed that Donne's monument 'seemed to breathe faintly, and posterity shall look upon it as some kind of artificial miracle'.[23] It was certainly unusual in surviving the Great Fire of London. Another striking example of an urn monument is that to **George Villiers**, the Duke of Buckingham, in Portsmouth Cathedral, which in his case (as in others) afforded the opportunity for a second memorial.

Urns were considered most famously in ***Urne-Buriall*** of 1658 in which Thomas Browne was prompted by the excavation of over forty Roman urns ('sad and sepulchral pitchers') in nearby Walsingham to muse on the forms of commemoration. Most contained bones, and some artefacts too.

...

closed

165. Monument to George Villiers, Duke of Buckingham, 1628

166. Thomas Browne, dedicatory spread from *Hydriotaphia, Urne-Buriall*, 1658

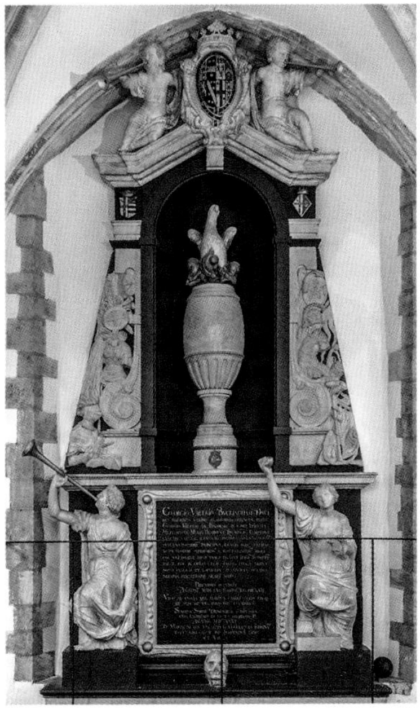

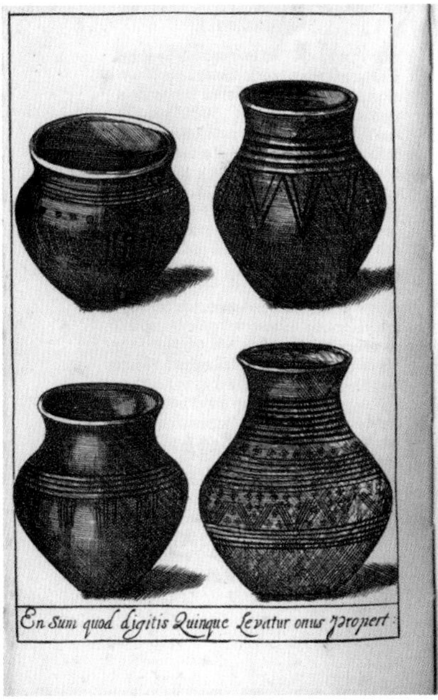

Dedicatory.

old, to be wrapt up flowers and garlands.

Nullum sine venia placuisse eloquium, is more sensibly understood by Writers, then by Readers; nor well apprehended by either, till works have hanged out like Apelles his Pictures; wherein even common eyes will finde something for emendation.

To wish all Readers of your abilities, were unreasonably to multiply the number of Scholars beyond the temper of these times. But unto this ill-judging age, we charitably desire a portion of your equity, judgement, candour, and ingenuity; wherein you are so rich, as not to lose by diffusion. And being a flourishing branch of that [k] Noble Family, unto which we owe so much observance, you are not new set, but long rooted in such perfection; whereof having had so lasting confirmation in your worthy conversation, constant amity, and expression; and knowing you a serious Student in the highest arcana's of Nature; with much excuse we bring these low delights, and poor maniples to your Treasure.

[k] Of the most worthy Sr Edmund Bacon prime Baronet, my true and noble Friend.

Norwich May 1.

Your affectionate Friend

and Servant,

Thomas Browne.

It is more usual to find urns featuring as supporting components in monuments, representing memory and loss in rather elastic ways, rather than being tied to actual bodily remains. In the late seventeenth century **Viscount Campden** was commemorated with his fourth wife by Grinling Gibbons with an urn on a pedestal between them. Further urns sit atop the flanking obelisks. Henry Cheere's monument to the second **Duke of Ancaster** shows the Duke rather nonchalantly leaning on an urn with his wife's profile beneath it.[24] Here we have figurative and abstract representations of the living and the dead body, as well as its pictorial representation.

...

167. Grinling Gibbons, monument to the 3rd Viscount Campden, 1686

168. Attributed to Henry Cheere, monument to the 2nd Duke of Ancaster, 1741

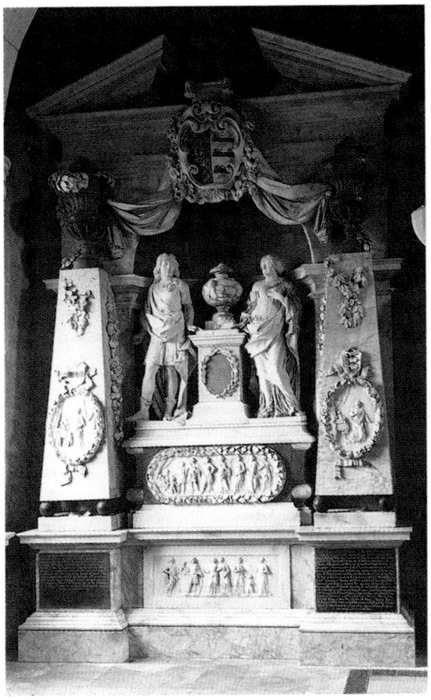

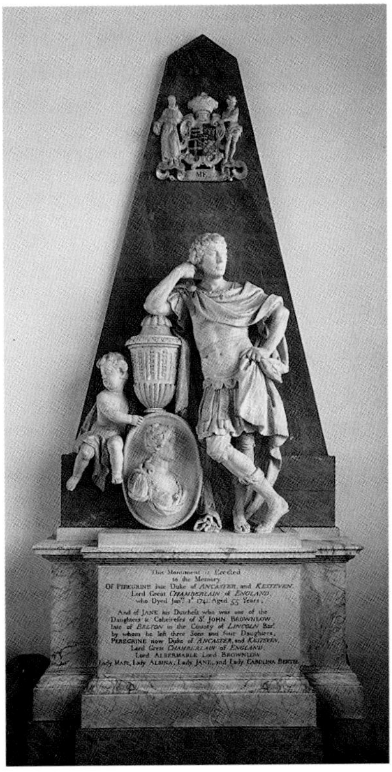
This Monument is Erected
to the Memory
Of PEREGRINE late Duke of ANCASTER and KESTEVEN
Lord Great CHAMBERLAIN of ENGLAND
who Dyed Jan. 1 1741 Aged 55 Years;
And of JANE his Dutchess who was one of the
Daughters & Coheiresses of Sr JOHN BROWNLOW
late of BELTON in the County of LINCOLN Bart
by whom he left three Sons and four Daughters,
PEREGRINE now Duke of ANCASTER and KESTEVEN
Lord Great CHAMBERLAIN of ENGLAND,
Lord ALBEMARLE Lord BROWNLOW
Lady MARY, Lady ALBINA, Lady JANE, and Lady CAROLINA BERTIE

By contrast, Joseph Nollekens's memorial to **Bennett Noel** shows the image of the Lieutenant General on the urn, with his widow at its side. The urn may represent the deceased, or the mourner, or neither, or both; it may be, as it were, empty or full; its lid realistically configured to suggest its interior.

Carlo Marochetti's tomb to **Ugo Foscolo** in Chiswick is a tomb chest in form, a cenotaph in content. Foscolo, whose remains were returned to Italy after his burial in 1827, was, perhaps ironically, the author of *Dei Sepolcri* (1807), which laments the loss of wooded cemeteries, where trees shaded 'urns in perennial remembrance, and precious vases held the suppliant tears'.[25] Foscolo even suggests that the urns themselves are comforted by weeping, and that they might be embraced and questioned. There is here more than a suggestion that there is something inside the urn, a spirit, a sensitivity, a knowledge. The quality of the closed suggests that there is something inside: that the urn not only might enclose the remains of the defunct, but also gather tears and provide for the congregation of memory. Browne certainly lamented the fact that his urns were silent, rather than being the 'Theatrical Vessels' of the Roman world, when they were used to project the voice.

...

173. Joseph Nollekens, monument to Lieutenant General Bennett Noel, 1787

174. Carlo Marochetti, tomb of Ugo Foscolo, 1827

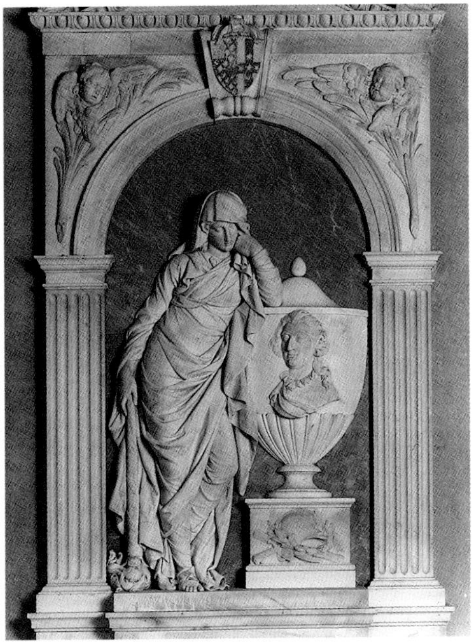

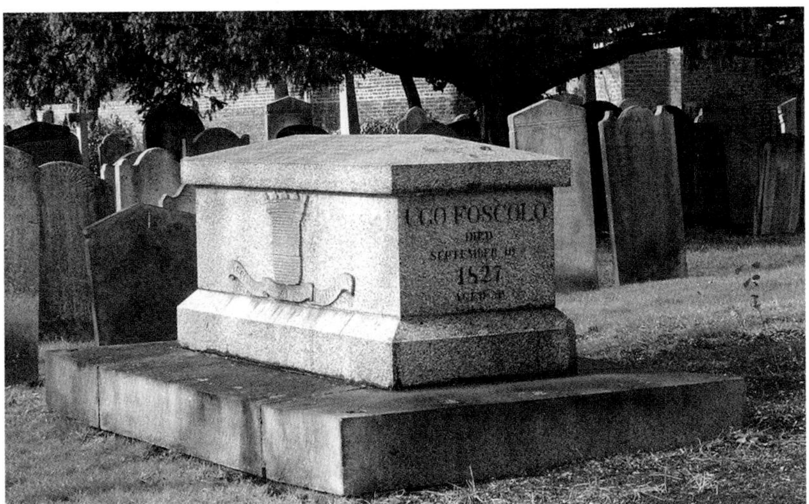
UGO FOSCOLO
DIED
1827

The notion of the inside of sculpture was slow to be explored, and perhaps the continuities are obscured by the fact that we have focused more on the openness of modern sculpture than on its closedness; more on the inside and less on the out. But the endlessness of the urn as sculptural device finds an echo in the immediate post-war work of Barbara Hepworth. In these years Hepworth uses the spiralling symmetry of the urn to create an effective symbol of change and stasis combined. Even if titles are treacherous, it is tempting to see the link between a work such as ***Helikon*** and the mountain of the same name (Helicon), where the muses were refreshed by fountains, and the notion of the urn, which represents both death and life, fire and water, the past and the future.

176. Barbara Hepworth, *Helikon*, 1948

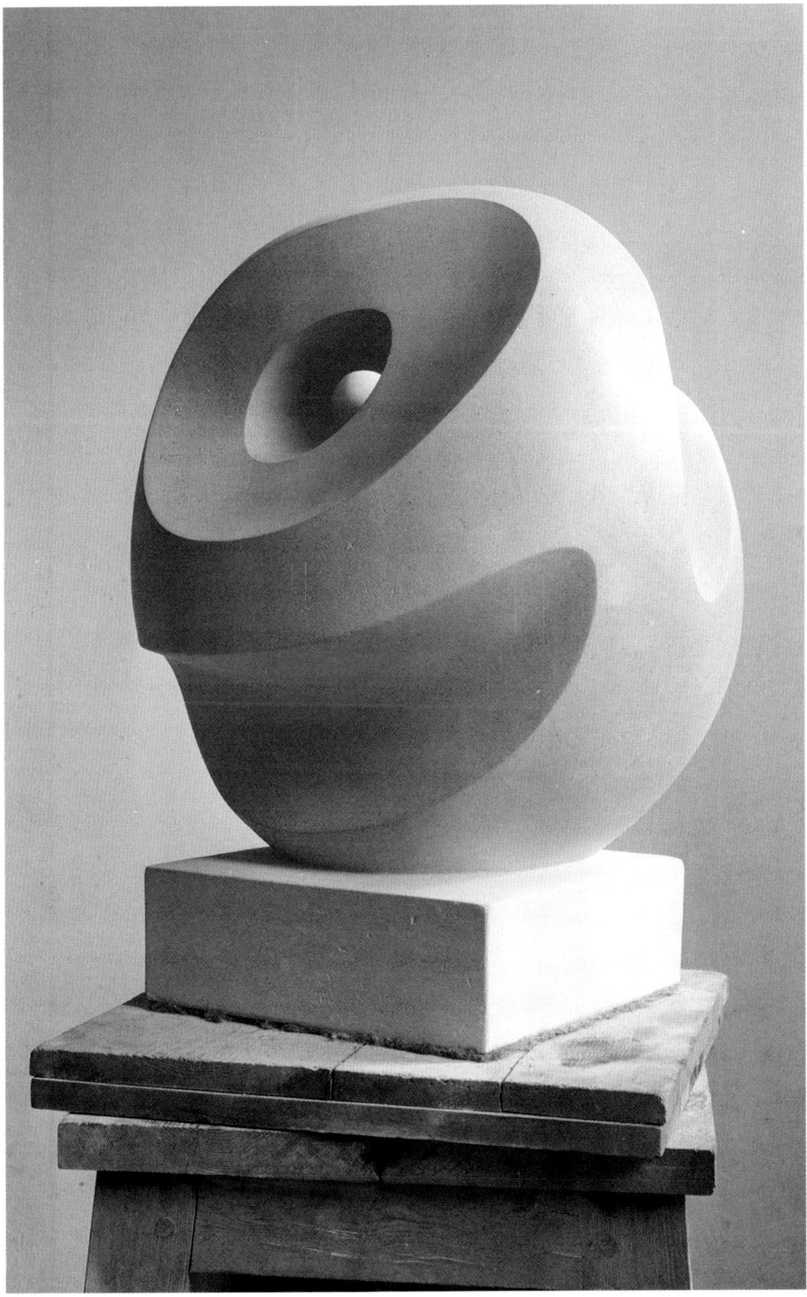

In the previous chapter, by considering the closed, we looked by and large at the preservation of content, physical and conceptual. This was content that would remain the same, across time. By contrast, with the open form, we touch on sculpture as a place of change. **'Welcome'**, proclaims Ceal Floyer's doormat, and I extend the same invitation, as we step in.

Martin Creed's neon work ***Work No. 203: EVERYTHING IS GOING TO BE ALRIGHT*** was first designed for the portico of what was left of the London Orphans Asylum in Clapton, made to fit its tympanum, like many such inscriptions before it. Creed's interest in the entrance, the nature of passage, is displayed in other pieces that also inhabit doorways, such as his *Work No. 132: Door opening and closing and a light going on and off* (1995) and *Work No. 990: Curtains opening and closing* (2009), which both invite and deny egress.

...

177. Ceal Floyer, *Welcome*, 2011

178. Martin Creed, *Work No. 203: EVERYTHING IS GOING TO BE ALRIGHT*, 1999

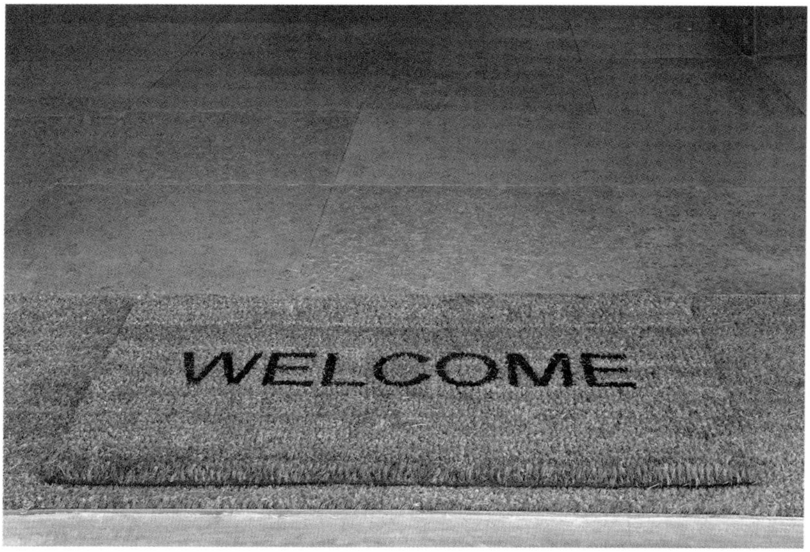
WELCOME

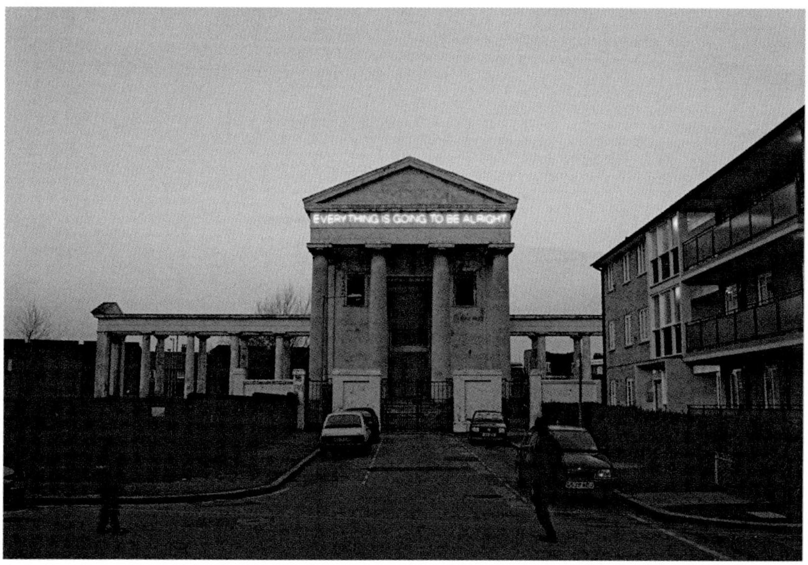
EVERYTHING IS GOING TO BE ALRIGHT

Such imagery is part of a tradition in which curtains are pulled together (or back) on monuments, with tombs from the early seventeenth century adopting this lively theatrical device, as in Maximilian Colt's **Chamberlayne** Monument. Monument-makers in the age of Louis-François Roubiliac used the curtain too, though it may now also be read as a funeral shroud or sacred cloth. Roubiliac used it routinely, but in different ways, as in his monuments to the **Myddeltons** and to **Richard Children**.[1]

...

open

179. Maximilian Colt, monument to Robert Chamberlayne, 1615

180. Louis-François Roubiliac, monument to Thomas Myddelton and Arabella Myddelton, c.1756

181. Louis-François Roubiliac, monument to Richard Children, 1753

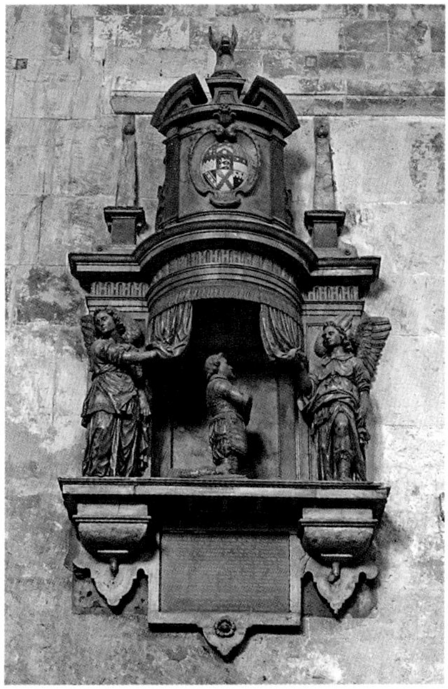

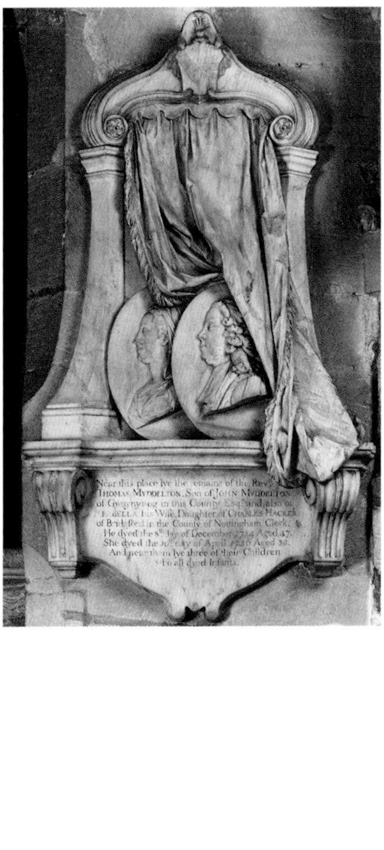
Near this place lye the remains of the Rev.
THOMAS MYDDELTON, Son of JOHN MYDDELTON
He dyed the 8th day of December
She dyed the
An near them lye three of their Children
who all dyed Infants.

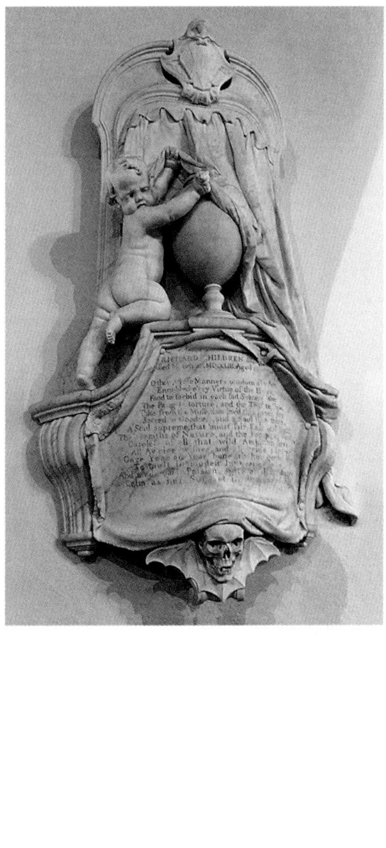

Time and Fortune Draw a Curtain Over Temple Bar, by Charles Mabey, marks the end of the last of the eight gateways into the city of London. The curtains close the gateway. The relatively late construction of Temple Bar, believed to be by Christopher Wren, in 1672, followed the Great Fire, and was a royal commission that included four royal statues. **Temple Bar** stood across Fleet Street for two centuries until it was dismantled in 1878 and later removed to a private park, before its recent return to the city. The Temple Bar **Memorial**[2] marks the spot where the arch had stood; solid pedestal replacing pierced arch. No longer practical, largely meaningless symbolically and functionally, the curtain has been lowered.

...

open

182. Charles Mabey, *Time and Fortune Draw a Curtain Over Temple Bar*, 1880

183. Christopher Wren, Temple Bar Gate, 1672

184. Horace Jones, Temple Bar Memorial, 1880

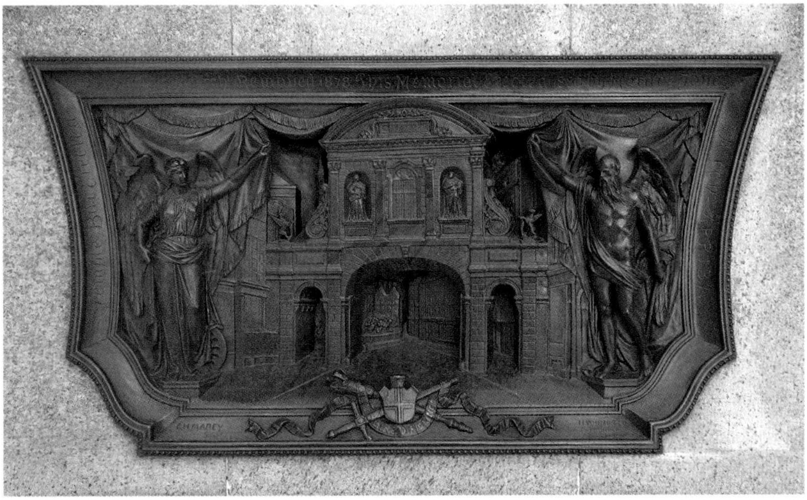

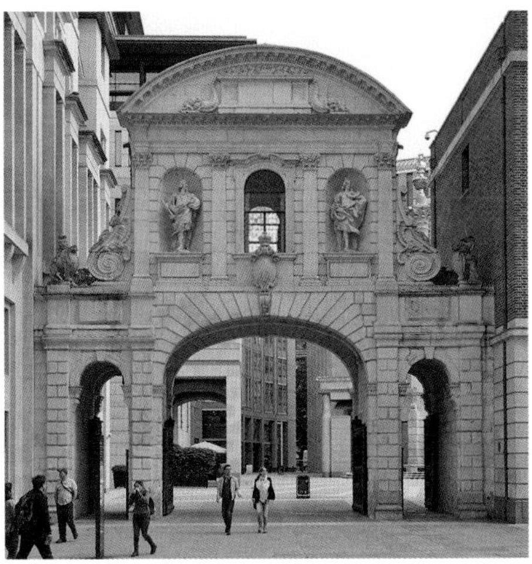

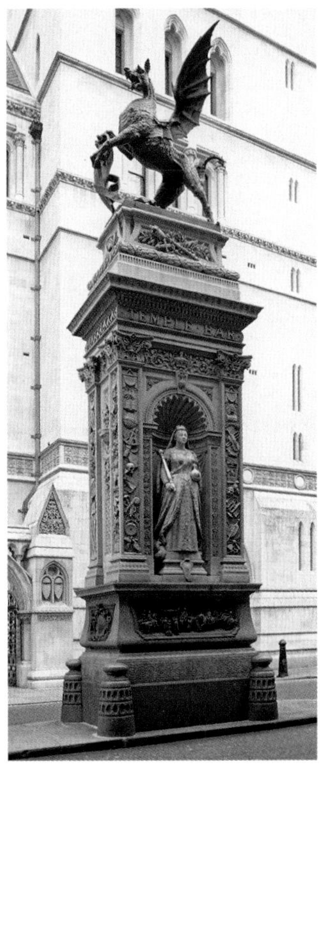

London is less known than Rome or Paris for its gateways and arches; the ones we know today were mostly erected in the 1820s and 1830s, associated with the remodelling of Buckingham Palace and the advent of the railways,[3] and all of them have since been moved. The most recent arch, and the only one through which traffic still flows, even if a hotel now sits above, is the Edwardian Admiralty Arch.[4] London's other arches have little function in the present day, and their re-positioning often obviates this very possibility.

Robert Adam and John Soane were among the architects who proposed designs to mark Hyde Park Corner's strategic importance at the west. It was, however, the revised design of Decimus Burton that was approved in 1826 for what was originally styled the **Green Park Arch**.[5] Although for fifty years it made sense in relation to Buckingham Palace, since 1962 it has been isolated as now. Similarly adrift is John Nash's **Marble Arch**, close in date and originally even more closely associated with the palace, until its removal in 1850. Both arches had included more figurative sculpture[6] in their original designs; both schemes were scrapped as they overran their budgets. Nonetheless, even as gateways, or indeed, just because they are gateways, they have a sculptural quality.

185. Decimus Burton, Green Park Arch, 1826–30

open

- - -

186. John Nash, Marble Arch, 1826

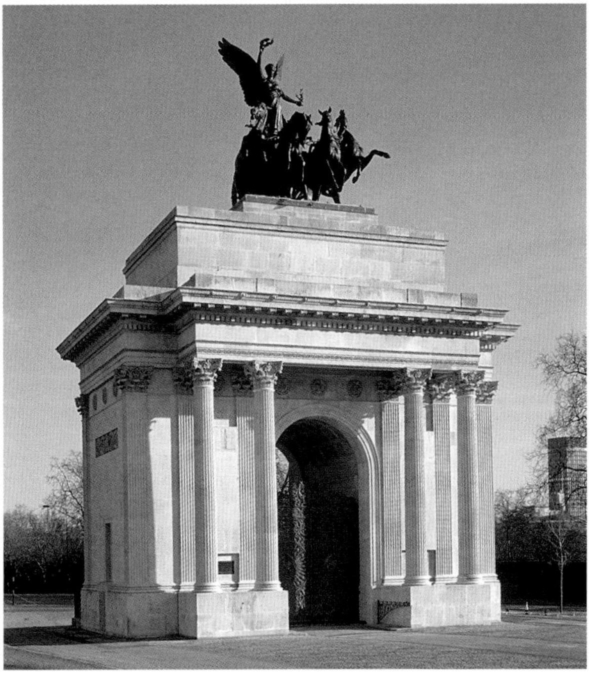

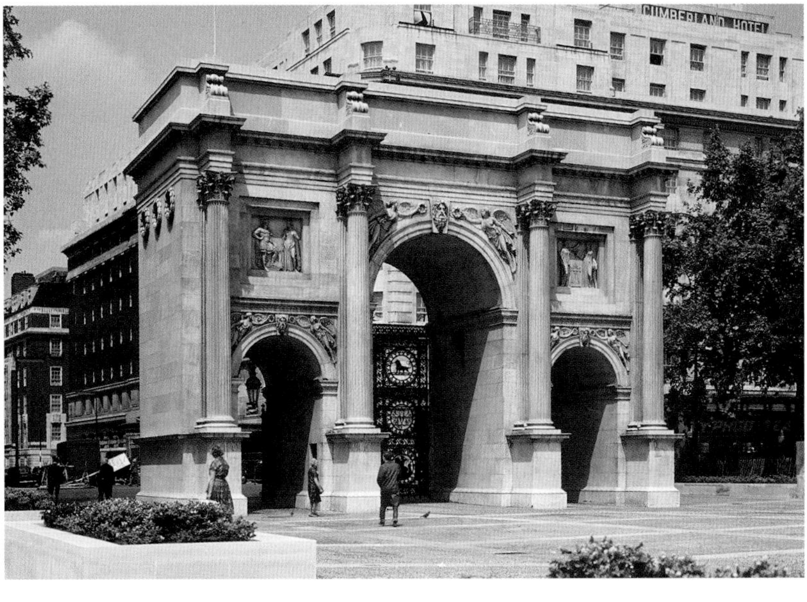
CUMBERLAND HOTEL

The arch is always open; the door is more mutable, more clearly transitional. Even when a door is closed, its meaning is also about its opening. Some of the most significant church doors were opened only rarely, but nonetheless display scenes such as the Visitation or the Annunciation, which denote the moment of change within a narrative; at the crux of before and after. The bronze or iron door traditionally marks the treasure house or sanctuary; the vault or safe place. Bronze doors to cathedrals are more common in continental Europe than in Britain, and date back to the ninth century.[7] British examples, such as these in Nottingham, by **Henry Wilson**, are a much later reprise, reflecting Wilson's Arts and Crafts background. These huge undertakings have a double signification: representing both interior and exterior, they cast the church into its role as both giving and needing protection.

187. Henry Wilson, bronze doors, 1905

188. Eric Gill, *Prospero and Ariel*, 1933

The cathedral porches of Europe act as spaces of transition, with their tympana and lintels carrying composite scenes, and their jambs and columns bearing individual figures, generally in series. **Eric Gill**'s *Prospero and Ariel*, on British Broadcasting House, reminds one of these threshold figures, as do **James Woodford**'s contemporaneous pylon figures at the Royal Institute of British Architects, at either side of his great bronze doors.

open

These prompts to reflection, at the building's portal, might be linked to earlier gateways, such as those at Gonville and Caius College, Cambridge, where **gates of Humility** lead to Virtue and thence to Honour.[8]

...

189. James Woodford, bronze doors, 1934

190. Gates of Humility, 16th century

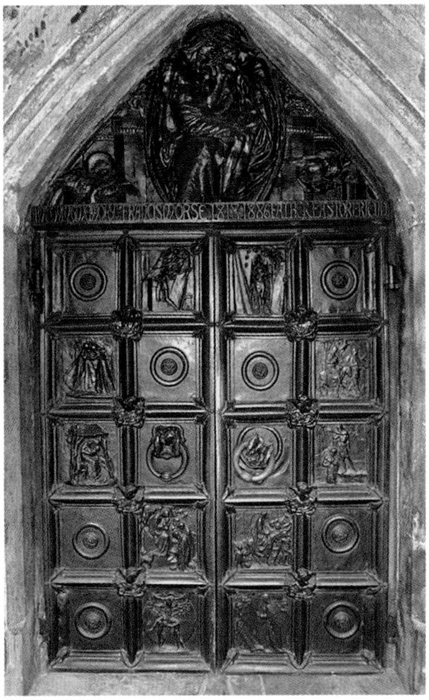

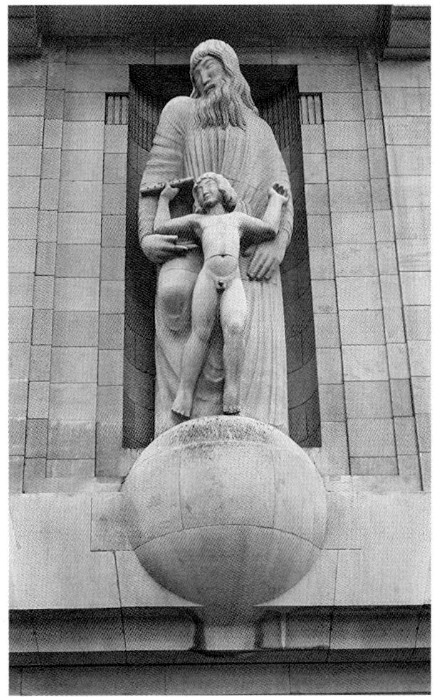

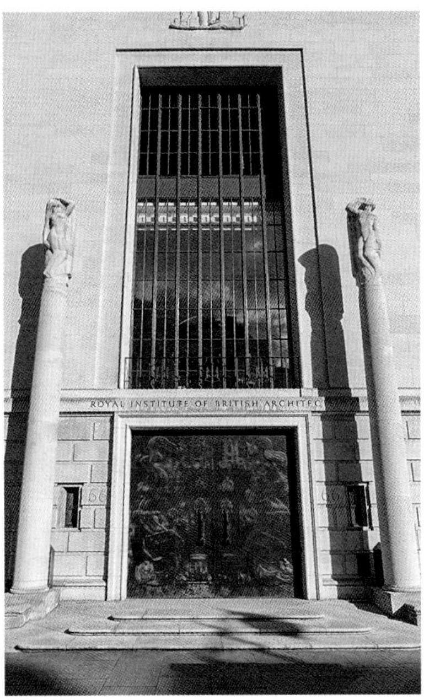
ROYAL INSTITUTE OF BRITISH ARCHITEC

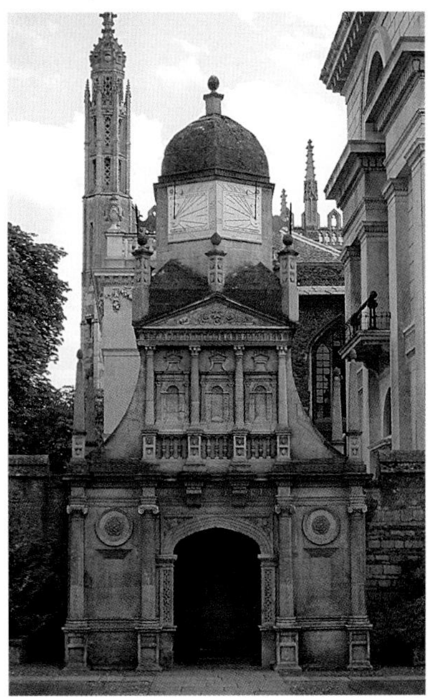

The portal or gateway has been developed as a concept, and as a physical stage, by a number of artists in recent years. Central to their work is an auratic quality denoted through illumination and suggestive of a kind of heavenly sanctuary. **Martin Creed**'s golden doors for the Johnen Galerie in Berlin announce something of what is inside; they make one think of **John Frankland**'s golden lift doors, first shown in Hales Gallery, and then at the Saatchi. They reflect us in their insubstantial polythene surface, and almost deceive; they speak of us as viewers and of our possible translation to a higher level. Frankland's later project for PEER in Hoxton St extended the concept across the gallery façade, making the whole building into a sculpture. **Rose Finn-Kelcey**'s *Pearly Gate* made explicit, in its title, and with its latch unclasped, the potential for celestial access.

...

open

191. Martin Creed, *Work No. 1432: Gold leaf on door*, 2012

192. John Frankland, *You Can't Touch This*, 1992–3

193. Rose Finn-Kelcey, *Pearly Gate*, 1997

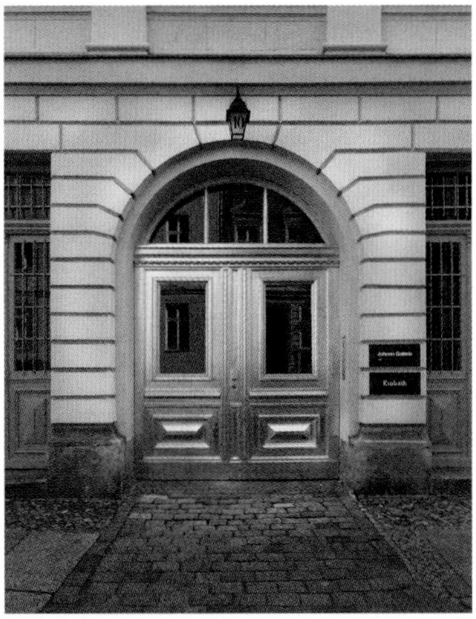

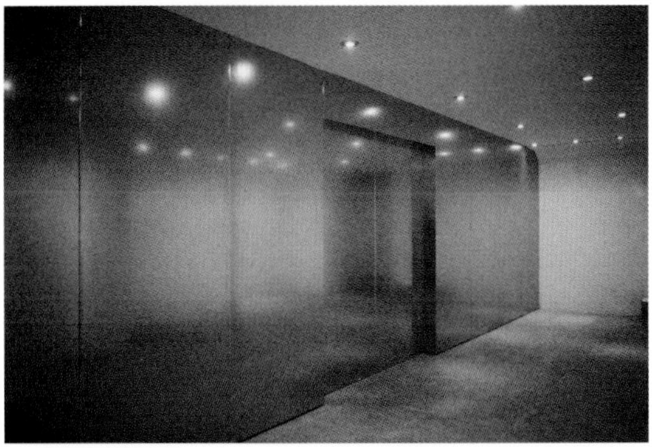

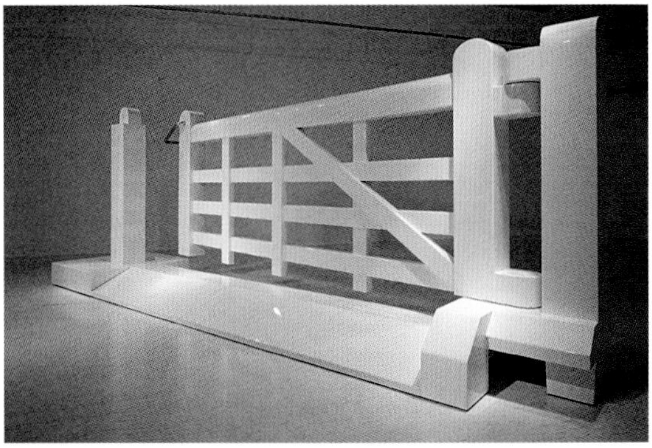

Thinking of sculpture as a frame, through which we might enter, takes us interestingly to other framing devices. Barbara Hepworth's ***Four Square (Walk Through)*** allows its viewers to step through; it is indeed like a ceremonial gate, a porch or belfry. Going further than her earlier holed works, in which one can imagine being in the interior, this work invites and holds the viewer briefly inside, as he or she moves in and out, crossing its threshold repeatedly.

...

open

194. Barbara Hepworth, *Four Square (Walk Through), in situ* at the Trewyn Studio, 1966

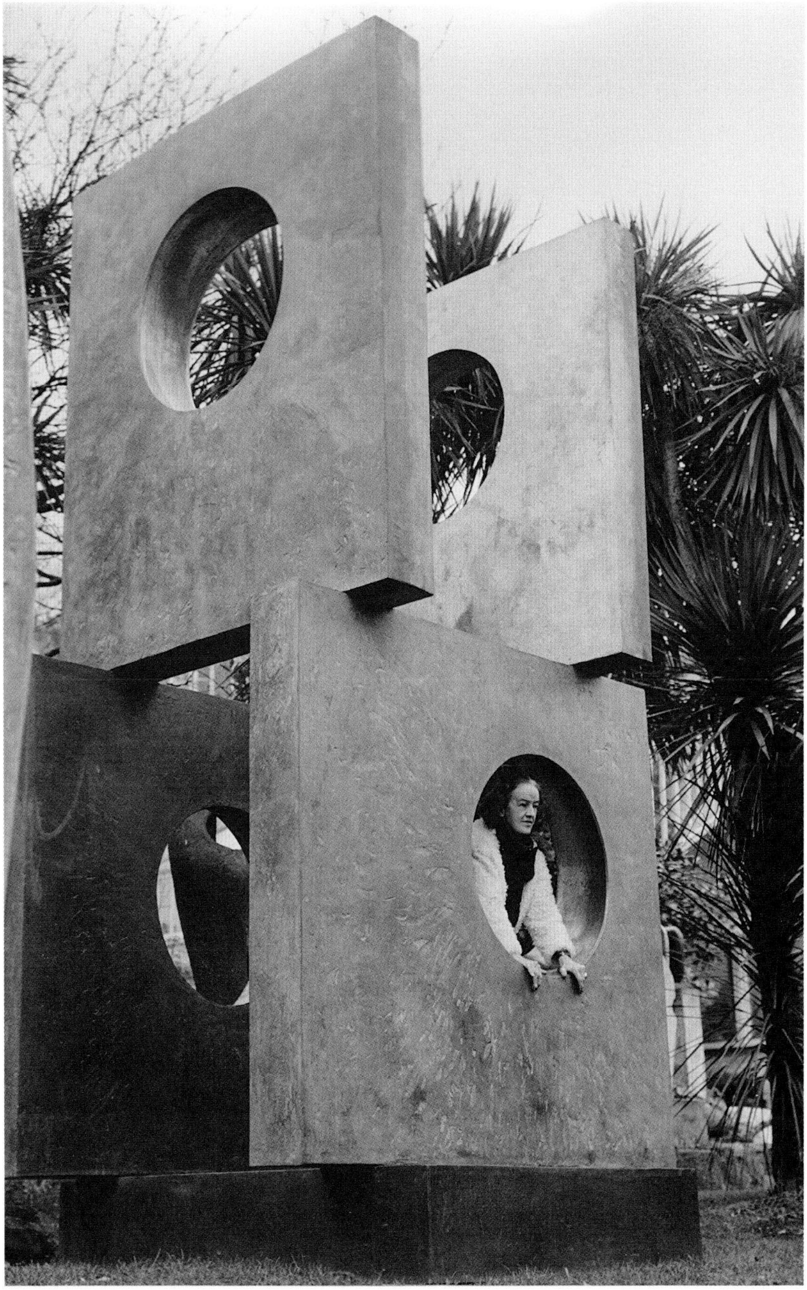

The step over the threshold requires a shift in behaviour: a greeting, a change of clothes, a different attitude. This is obviously the case with the entrances to places of worship, and of education, and contemporary artists play on this with their installations. Nathan Coley's ***Threshold Sculptures*** measured and marked their own beginning and end. Adam Chodzko's ***Untitled Stile*** and Lucy Gunning's ***Gate*** might also mark their viewer's entrance, however they chose to proceed, as if into an unbounded space.[9]

...

open

195. Nathan Coley, *Untitled (Threshold Sculptures)*, 2007

196. Adam Chodzko, *Untitled Stile (Teenage Version)*, 1992

197. Lucy Gunning, *Gate*, 1996

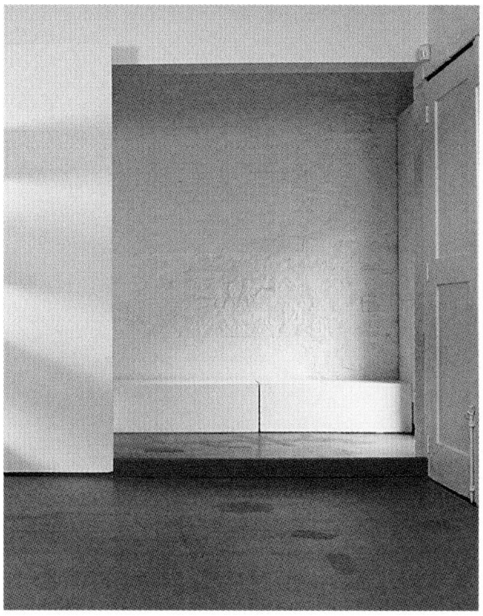

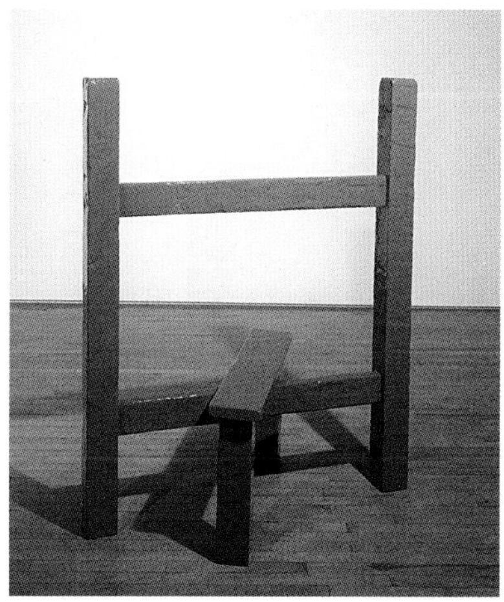

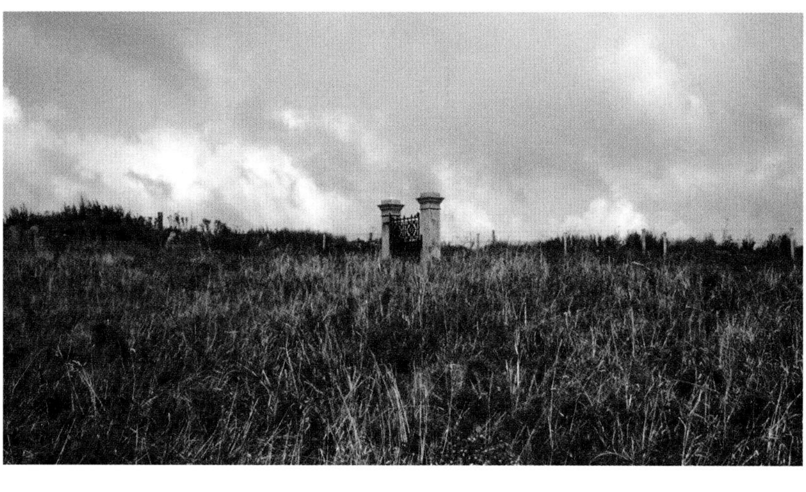

Ceal Floyer does something similar, but larger, with her ***Vorsicht Stufe*** on the steps of the Humboldt University in Berlin. Her repeated warnings precede, physically and conceptually, the monumental quotation from Marx:

> Philosophers have only interpreted the world in various ways: the point is to change it.[10]

Beware of the step. To enter is often to beware as well as to be aware. Ryan Gander's *I Need Some Meaning I Can Memorise: The Invisible Pull*, installed at the entrance to the Fredericianum in Kassel, effectively marshalled these forces, combining arrival with event, as visitors came to realise that the work was the stiff breeze that greeted them as they entered.

...

198. Ceal Floyer, *Vorsicht Stufe*, 2009

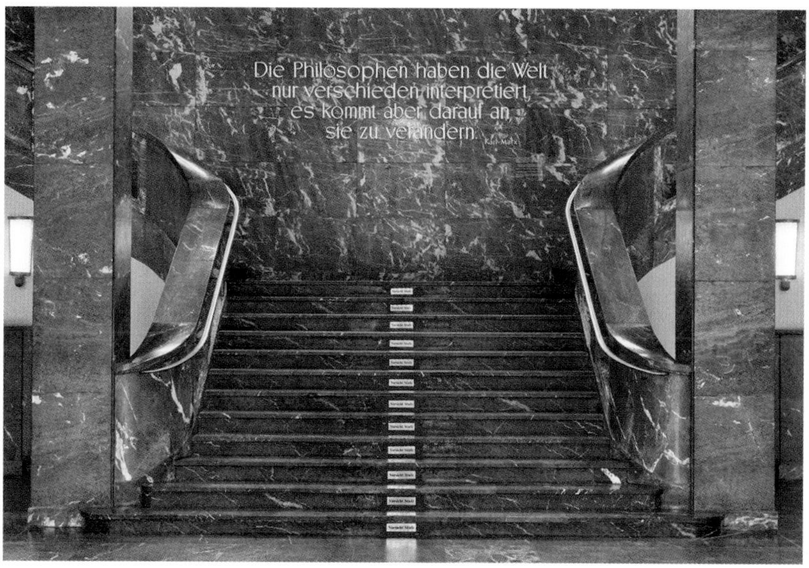
Die Philosophen haben die Welt
nur verschieden interpretiert,
es kommt aber darauf an,
sie zu verändern.

The doorway sounds, heralding the arriving visitor. A. K. Dolven's ***Out of Tune*** made very apparent the magic of the bell (in this case from Scraptoft Church in Leicestershire) by demonstrating its quite particular amalgam of weight and height. Like a huge gateway on the beach, the bell, when rung, seemed to ground the structure and, with it, we announced our arrival. The bell also marks transformation: the wedding or the funeral. It invites or repels: calling to prayer or warning off ships. It can be a beacon, or mark the rite of passage. It can be alone, or in company. Part of Dolven's point, in this particular piece, is the isolation of the single bell, removed from the peal because it did not harmonise.

Bells are as central to the language of the foundry as armour, necessarily made by casting. They more particularly represent this essential duality, with their inversion as mortars a reminder of their potential doubling, and of their alchemical roots. Fiona Banner's bell, ***Tornado***, makes explicit in its title its journey from military hardware, and was cast, like many bells, at John Taylor's,[11] the Loughborough Bell Foundry. Unusually, however, her bell was made from the aluminium retrieved from the plane, rather than from bronze, and is untuned.

open ---

199. A. K. Dolven, *Out of Tune*, 2011

200. Fiona Banner, *Tornado*, 2010

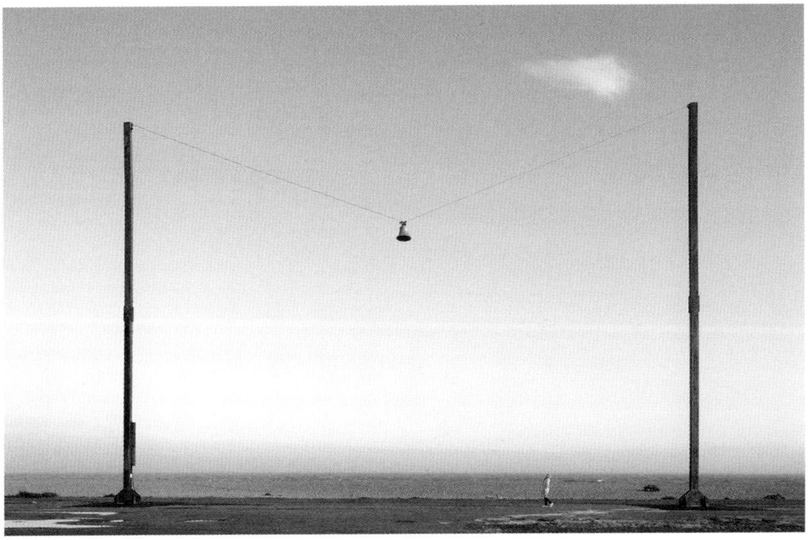

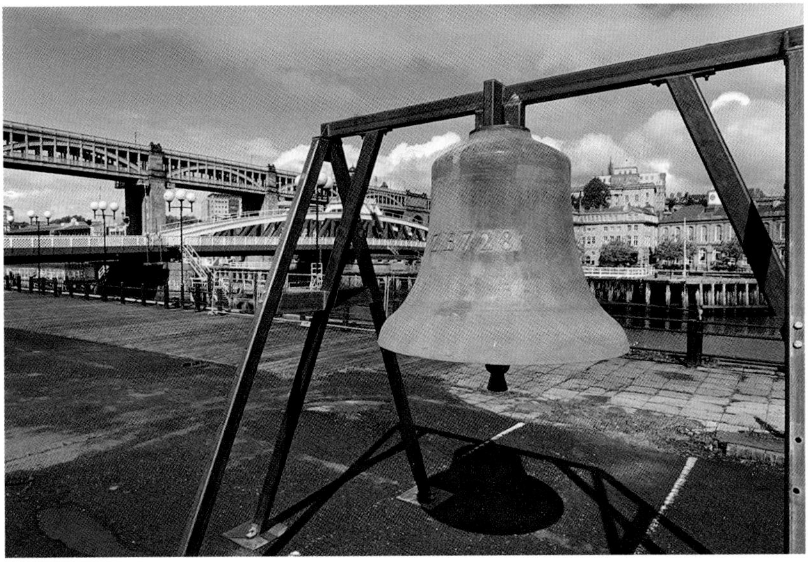

The doorway becomes the frame for sound. The **Sanctuary Ring**, from the door of Durham Cathedral, signified safety and protection from secular persecution for the person knocking. Founders have traditionally made knockers for doors as part of their repertoire, or, on occasion, cast those more particular designs of sculptors. Alfred Stevens made **doorknockers** for Westonbirt House, and all the door furniture for Dorchester House, London; Jacob Epstein made the door handles for ecclesiastical commissions, and Gertrude Hermes had a speciality in making doorknockers, including a brass frog.[12]

...

201. Sanctuary Ring knocker, copy of 12th-century bronze original

open

202. Alfred Stevens, doorknocker, c.1865

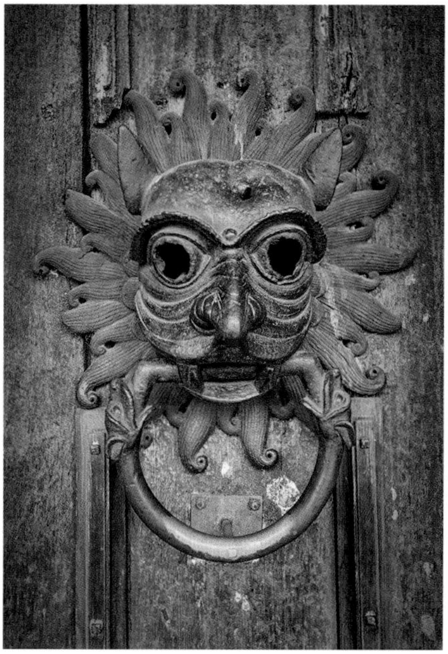

203

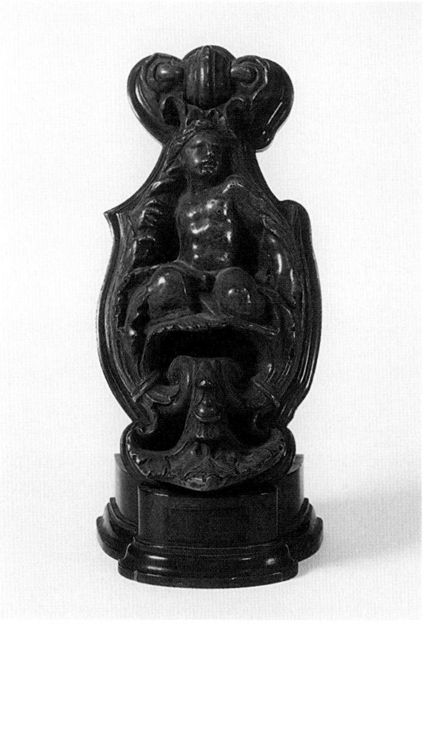

The threshold is notably associated with metalwork; the doorknocker, the bell, the railing. The foundry seems at home here, in this place between in-doors and out. Metalwork is strong enough to protect while at the same time opening up to view; inside the church, where grilles were as much about denying as enabling access, their open-work character allowed sight of the objects they protected. They were particularly used to protect and screen altars and tombs, and signal the presence of something of great importance, usually the body of a king or a saint. More commonly of course railings have a more banal function, keeping children out and their footballs in, as pictured by Keith Wilson in his ***Football in Railings***.

...

open

203. Keith Wilson, *Football in Railings*, 1998

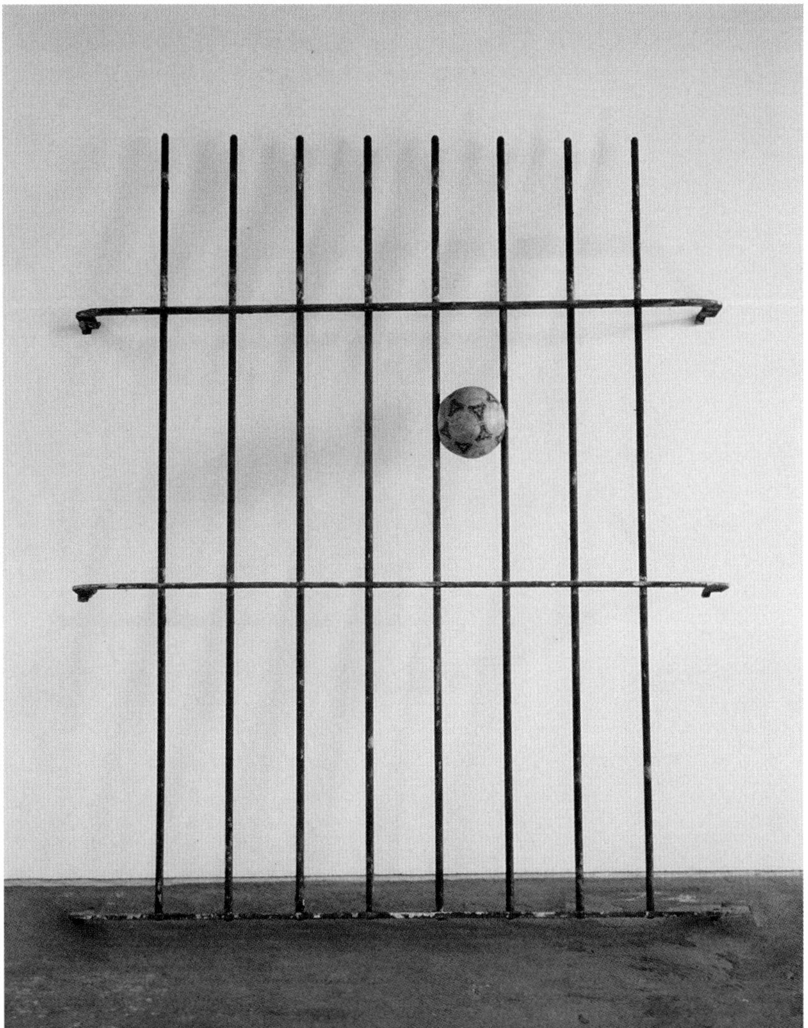

205

Surviving grilles are rare; the **Chichester Grille** is thought to have screened the tomb of Saint Richard in the choir of Chichester Cathedral. Westminster Abbey deploys a number around its tombs, including that of Queen Eleanor. The small **grille** now in the Victoria and Albert Museum may well have come from St George's Chapel, Windsor, where the **gates of Edward IV**'s chantry chapel represent unusually magnificent ironwork, made by John Tresilian, the late king's 'principal smith' between 1477 and 1484.

...

open

204. Chichester Grille, c.1250

205. Wrought-iron grille, 1480–1500

206. John Tresilian, gates to Edward IV's chantry chapel, 1477–84

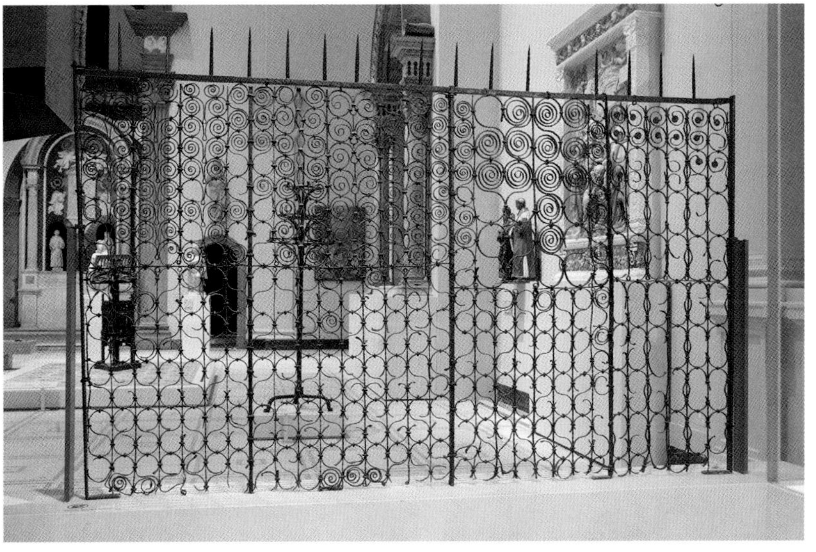

207

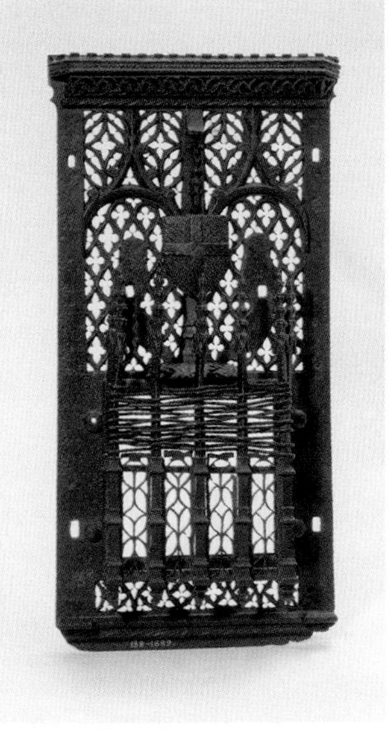

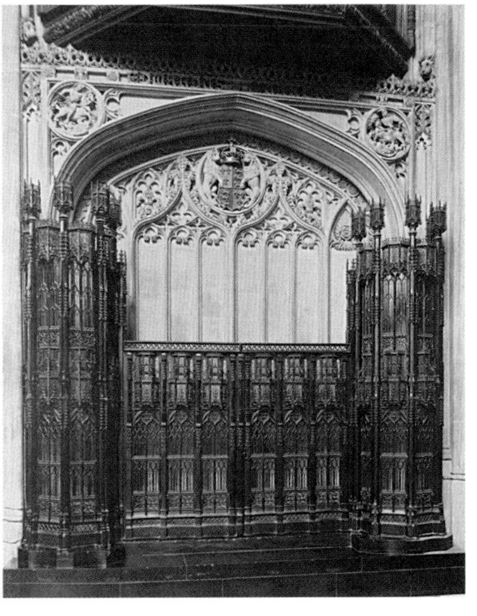

Alfred Gilbert may have been inspired by the exceptional quality and design of the late medieval ironwork in the Windsor grille (he was after all working there on the Clarence Memorial, where a fine bronze screen is punctuated by figures of saints) in his unusual late memorial to **Queen Alexandra**. Here, however, the grille is reversed, acting as foil to the figures (Faith, Hope and Charity), protecting them rather than us, but nonetheless carrying the vestige of the idea of the medieval shrine, even on a London street. The fact that this memorial is also a fountain links back to a pre-classical trope, of a sacred spring or protected place.

207. Alfred Gilbert, Queen Alexandra Memorial, 1926–32

- - -

One of Gilbert's most extraordinary works is the **chimneypiece** he designed for Rutland Lodge, the home of Leeds textile manufacturer and art collector Sam Wilson. Hard to interpret in any way as a utilitarian object, the chimney-piece nonetheless derives much of its power from the fact that it was designed to hold fire. Cast in sections, each perhaps more closely related to the work-manship associated with woodcarving, with their linen-fold panelling and highly sinuous female figures, it comes complete with an inset painting. Three and a half metres high, it sits oddly now in the Leeds City Art Gallery, its bronze forms apparently melting, its wooden appearance highly combustible, its apertures suggesting the piercing of the wall and the potential for communion with another, less stable, world.

open

208. Alfred Gilbert, Sam Wilson Chimneypiece, c.1908–14

...

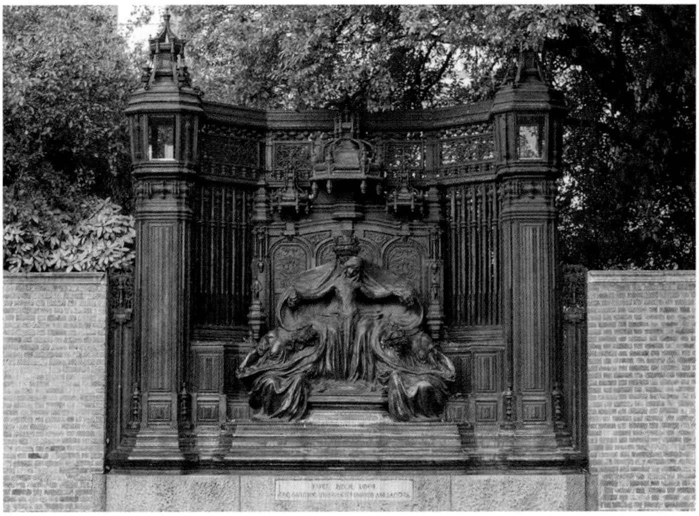

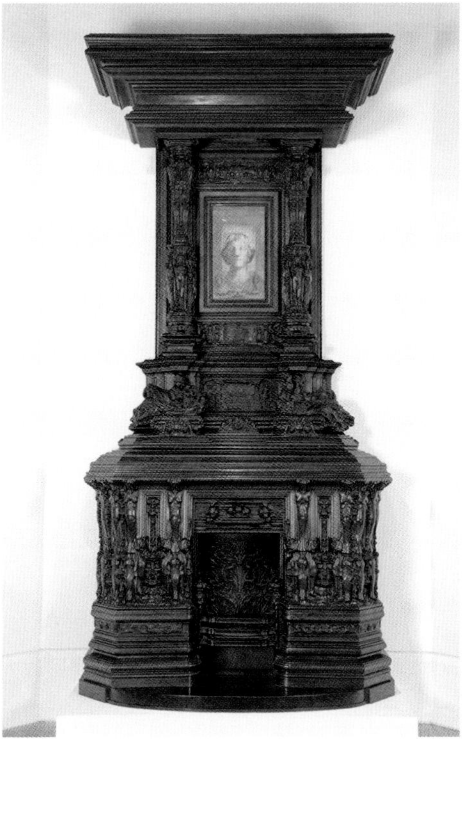

Even less highly bespoke fire furniture drew on the rich symbolic associations of the fireplace. During the 1850s Alfred Stevens was chief designer to the Sheffield manufacturers Hoole & Co. and in the Victoria and Albert Museum are numerous plaster sections of his designs, including angle pieces, corner pieces and spandrels, all furniture and fittings for the fire. At the Great Exhibition he exhibited, for Hoole, a 'console stove'[13] and a fireplace known as the 'Boy', which greatly increased their business, and that of Stevens. Stevens's work was often realised in multi-media compositions, using various metals, including bronze, brass and steel. The figuration he used is inventive, but not innovative. Figuring the fireplace was a long tradition, and figures such as the 'Boy' have a lineage that can be traced back to the Renaissance and beyond. The representation of the Elements (the boy holds his pitcher of water) is very much central to the repertoire.

open

In 1930 the sculptor C. S. Jagger produced one of the most arresting fire surrounds with his ***Scandal***. Originally made for the house of Henry and Gwen Mond in London's Smith Square, which was remodelled by Darcy Braddell, the relief depicts lovers oblivious to society, and the fire basket below uses two Egyptianate cats to support a central motif of two masks in profile with a bird perched at the centre. The clients' initials are inscribed on the three shields below. It is probable that Jagger had the work cast at the Thames Ditton foundry of A. B. Burton; the relief in bronze, the basket in iron.

...

209. Charles Sargeant Jagger, *Scandal* relief and firebasket, 1930

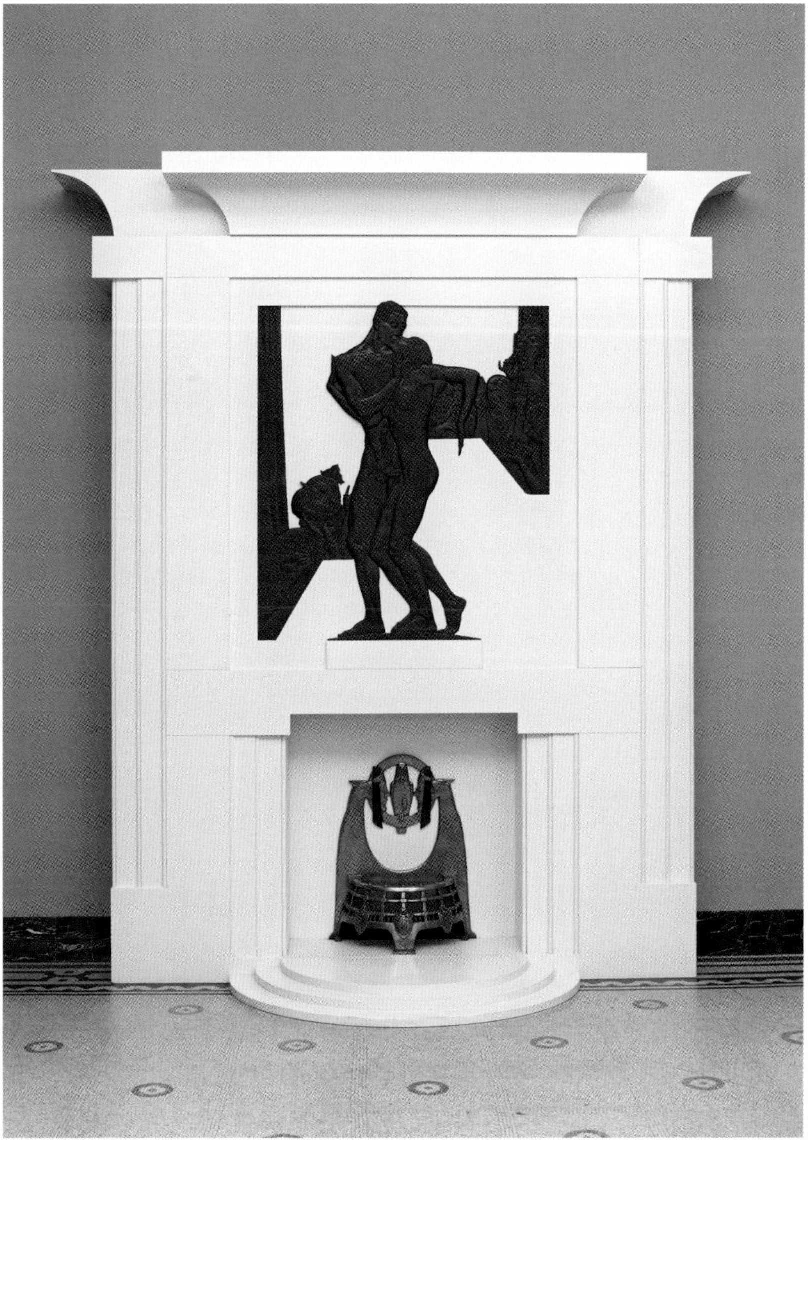

In the foundry are cast the iron grate and the bronze relief; fire makes them and they will carry fire. This close relationship, operating through the foundry, in which destruction and creation are co-dependent, is a rich theme for the sculptor, whether more or less explicitly. But the fireplace represents more than fire; symbolically and practically, with its access to a physical exterior, to the elements, it suggests more widely and more concretely a world beyond the walls of the room in which it stands. Such fireplaces were unique commissions, with highly personalised iconography that seems to link love and death with the place of the hearth. We are reminded of Alfred Gilbert's contemporary use of the phrase 'Mors Janua Vitae' ('Death is the gateway to life').

There is something of this piercing of the wall at play in the work of various contemporary artists, and not just Anish Kapoor, whose work also adds something of the male/female dynamic. Rose Finn-Kelcey's ***Just Minus*** fireplace, which introduced copper pipes carrying refrigerant through the fireplace and into the warmth of a Roman room, makes explicit the fireplace's transitional function as a place of exchange for heat and cold, for exit and entrance. Anna Barriball's ***Draw (fireplace)*** proposed that the fireplace was inhaling and exhaling, and with each intake the sheet of paper that covered the grate embraced its details, as if it were indeed a tracing or rubbing.

open

---

210. Rose Finn-Kelcey, *Just Minus*, 1994

211. Anna Barriball, *Draw (fireplace)*, 2005

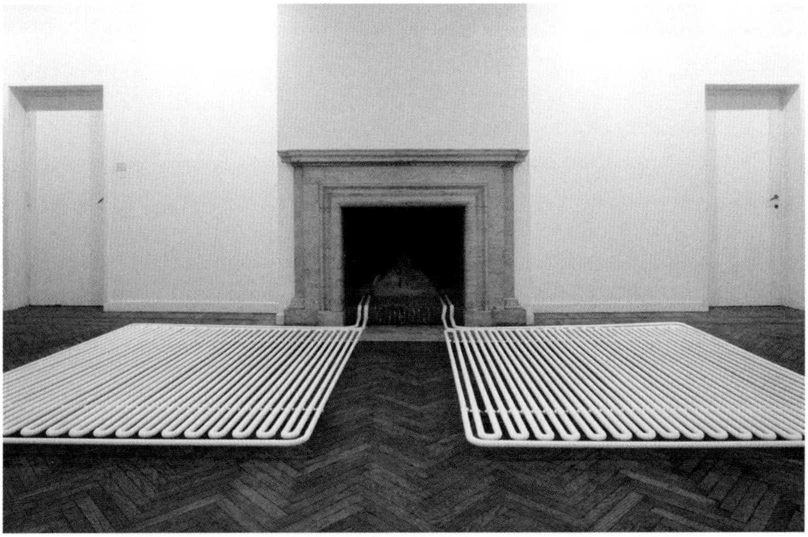

213

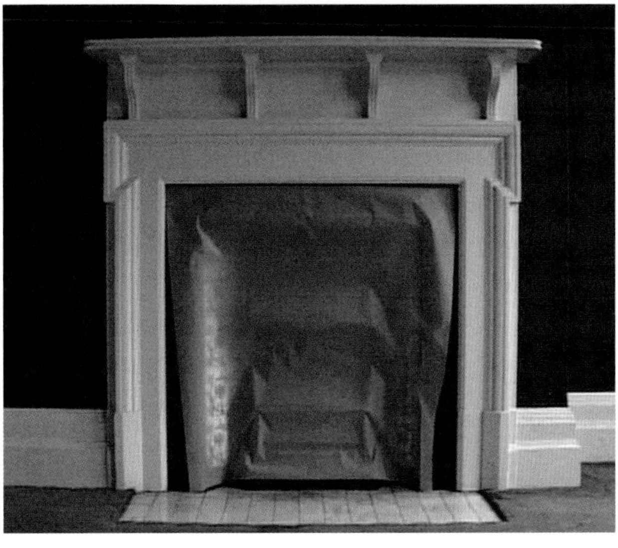

The fireback, the part of the whole ensemble that is nearest to the fire itself, seems to get closest to telling the story of its own production. The earliest dated fireback is of 1553, but they are likely to date back to the construction of the first blast furnace in the last decade of the fifteenth century. Such firebacks remind us of the proximity of fire to sculpture, and images of statuary being forged are an excellent model.

In William Adam's **Duff House**, Banff, there is a good example of a statue being struck as if out of the fire itself. This may show the Creation of Man by Prometheus, who, after all, had stolen the fire from Zeus. The representation of the creation of man is indistinguishable from the creation of a statue. Clay is, as it were, insufficient; heat is also necessary.

212. Duff House fireback, 1735–40

If not displaying a coat of arms, which is most common, or other kinds of more rustic stamps, firebacks also seem to be a site of choice for mythical scenes of transformation. Alfred Stevens's *Rape of Proserpine* shows Pluto in his chariot, plucking Proserpine from the ground to take her to Hades. Her return to earth marks the spring, but she is more strongly associated with the underworld and the spirits of the dead.

open

Biblical scenes are also found. In Bessie Surtees House, Newcastle, is a fireback apparently depicting the **Annunciation**.

...

213. *Annunciation* fireback, 17th century

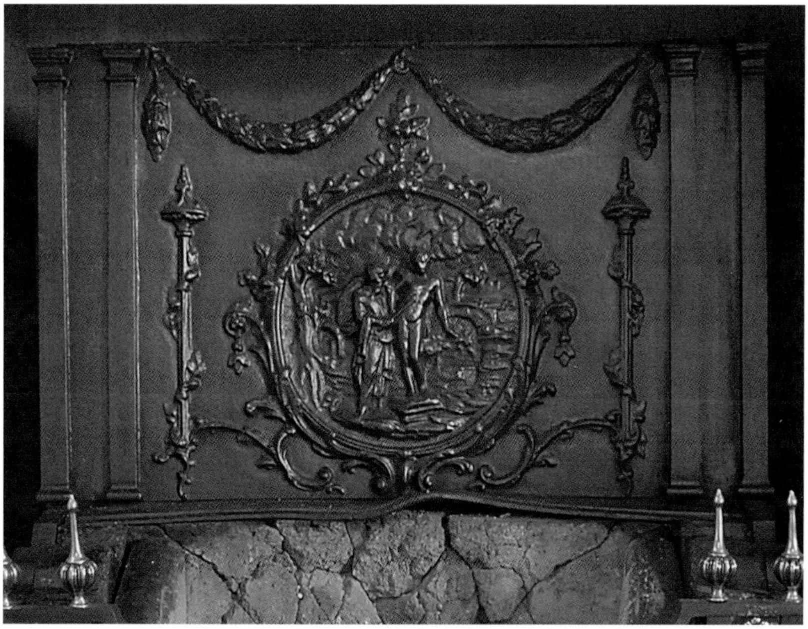

215

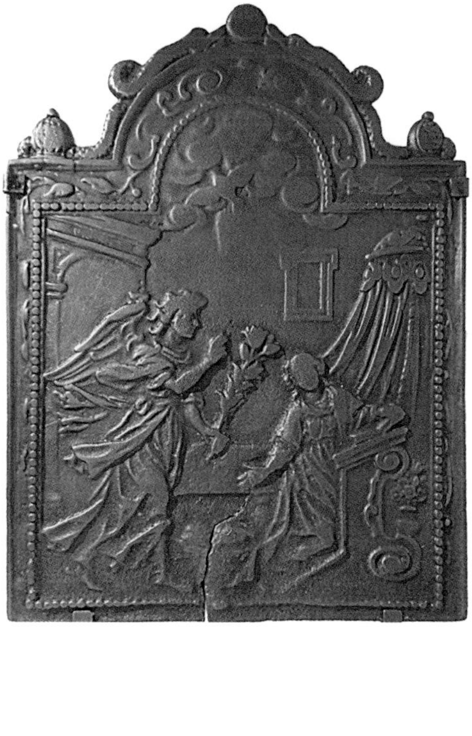

Others relate more particularly to the context of the fire and may denote confession. Good examples are found at the Anne of Cleves House Museum, which is devoted to the Wealden Iron Industry. An example from around 1600 represents **Protestant martyrs** being burnt at the stake. From the mid-seventeenth century we have scenes from the Bible such as the **Burning Fiery Furnace**, and the sacrifice of Isaac. A secular example, marked as of the Company of Blacksmiths, shows a phoenix suitably rising from the flames. An equally conceptual example has the fireback representing the **firedogs** in front.

---

open

214. Fireback depicting Protestant martyrs being burnt at the stake, c.1600

215. Fireback depicting the Burning Fiery Furnace, 1636

216. Fireback depicting firedogs, date unknown

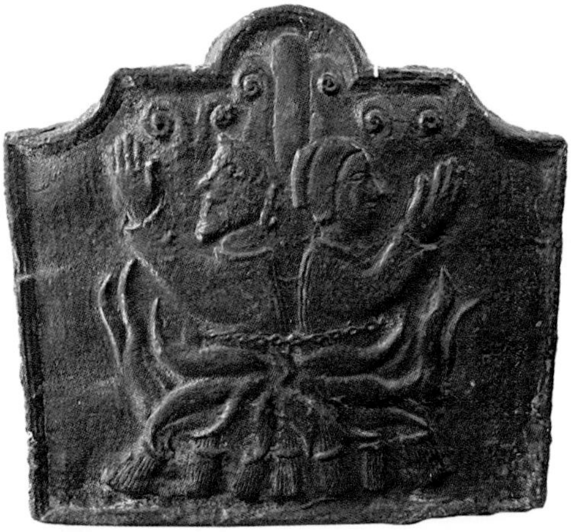

217

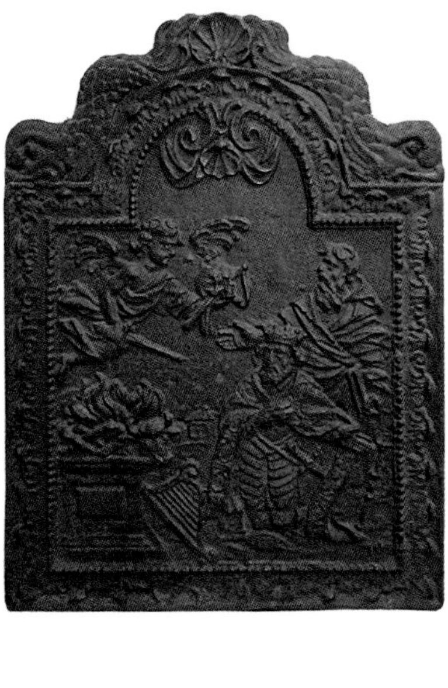

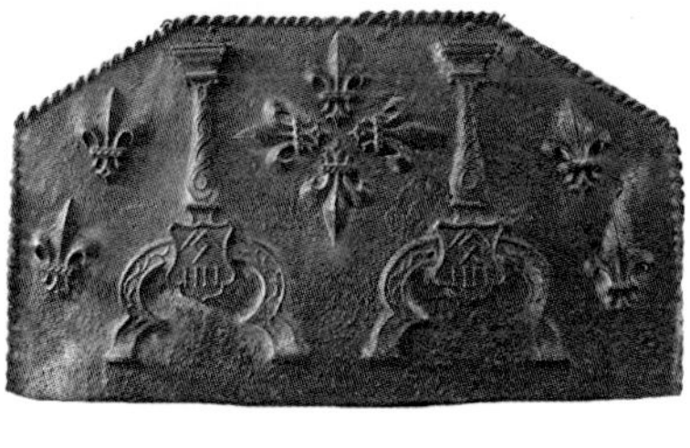

The accoutrements for the fireplace also allude to its significance as foyer; they too make the bridge between founder and fireplace, and between art and armour, as well as between our space and a space beyond. Anthony Hatch, working in London in the late seventeenth century, was part of the Armourers and Braziers Company and supplied the Company's chimneypiece. Most of the enamelled brasses that are now known are presumed to have emanated from his workshop. The blue and white enamel of his **firedogs** sets off the brass putti who play in the garlands, but perhaps more remarkable is the overall profile of the dogs themselves.

Another kind of vestigial marker of the fire (having originally supported the burning logs), firedogs remain on the hearth like a trace of a time past, or of the fire that made them. After the advent of the firegrate, the andiron or firedog survives essentially as a kind of doubling of the fire, acting both as prototype and advance announcement. It is a piece of threshold furniture that announces the threshold itself. Much simpler examples than those of Anthony Hatch abound, as in the National Trust's properties at Ty Mawr Wybrnant, where the **dog form** is quite clearly shown; Dudmaston (seventeenth century); Blickling (*c.*1860), by John Pollen; and Owletts (early 1900s), by Herbert Baker.

open

...

217. Anthony Hatch, firedog, 1650–80

218. Firedogs, date unknown

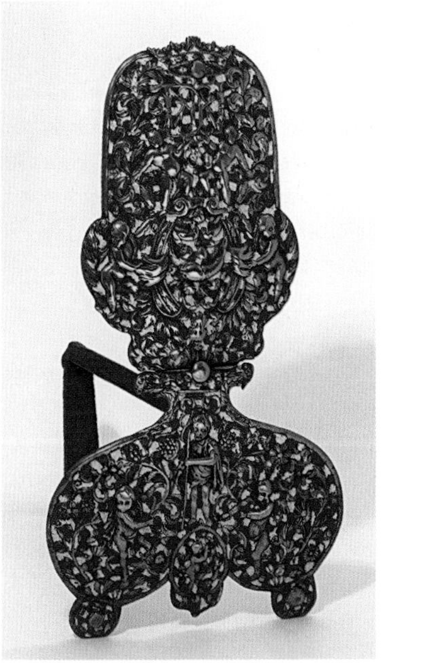

219

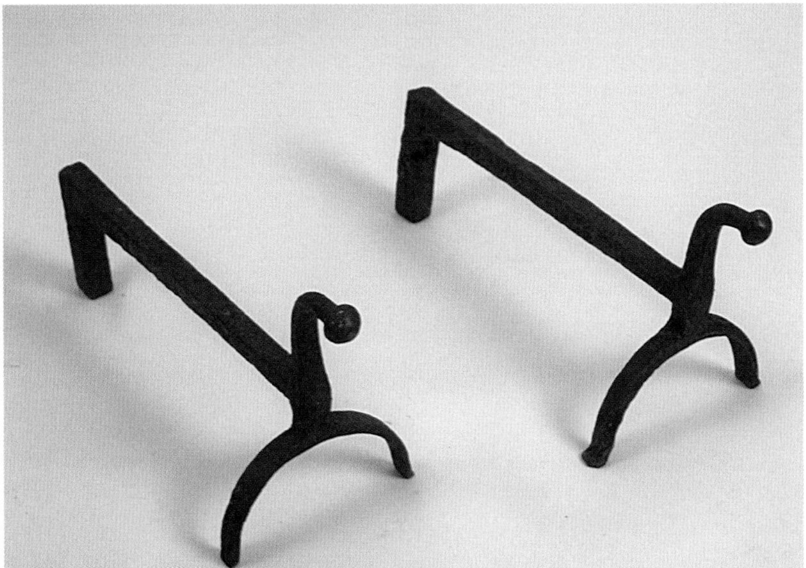

In France there was in the inter-war years a minor fashion for fire furniture, occasioned by the support of rich clients such as Marie-Laure and Charles de Noailles, who, working with interior designer Jean-Michel Frank, looked for opportunities in which modern sculptors such as Henri Laurens and the Giacometti brothers could integrate their work into the interior. They found embedded in the fireplace similar opportunities, allegorical and material. Some of these designs were inspired by contemporary and continuing discoveries as Howard Carter excavated the tomb of Tutankhamen; threshold objects placed in progressive order in relation to the body and its afterlife.

Occasional modern British designers, including **Charles Rennie Mackintosh** in his fireplace for the Willow Tea Rooms in Glasgow, effectively combine andirons, grate and fender to make a simple but striking composition that speaks clearly of the fire behind it. Geoffrey Clarke's iron couple, *Man* and ***Woman*** retain something of this sense of fireside furniture, in their material, their pairing, and in their form. Upright, annunciatory, made in the fire, vaguely functional, they also suggest the potential of the future.

219. Charles Rennie Mackintosh, fireplace, c.1904

- - -

open

220. Geoffrey Clarke, *Woman*, 1953

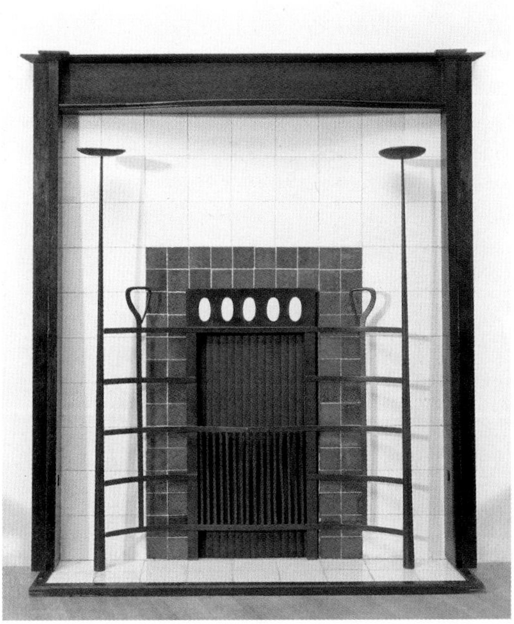

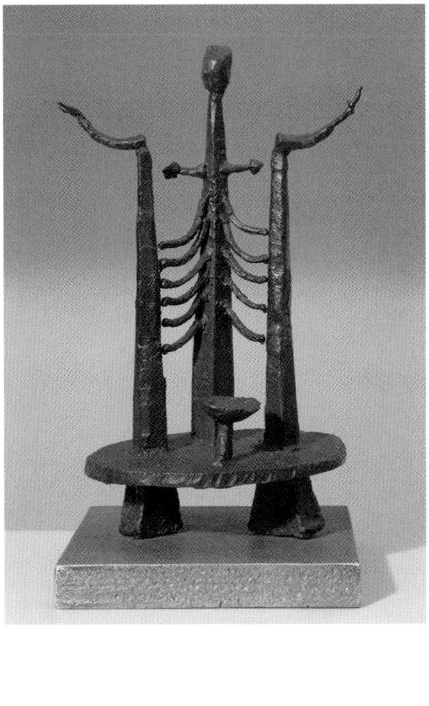

If the fire is the place of creation and metamorphosis, most especially in relation to sculpture, the fireplace surround has a related but different set of meanings. The chimneypiece is symbolic of the shift in form, but carries further in terms of the shift in time and place. Its stone construction removes it from the foundry and thus from the fire itself; it is a frame made from the material of the landscape, the cool frame for the fiery heat.

The chimneypiece, with its various components, is the perfect stage around which to construct this narrative, and it is indeed very often theatrical. Too often now only one part survives, in isolation, separated from its fuller spatial context. Magnificent as it is, William Chambers's splendid **chimneypiece** for Gower House, probably carved by Joseph Wilton, can no longer draw on its environment. Are its herms, who seem to represent lictors with their axes and bunches of fasces, an allusion to the firewood gathered outside?[14]

Similarly the **overmantel** relief by William Collins and Henry Cheere would regain meaning if it were reunited with its chimneypiece, where we would understand better why the shepherd girl is asleep. A similar conceit might be evinced by Anne Seymour Damer's ***Two Sleeping Dogs*** lying in front of the fire, which might be lit in John Bacon's chimneypiece in the Tapestry Drawing Room at Goodwood. More soberly, in George Richardson's church at Stapleford, the ***Sacrifice of Isaac*** is carved into the gallery mantelpiece, a small brazier figured alight above the real flames below.

open

...

221. Attributed to Joseph Wilton, chimneypiece, c.1775

222. William Collins and Henry Cheere, *Shepherd and Shepherdess*, c.1761

223. Anne Seymour Damer, *Two Sleeping Dogs*, 1784

224. *Sacrifice of Isaac*, 1783

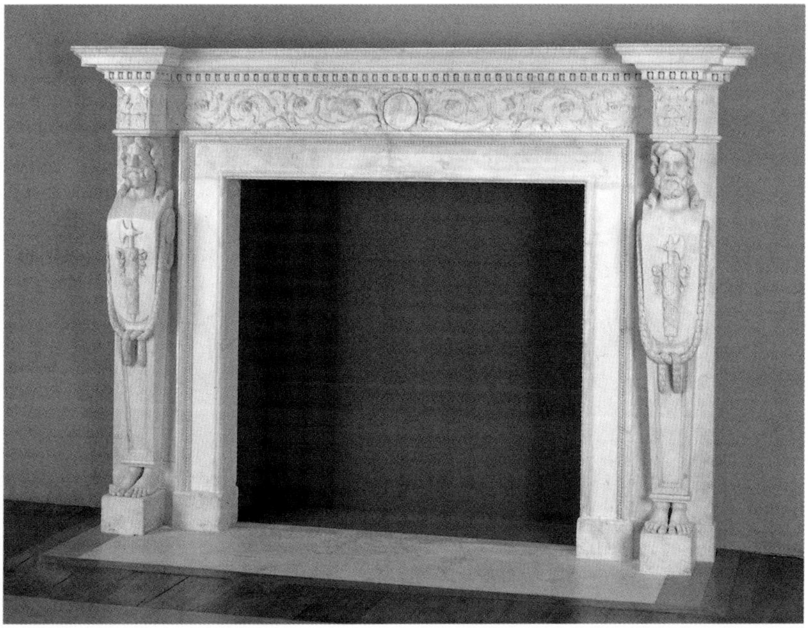

223

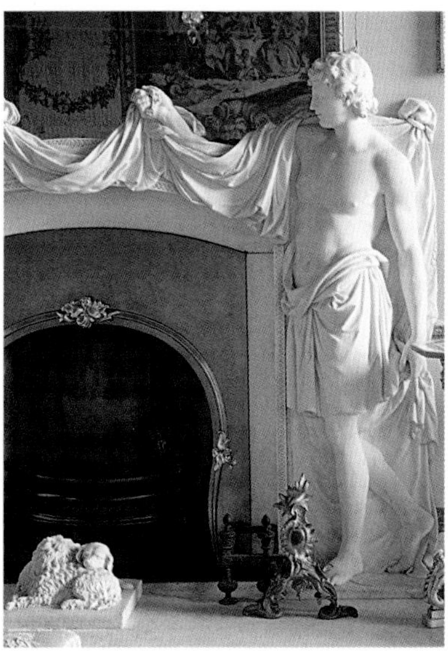

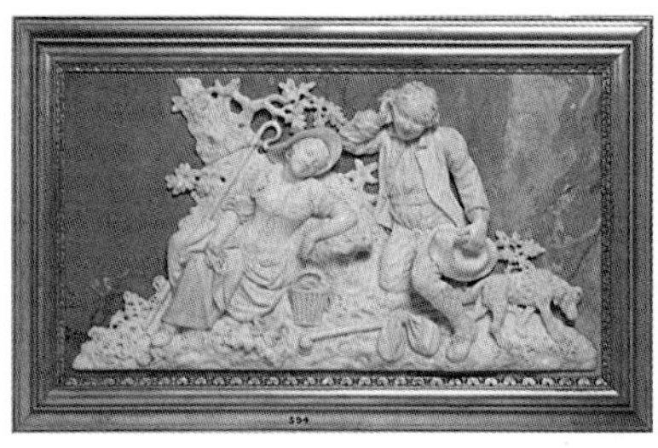

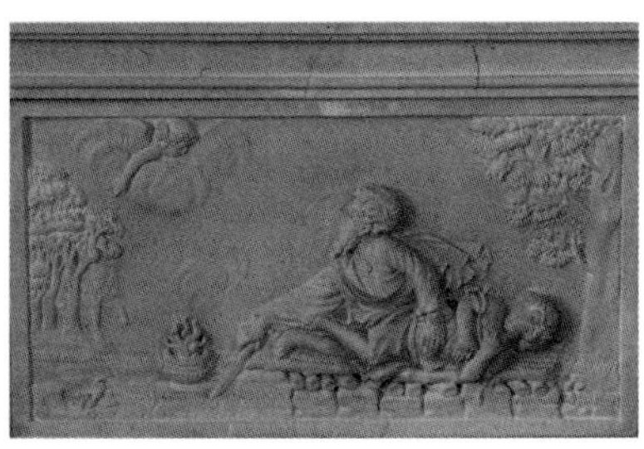

A work by Lucy Gunning, entitled ***Peeling the Apple***, uses the space of the chimneypiece for its effect, hinting at a biblical transgression. The video monitor is concealed within the chimney and the image could only be seen on a mirror placed on the hearth. The short film, a close-up of a woman peeling and eating an apple, also included the sound of bird song, again bringing the outside in, as if through a hole. This kind of triangulation of viewpoint, as the artist describes it, represents more explicitly what I have been describing above, with the site of the fireplace a miniaturised theatre of action, with its proscenium arch and noises off, and sense of narrative time.

- - -

open

225. Lucy Gunning, *Peeling the Apple*, 1996

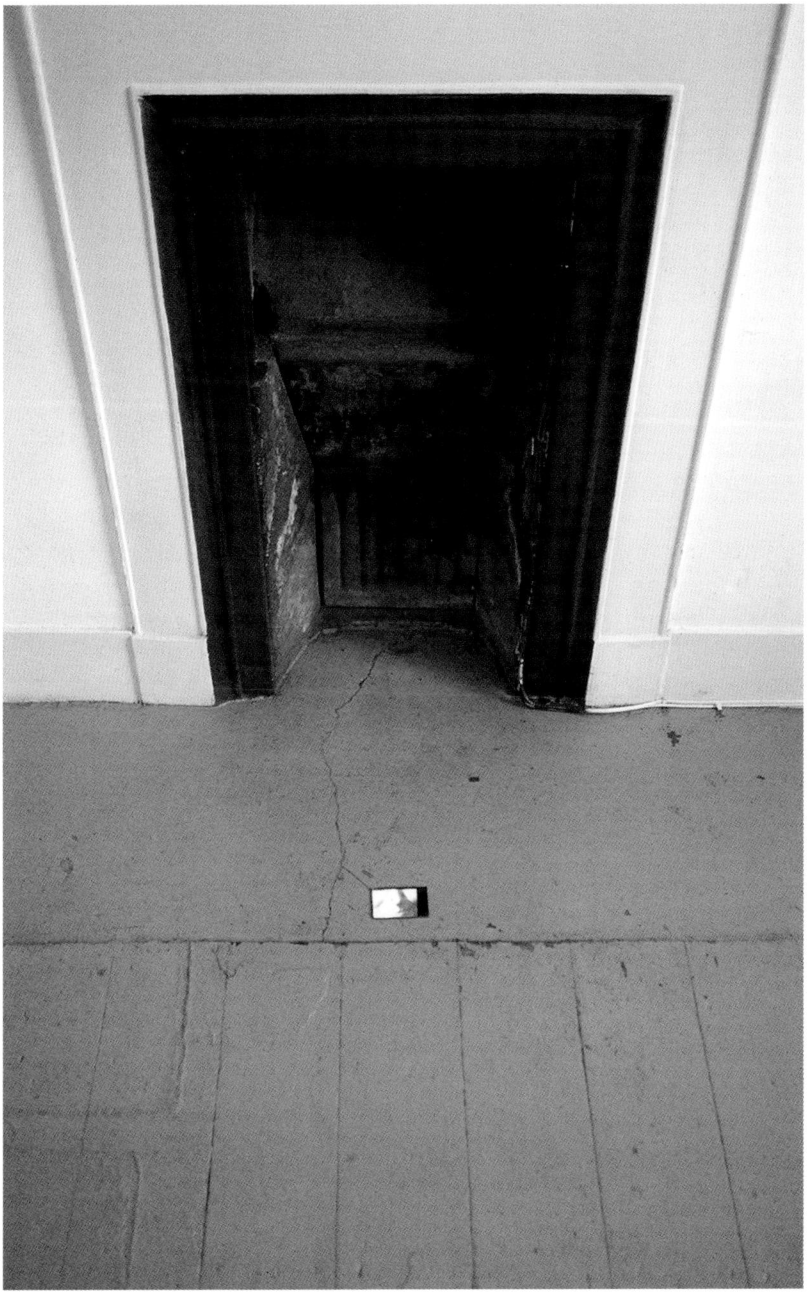

Overmantels may depict specific allegorical subjects, but the place is more often reserved instead for a mirror. There is a different kind of potential here, which seems perhaps to suggest the combination of mind and body, the conceptual and the physical, the here and now (the physical body's need for warmth), combined with more cerebral reflections on the future and even of the afterlife (of the fires of redemption).

Mirrors hang, quite literally, on the threshold between object and image, between two ways of apprehending. Mid-eighteenth-century mirrors of the quality of those made by and after **Thomas Johnson** are more than mere frames, and have a transcendent nature that takes the viewer well beyond him or herself, and their immediate surroundings. So well do such mirrors blend in with the material decoration of the room more generally, and so shallow is their depth, that they seem to offer not just reflection, but actual transparency or piercing of the wall.

Another mid-century example, by or after **Thomas Chippendale**, seems almost to enclose a hole. **John Frankland**'s so-called 'brown works', which go as far as works can in stripping back illusion, are the frames without the skin, similarly enclosing a space on the wall. Such works take us close to demonstrating what happens with the mirrors.

open

...

226. Thomas Johnson, mirror frame, 1750–60

227. By or after Thomas Chippendale, mirror, c.1765

228. John Frankland, *Untitled Brown Work*, 2005

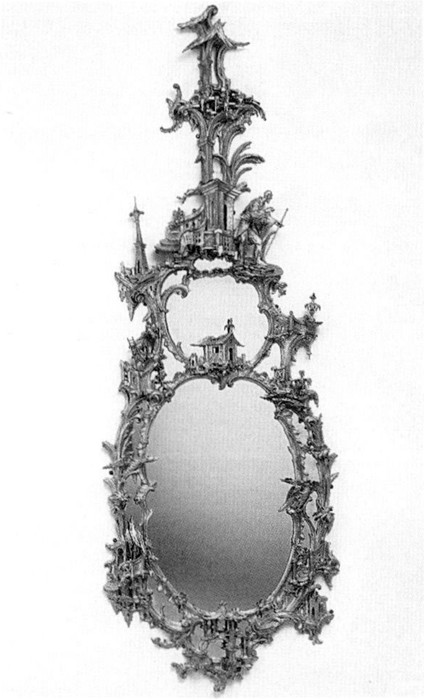

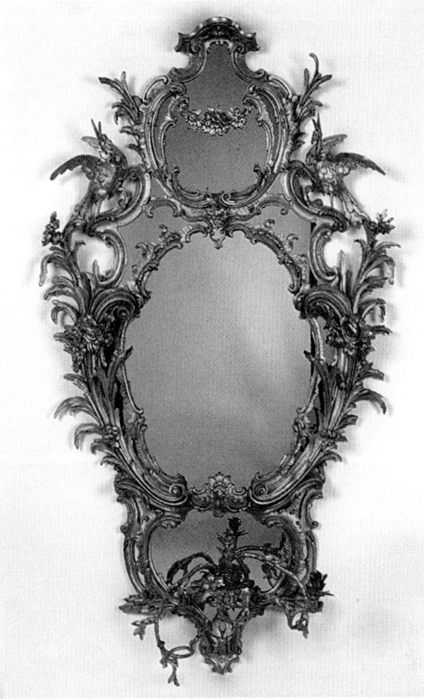

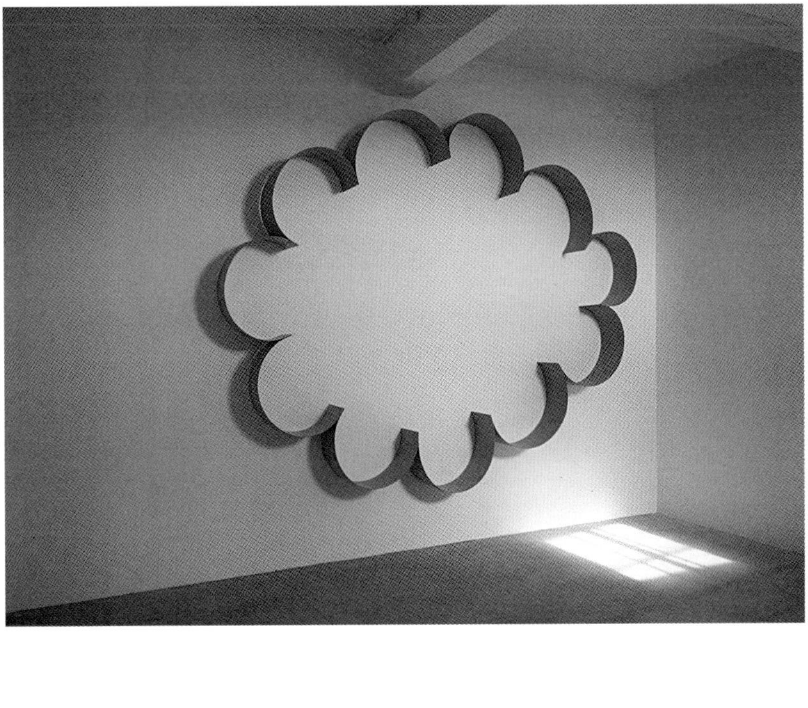

Thomas Sheraton's *Cabinet Dictionary* of 1803 only includes convex mirrors, noting their 'agreeable effect' over and beyond their convenience of holding lights. This fashion coincided with the technical improvements made by the Ravenhead glass works at St Helens. An **example** in the Victoria and Albert Museum shows the basic form with various decorative extras. Early works by Hermione Wiltshire, like ***Puff***, quote from the abundant gilding of the Rococo interior to allow themselves entry into such rooms and to reveal their subliminal bodily aspect. Her teacher Helen Chadwick also played on the Rococo interior to point up its inherent sexuality in her ***Vanitas II*** self-portrait.

...

open

229. Convex mirror, c.1800

230. Hermione Wiltshire, *Puff*, 1996

231. Helen Chadwick, *Vanitas II*, 1986

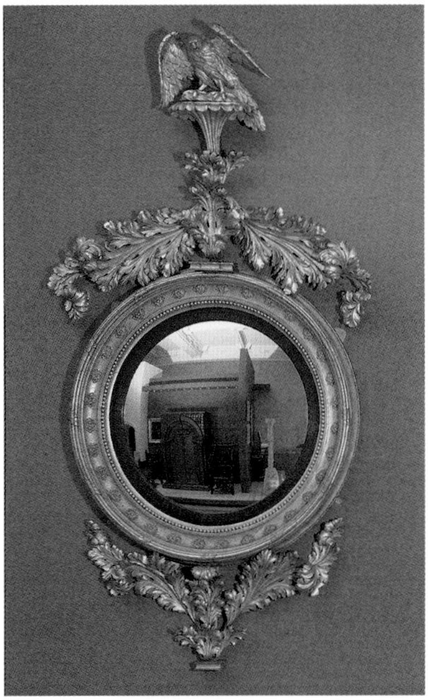

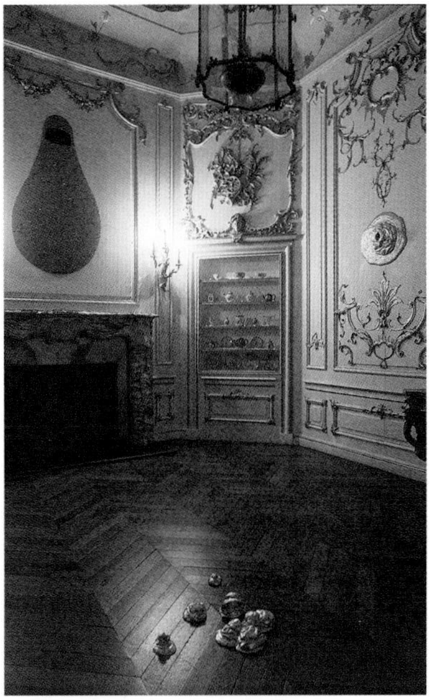

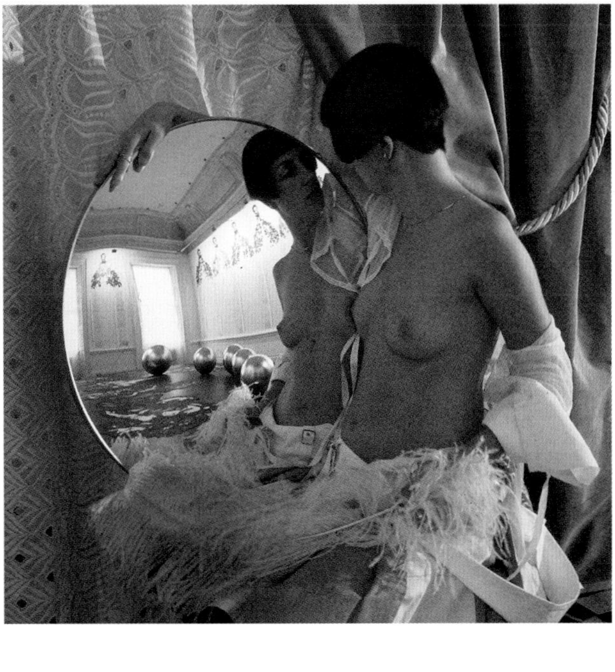

Whereas Chadwick represents the mirror, Anish Kapoor used the mirror itself. His ***Turning the World Upside Down*** does what it promises, and delights in doing so. In 1996 the artist Cerith Wyn Evans showed, in his first solo exhibition at the White Cube gallery, his ***Inverse Reverse Perverse***. Although Evans has gone on since to make many more complicated mirror installations, the very simplicity of this first piece represents the mirror's basic fascination and its interest to artists and designers.

...

232. Anish Kapoor, *Turning the World Upside Down*, 1995

open

233. Cerith Wyn Evans, *Inverse Reverse Perverse*, 1996

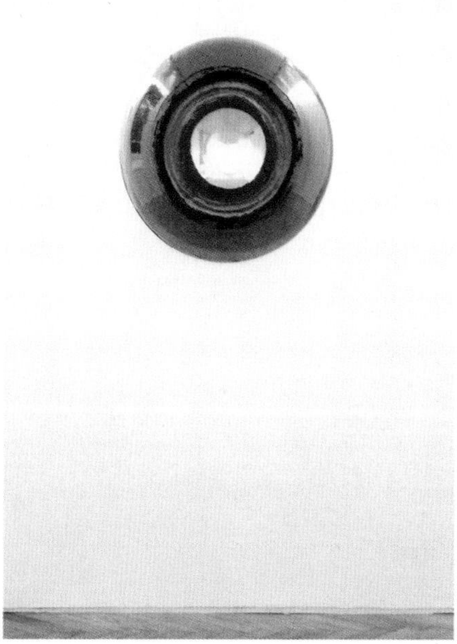

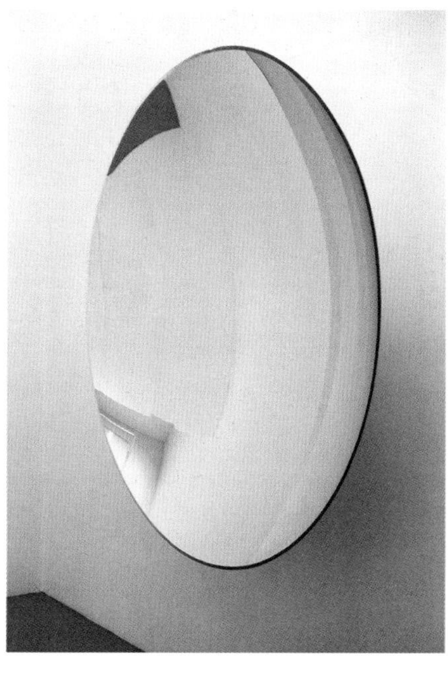

The ubiquity of Kapoor's mirrors has perhaps come to deny them their intrinsic significance as works that speak similarly of eye and body at the same time, allowing their viewers to merge with their environment and, as it were, to walk through walls. ***Double Mirror*** is analogous to earlier works by Bruce Nauman, Dan Graham and Michelangelo Pistoletto, which played on our delight in being endlessly reconfigured. Dan Graham's central subject is recent time, or, as he styled it in an early work, *Present Continuous Past(s)*, and perhaps we might go so far as to link recent mirror works with a model that goes back at least to the developing understanding of the role of the observer in any interpretation of the physical world, as understood by the scientists developing atomic physics in the years leading up to the Second World War.[15] This certainly fascinated Barbara Hepworth in the 1940s and her work too oscillates similarly between two places and two different experiences, fascinated as she was by the observer's relationship to the observed. One might see **Mark Leckey**'s repeated return to work set in his studio in London's Windmill Street, seen through a convex mirror, as representing that kind of self-reflexive circularity.

...

open

234. Anish Kapoor, *Double Mirror*, 1998

235. Mark Leckey, *Made in 'Eaven*, 2004

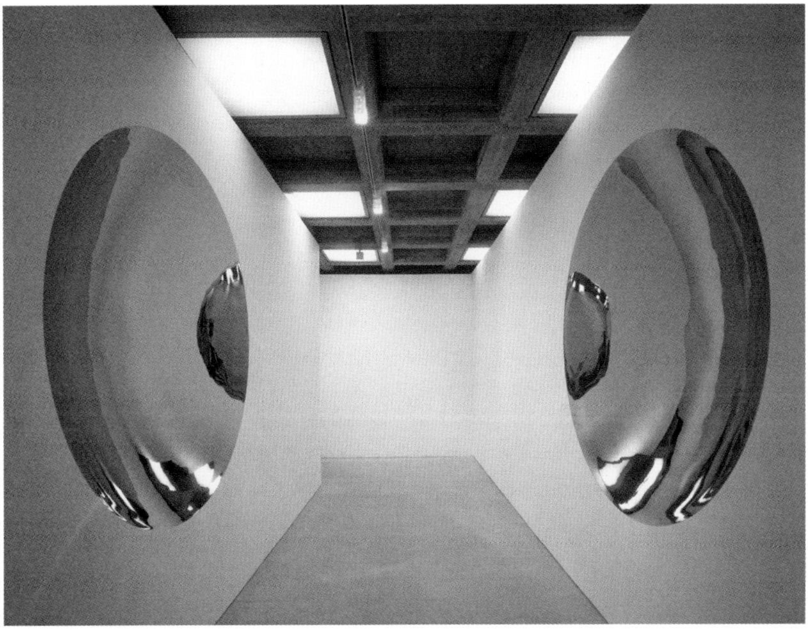

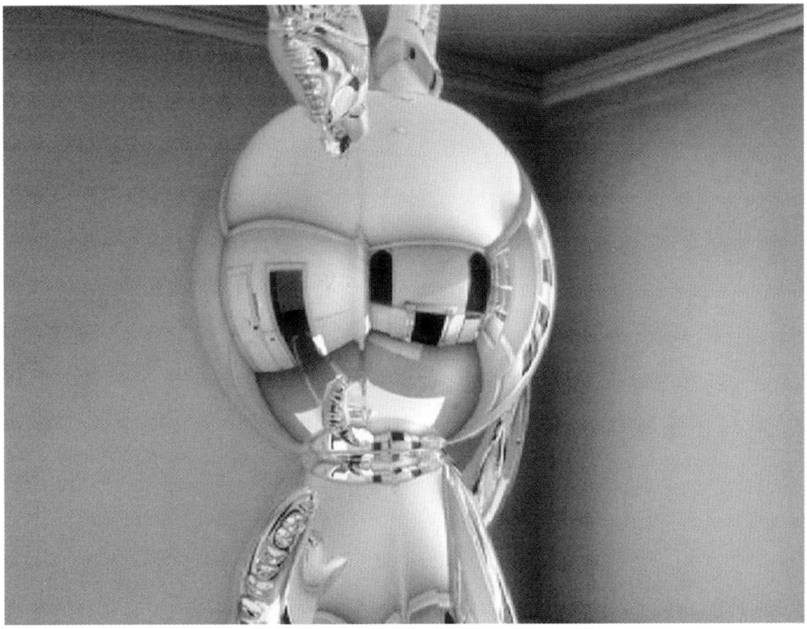

The very particular **combination** found in a remarkable work of c.1720, which combines a mirror with a barometer and a thermometer, and a support for a clock, ties us back to the conditions of our physical environment and the ways in which we measure them. On the wall in front of us we see ourselves, within the room where we stand. We look up or to the side and register the time, the heat and the air pressure, and back to our own reflection. We are image and object, changing, minutely, along with the environment around us.

Why is this object so fascinating? I think both because it provides a frame for the unframeable: for time, weather, wind, smoke, pressure, and because it creates a sculptural passage, a kind of egress, out from the confines of the drawing room. Somehow the inverse of a Temple of the Winds, which is outside rather than in, it too 'captures' the invisible and provides it with a face. A Janus-like arrangement, it arrests us on the threshold, physical and conceptual, of the point at which we stand.

---

open

236. Mirror, c.1720

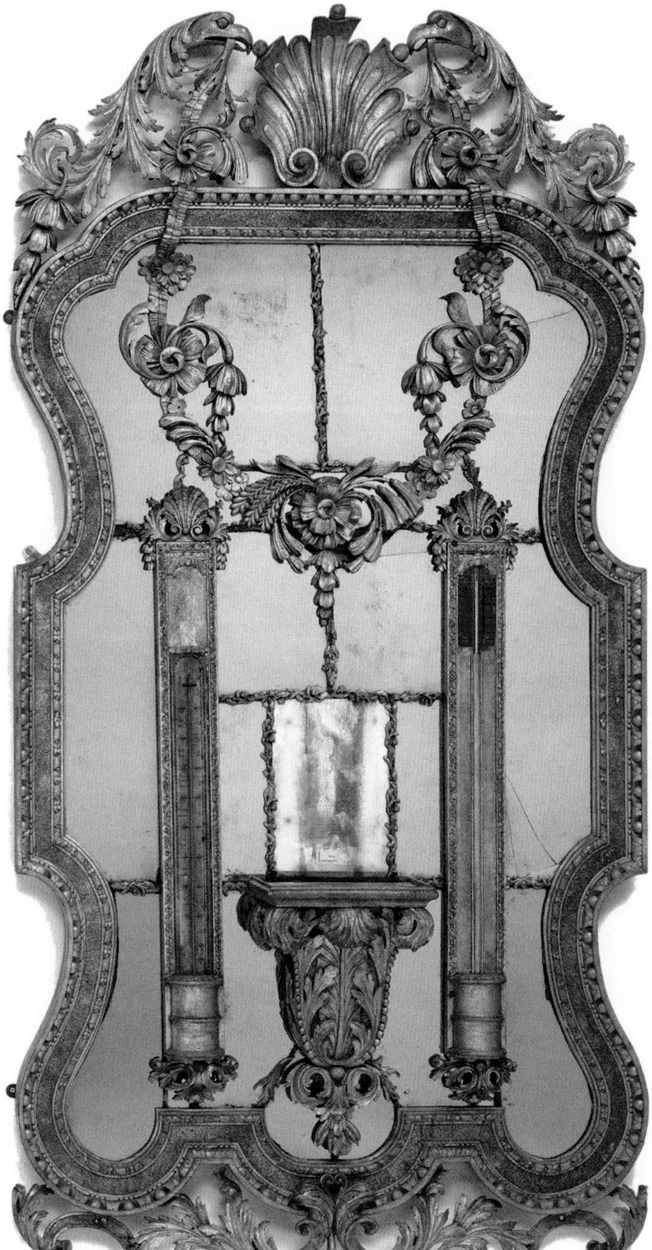

It is a leap, but a plausible one I want to suggest, from the fireplace ensemble to that of the monument. A particular example is given us in the Easter Sepulchre (surviving where it does as at **Heckington**, Lincolnshire), a place of ritual transformation. But this occurs even in the post-Reformation period, when such fittings, notably the chantry chapel, were no longer liturgically acceptable and when the walls of the church were the space of artistic invention. Their compositions bring together the upright and recumbent bodies that we have examined, along with the casket or container, and the framing portal, to create an ensemble that brings the viewer to the threshold of sculpture, and to that of a world beyond.

...

open

237. Easter Sepulchre at Heckington, 14th century

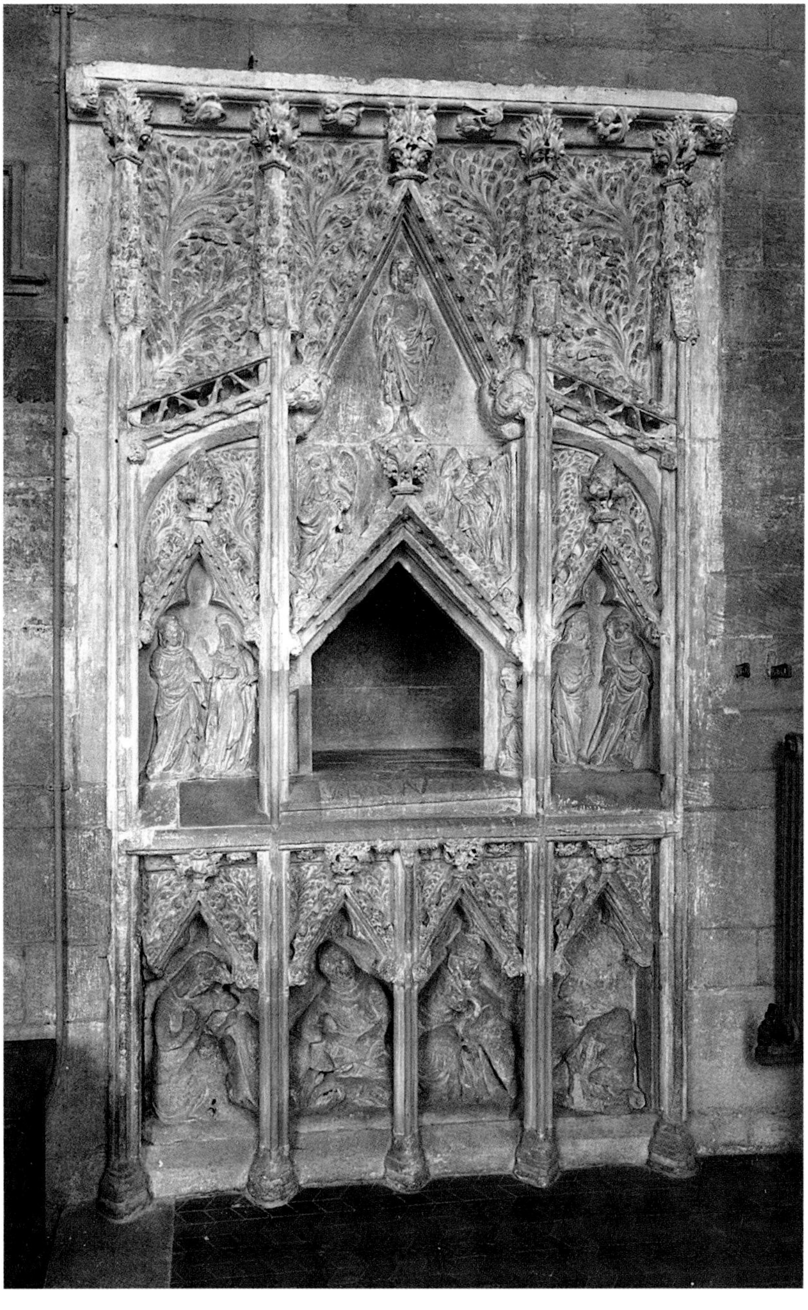

237

Monuments such as that to **Richard Bertie** at Spilsby contain all these elements, if somewhat incongruously: the sealed tomb chest, the upright figures, the portal-like niches. There is a sense here of the space on the other side, beyond the wall of the church. This is a kind of theatrical façade or gateway that protects but also suggests the world beyond. One might compare this to the later **Kinnoull Monument** of 1634 in Perth, in which the setting and figure of the Earl seem to reference the **frontispieces** to books (and in this case Sir Walter Raleigh); comparable gateways to knowledge, with their columns dedicated to:

> Time's Witness, Herald of Antiquity
> The light of Truth, and Life of Memory[16]

...

open

238. Monument to Richard Bertie, 1582

239. Kinnoull Monument, 1634

240. Frontispiece from *The History of the World* by Sir Walter Raleigh, 1614)

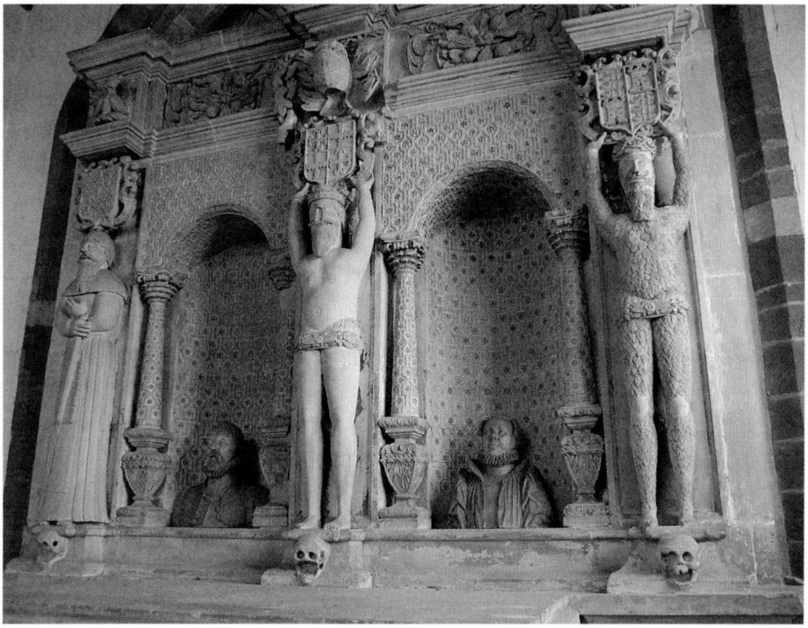

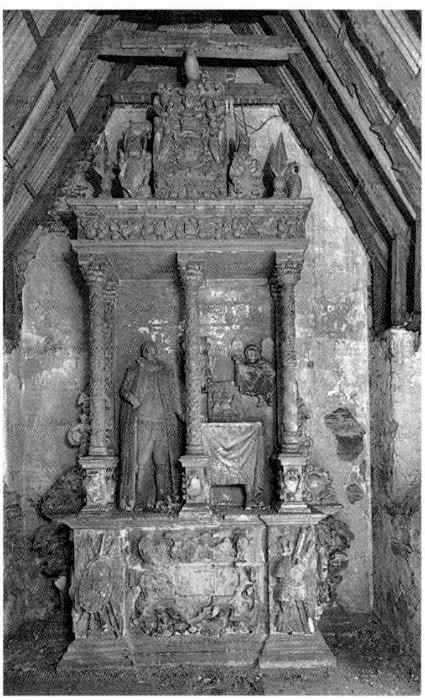

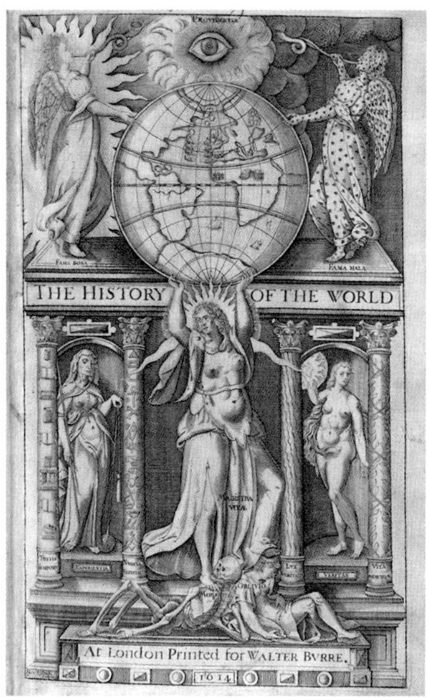
FAMA BONA
FAMA MALA
THE HISTORY
OF THE WORLD
MAGISTRA VITÆ
OBLIVIO
VERITAS
VITA
At London Printed for WALTER BVRRE.
1614

Only a few years later we have in Stapleford a monument to **Lord Sherard of Leitrim**; a composition combining obelisk, tomb chest with effigy, and a form remarkably reminiscent of the fireplace. The effigy lies under a chimneypiece-like frame suggestive of both the home and the church with their differing forms of threshold. In a sense the notion of the surround as a temple of fame comprises both readings.

The monument by Charles Harris to the third and fourth **Dukes of Ancaster** seems again almost to be mounted over a fireplace, temporarily closed as it were by the inscribed bronze plates. The contiguity with fire and smoke, with the solid turned to ashes, seems to bring the funeral pyre into the church in the disguise of a familiar domestic form. The breath of life, the sense of the portal or gateway, the fireplace with its urn, suggest the immortal.

...

241. Monument to Lord Sherard, 2nd Baron Sherard of Leitrim, 1640

open

242. Charles Harris, monument to the 3rd and 4th Dukes of Ancaster, c.1793

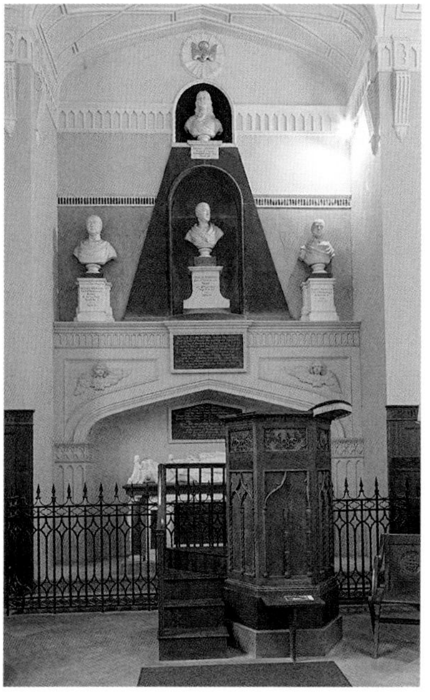

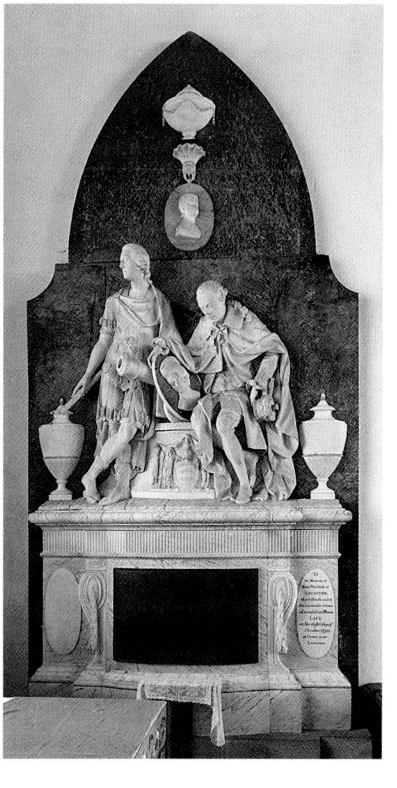

Even apparently uncontained fires, such as those made by Roger Hiorns (2003) and **Giorgio Sadotti** provoke a similar sense of boundary between two worlds.

My sense that mirror and fireplace belong together, and not merely in a domestic sense, but in the sense of something altogether grander, is reinforced by recent work by Rosemarie Trockel. In exhibitions like ***A Cosmos***,[17] works including doors, mirrors, shutters and fireplaces, all in glazed ceramic, occupied the walls like images, or icons, in shallow space, all representing things that might open, if in different ways. They hang like pictures, on the walls in front of us, but it is their depth and scale that allows them to function very differently from paintings, speaking instead quite literally, first of the fire that made them, and then of the space beyond the wall.

Trockel's wall pieces are barely reflective, and are closed. They are implicit rather than explicit. In contrast to Martin Creed's *Work No. 203: EVERYTHING IS GOING TO BE ALRIGHT* with which we started, one might end with Nathan Coley's illumination ***Heaven is a Place where Nothing ever Happens***. An artist who makes similarly declarative works, using found phrases and injunctions, Coley has produced a series that suggests endings rather than beginnings: *There will be no Miracles Here, Heaven is a Place where Nothing ever Happens* and *A Place beyond Belief*.[18] We have, as it were stepped over the threshold; we have arrived.[19]

open

243. Giorgio Sadotti, *Fire*, 2012

244. Rosemarie Trockel, *A Cosmos* exhibition, 2012

← 245. Nathan Coley, *Heaven is a Place where Nothing ever Happens*, 2008

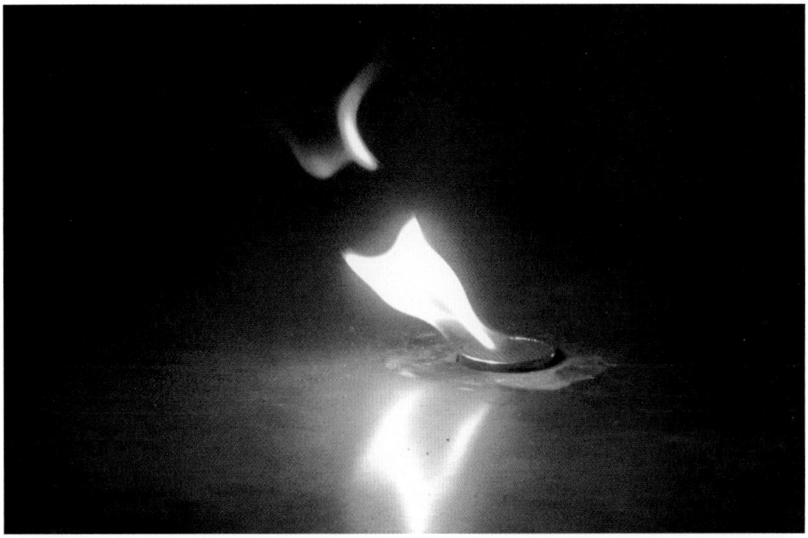

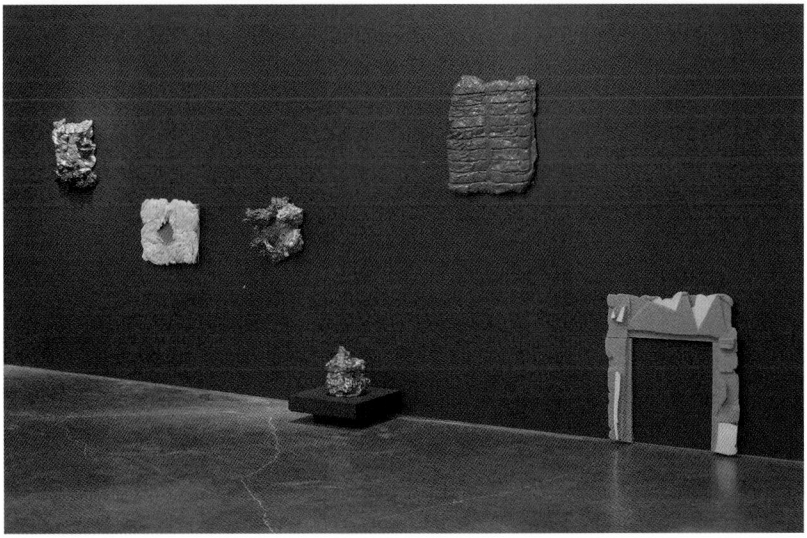

open

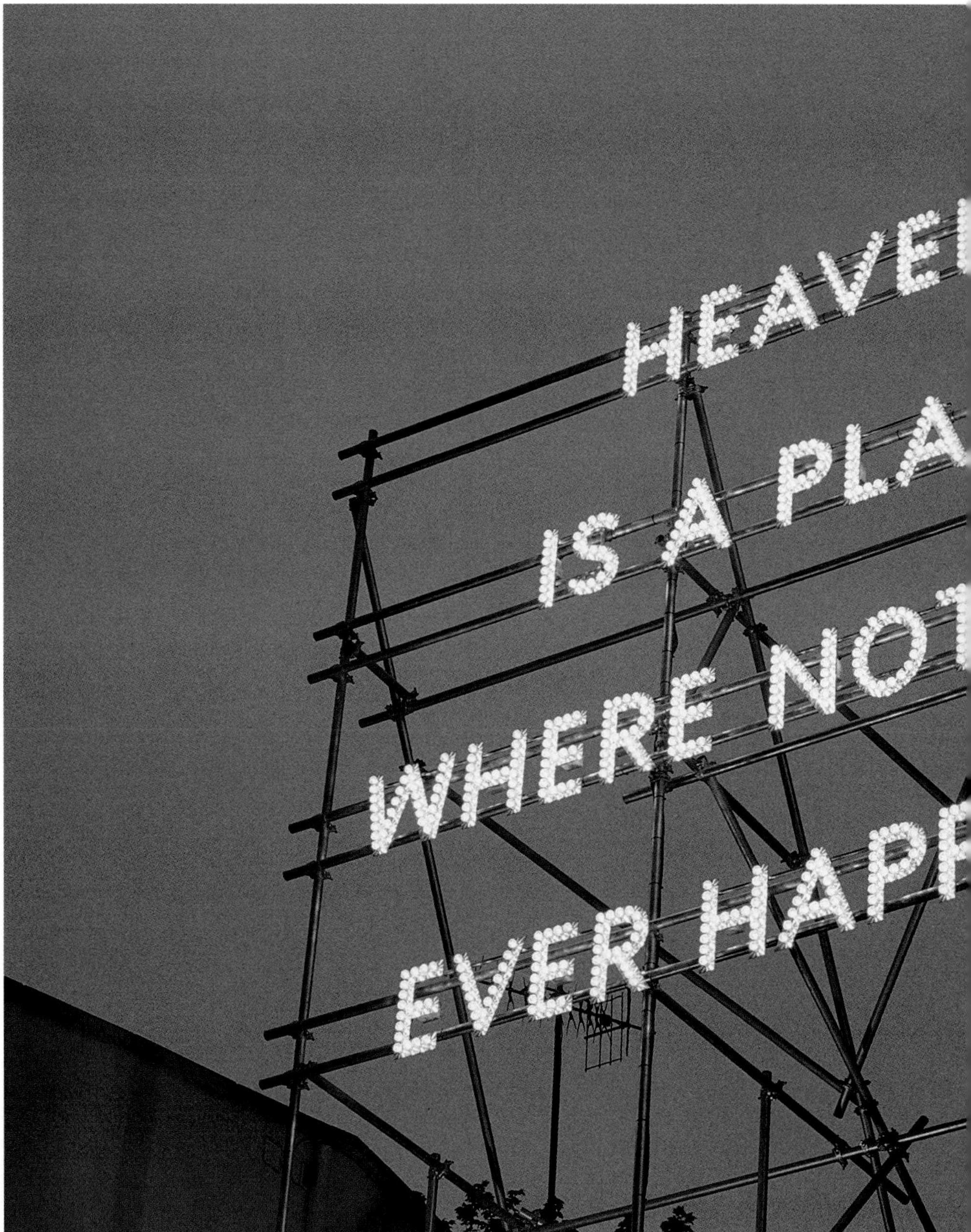

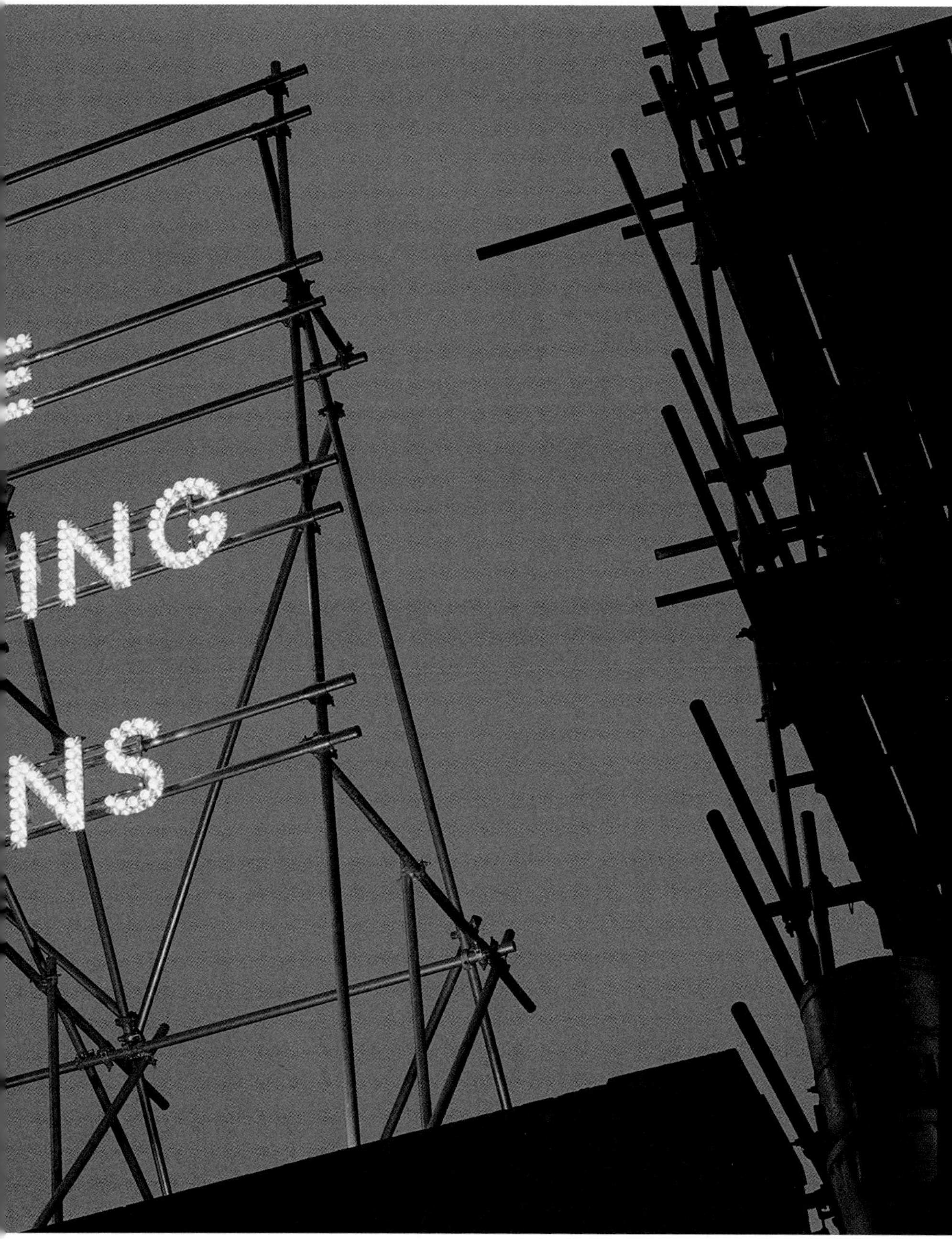
ING
NS

ensemble

V

ensemble

Over the last twenty years Bethan Huws has become known for a variety of work, but perhaps it is one of her earliest pieces that is best remembered, if necessarily imperfectly. This is ***The Lake Writing***, made for and installed in 1991 in the two upper rooms of the ICA, in Carlton House Terrace on Pall Mall. We have already touched on Huws's wooden floors, and she later wrote that in this piece she aimed:

> To make the exact equivalent of the *Floor* in writing.
> Now to replace the material *wood* with the material word.

Huws has since explained that 'Each time I visited the ICA I felt I entered a deep hole in the ground, one that is permanently in the shade…That is what made me think of a lake…'. She investigated a number of small mountain lakes in North Wales, where she grew up, and chose Llyn Idwal, which was 'closely surrounded on three sides by steep mountain slopes, with a river exiting it as its fourth open side'. In situ she recorded what she could see on a dictaphone.

…

246. Bethan Huws, *The Lake Writing* exhibition at the Institute for Contemporary Art (ICA), London in 1991

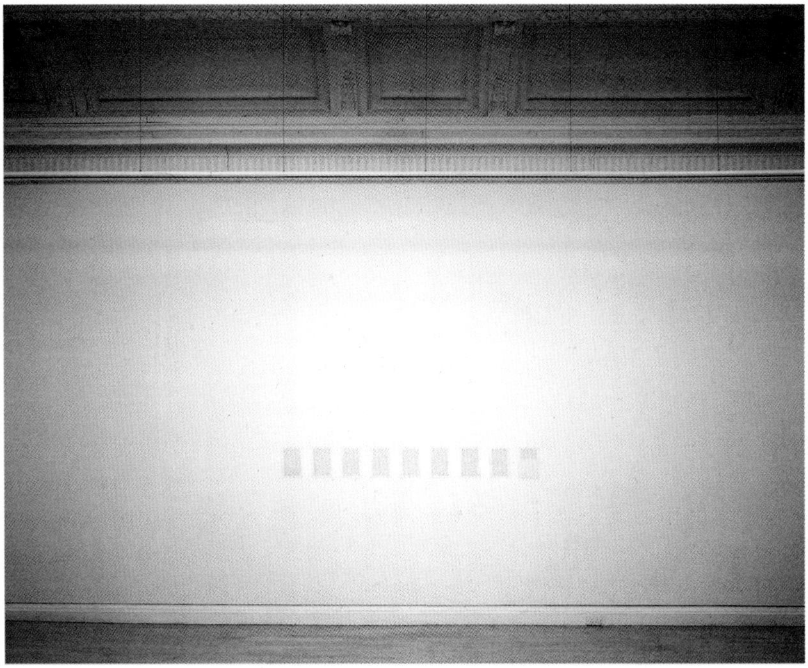

These impressions, over four walks, were written out **longhand** and fixed to the walls, in 'arrangements' that correspond to the 'arrangements of the lake. The vertical walls are the steep mountain slopes. And the two pairs of facing windows, the two rivers, the one that enters the lake at its open side and the one that enters it at its opposite side, down the mountain slope'.[1] For example:

> Today the lake is moving in different directions. To the left the lake is very brown and in the centre its very grey, a black grey and its white in the end. There's the sun catching the end of the lake and its shining like a mirror and the waves are catching light....

The attentive viewer moved around the room, reading the descriptions, hand-written in pencil on the walls, forgetting about London and transported to Wales, or, more accurately perhaps, poised somewhere between the two, by a lake in a gallery.

...

247. Bethan Huws, *The Lake Writing* exhibition at the Institute for Contemporary Art (ICA), London in 1991

The lake to the right is a sandy brown colour going towards the shingle beach. Its shining towards here and then its opaque but its totally blue in the rest of the lake, the edges here are brown and then to the left its brown blue again. The sky is blue in one part, the rest is cloudy and its very windy and there are large boulders along the lake here and its very blue mixed with brown where you can see the rocks underneath the water. By the edges and then in the rest of the lake there are blue lines and the wind has gone down now. Towards the brown part of the lake its a mousey greyish brown and the blue part is going into the brown part. There are very large grey boulders with green lichen. The lake is quieter now and is quite gentle and the noise of the water is deep in this part where its hitting very gently and very fully against the rocks. Looking across to the left, is the back of the river where the rocks have fallen down, its a gentle brown and to the right its a totally pure gentle brown with a tinge of green. And the lake at its furthest part is totally opaque and very dull and the front part is very shiny and the dull part is moving towards here across the lake quite quickly now making the lake dull. The dull part is also reflecting blue and coming in towards the brown bit. Its all becoming opaque at the edges at the brown edges the blue is coming over right over the brown. And here the waters lapping very gently and very fully on the rocks and there is gravel on the floor in this part where its like a small beach. The water is making a very hollow sound and here the water is shallow with a small rock in the water and then another small rock which looks as if they are equally placed along the edge of the lake. There is another small rock and there are very small bits of gravel, almost sand-like gravel round the edge of the lake and. looking here the lake looks as if the blue is carrying towards the brown and in the furthest part there are a lot of white waves and its intensly blue and the clouds are coming across to the right. The sky is very blue and then the waves here on the edge are totally dull. The waters moving quite fast now. The grit here is made up of blue

Lucy Gunning's ***Mirror Event*** also related to a particular setting in the natural world. It too attempted to capture within an artwork the encircling amphitheatre of mountain slopes around a lake. Made for the Wordsworth Trust in 2007, it was staged on the five peaks around Lake Grasmere: Loughrigg, Stone Arthur, Helm Cragg, Silver Howe and Alcock Tarn. The mirrors reflected the natural world behind the participants who carried them on their backs on the walk up the five peaks, and then held them up in front of themselves and across to their counterparts on the other side of the valley. Like gaps or gashes in the fabric of the world around them they moved to become pure light, signals of presence across space. The only person to see the glints of light from all five peaks was the canoeist on Lake Grasmere below; most of the participants could only see a part.

The self-referential nature of Gunning's larger project, entitled *The Archive, the Event and its Architecture*, was released, as it were, by a multi-part simultaneous event with many actors. In the larger scheme of things, Gunning's mirror piece might be seen as hardly strictly sculptural in that it was so pluralistic, so much a changing spatial event. However, I want to suggest that sculpture as event, and as architecture, is not so unusual, and I want also to propose that it is our performance within its space that reveals its three dimensions most fully. Their configuration, I will suggest, is more historically rooted than we might commonly think.

In attempting, in this last chapter, to understand how the previous four come together, I have chosen to look at the ways in which they intersect; in which horizontal crosses vertical, and open joins closed. Another way of defining the topic would be to invoke the fourth dimension, and while these chapters have already related time to place, now they do so more explicitly, in considering questions of the spectator's movement: procession and progression, address and circumnavigation.

---

248. Lucy Gunning, *Mirror Event*, 2007

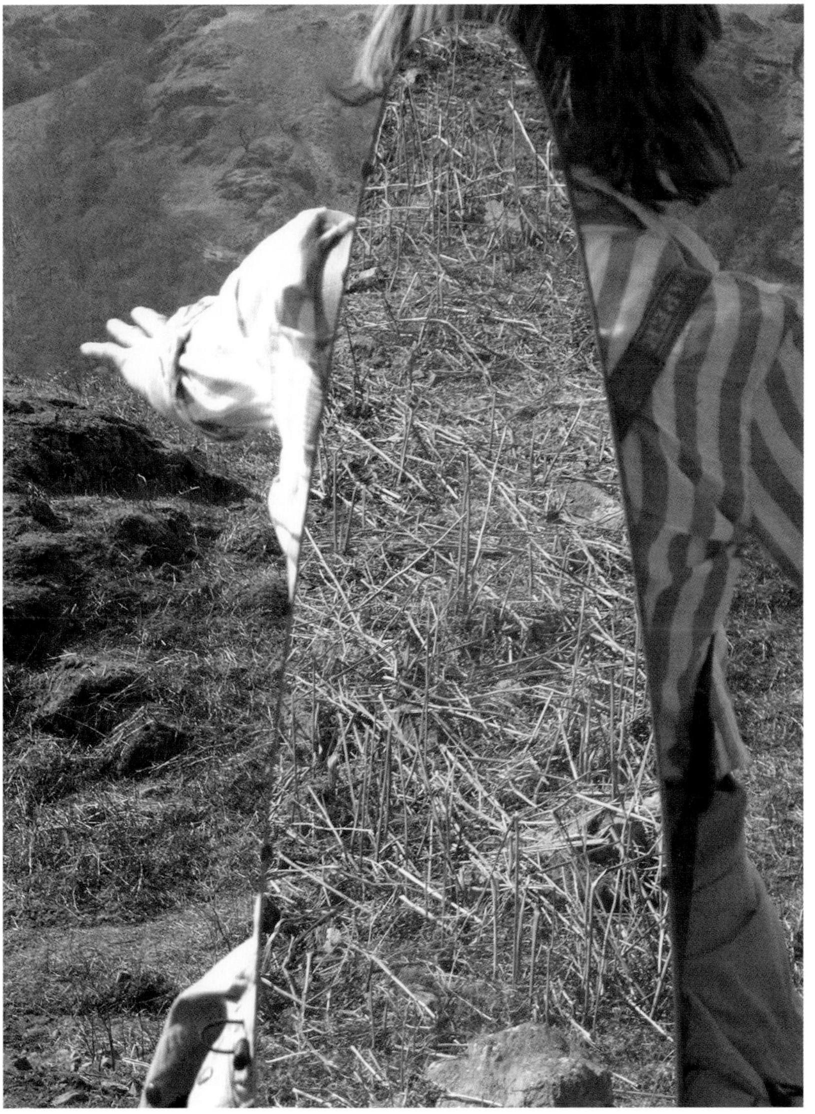

As with Bethan Huws, Gunning made a piece early in her career for which she is still perhaps best known: ***Climbing Around my Room***, a video installation shown on a high monitor as if it were a window. For seven and a half minutes a performer in a red dress (not the artist) climbs around the artist's empty studio without putting her feet on the floor. Her careful, deliberate, but to all intents, pointless, exercise loops around the room and the video like an unending Sisyphean task, and we are pulled into that clearly three-dimensional space as if we were at its centre, looking up. Gunning has interrogated exterior and interior space, looking at being in the round, using mirrors if they help, conveying the variously synthetic or fragmented experience of space.[2] Whereas the Grasmere work was centrifugal, the *Climbing* piece is centripetal.

...

249. Lucy Gunning, *Climbing Around my Room*, 1993

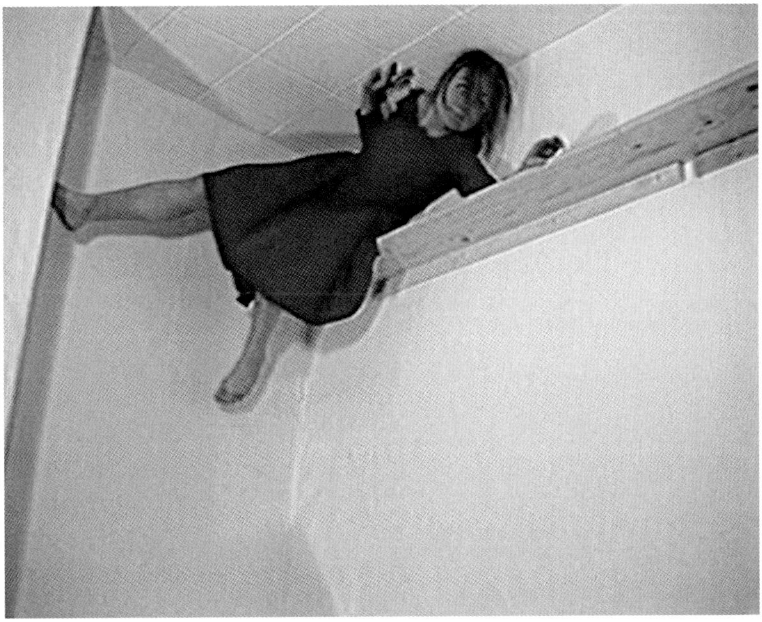

The use of the room as the material of the work, subject and object, and as both stage and plinth, is exemplified by a number of artists who use very reduced means to emphasise the physical space within which their works are situated. Mel Bochner's practice has, since his *Measurement Room* of 1969, refined this approach most succinctly. Measuring the dimensions of every surface, Bochner lays out for us the size of what we are looking at and its scale in relation to every other surface. The measurements are applied to the walls at the eye-height of the artist (who is tall).

Other similarly simple strategies by recent British artists also underscore the spaces where they are found, including Martin Creed's ***Work No. 227: The lights going on and off***, which illuminated the gallery for five seconds in every ten; Susan Philipsz's *Lowlands Away*, sung in a recording by the artist and presented, on occasion, in an empty gallery (2010); and Ryan Gander's *Invisible Pull* (2012). Whether with light, with sound or with air, each one of these artists made notably successful works that, in different ways, re-awoke their audiences to the places where they stood.

- - -

250. Martin Creed, *Work No. 227: The lights going on and off*, 2000

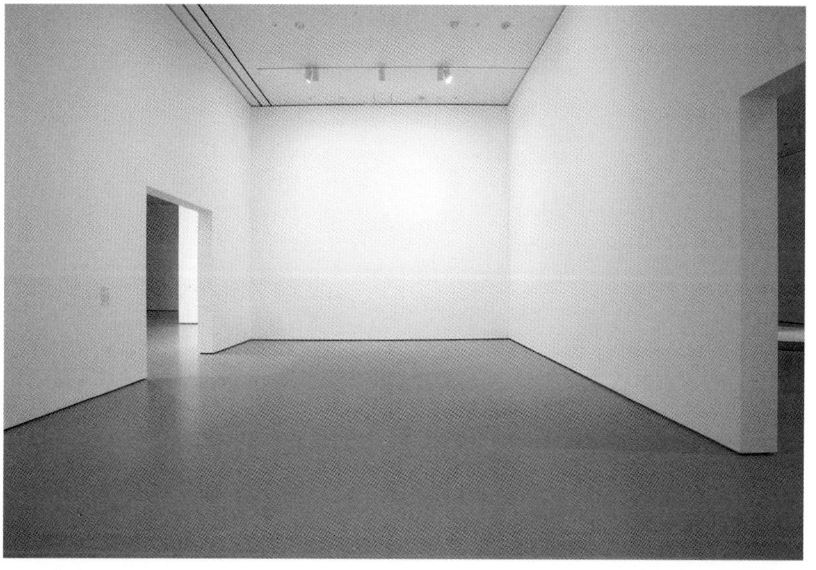

All these works use the senses to activate their space as well as making it their subject. They call to mind John Vanbrugh's **Temple of the Four Winds** at Castle Howard, which seems to suggest its own activation, as well as its reason for being, a shelter but also a conduit, or agency of external forces. Garden buildings, such as temples, grottoes, belvederes and cascades, suggest not only the elements of earth, wind and water that surround us, but our activation of them through the activity of our senses: sight, obviously, but hearing and feeling too. They are very often platforms from which we survey the view, or that catch our surveying gaze at the end of a vista. They mark the boundaries, high and low, vertical and horizontal, and allow us to see and feel them more fully. The feature at Castle Howard known as the **Four Faces** seems, in its very title, to declaim its cardinal points – the compass, the winds, the seasons, their intersection – over and above its merely decorative effect.

...

251. John Vanbrugh, Temple of the Four Winds, 1724

252. Nicholas Hawksmoor, Four Faces Monument, c.1720s

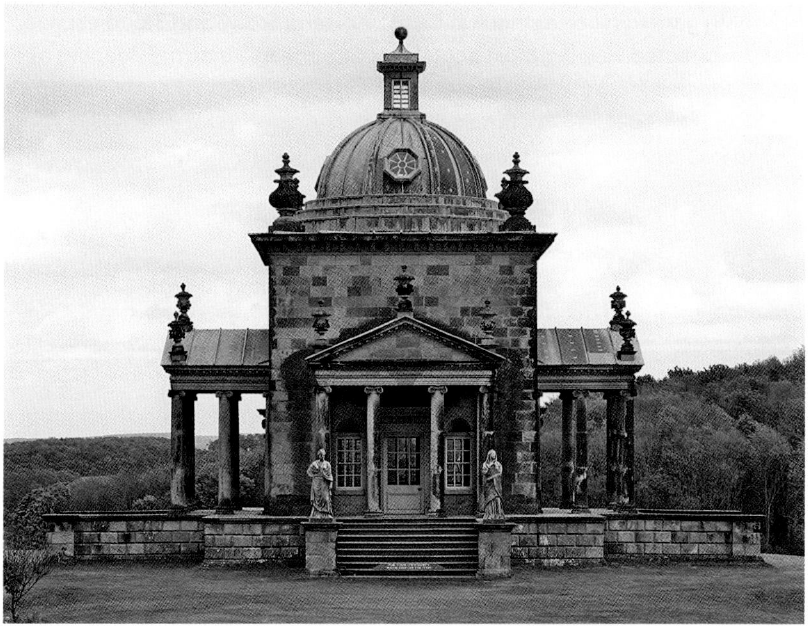

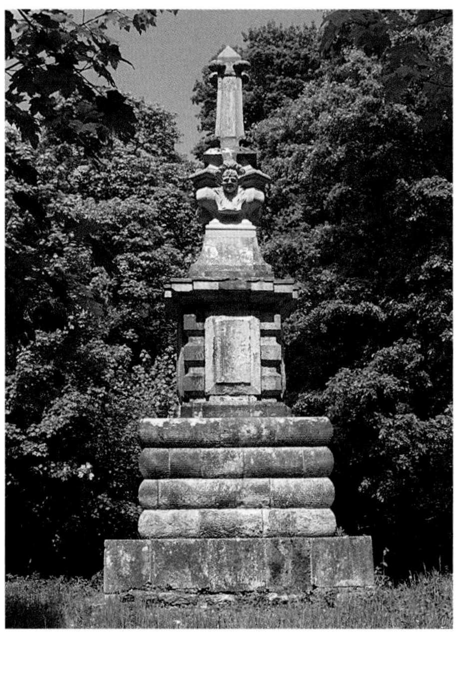

Ariadne, or the poet, asks us to be quiet, to moderate the impact of the senses. The landscape's features are offset by the architectural features of the temple in which the figure sleeps, but enhanced with a sexual charge.

Other sleeping statues, such as the cast of the ***Borghese Hermaphrodite*** at West Wycombe Park, seem similarly in command of their space: able to slow, stop or otherwise chasten those who intrude upon their silence, however knowingly.[4]

- - -

This neo-classical context, playing both on archaeological evidence and on the landscape garden tradition, in which the park is the stage for physical markers and activities, was masterfully re-ignited by **Pierre Huyghe** in the Karlsaue Park in Kassel at documenta 13. Huyghe combined the park's composting depot with various things made and unmade, unnatural and natural, including a National Socialist-like version of an Ariadne-like figure, her head surrounded by bees, set within a nearly dry pool. The reclining figure at the centre of this anti-park was perhaps an anti-monument, but nonetheless retained her status as the centre of the work, lying immobile on her plinth. Even if her currency was brought into question by the infestation of bees, they lent an aura of gilded fertility, not unlike a Danaë figure, perhaps, and also suggested the cleft rock or grotto where the bees would swarm. The statue's apparent durability gave her a position over and above the changing ecology of the environment in which she was placed. Her blindness was reminiscent of other sleeping sculptures, absorbing our gaze rather than returning it.

...

255. *Borghese Hermaphrodite*, 18th-century copy

← 256. Pierre Huyghe, *Untitled*, 2011–12

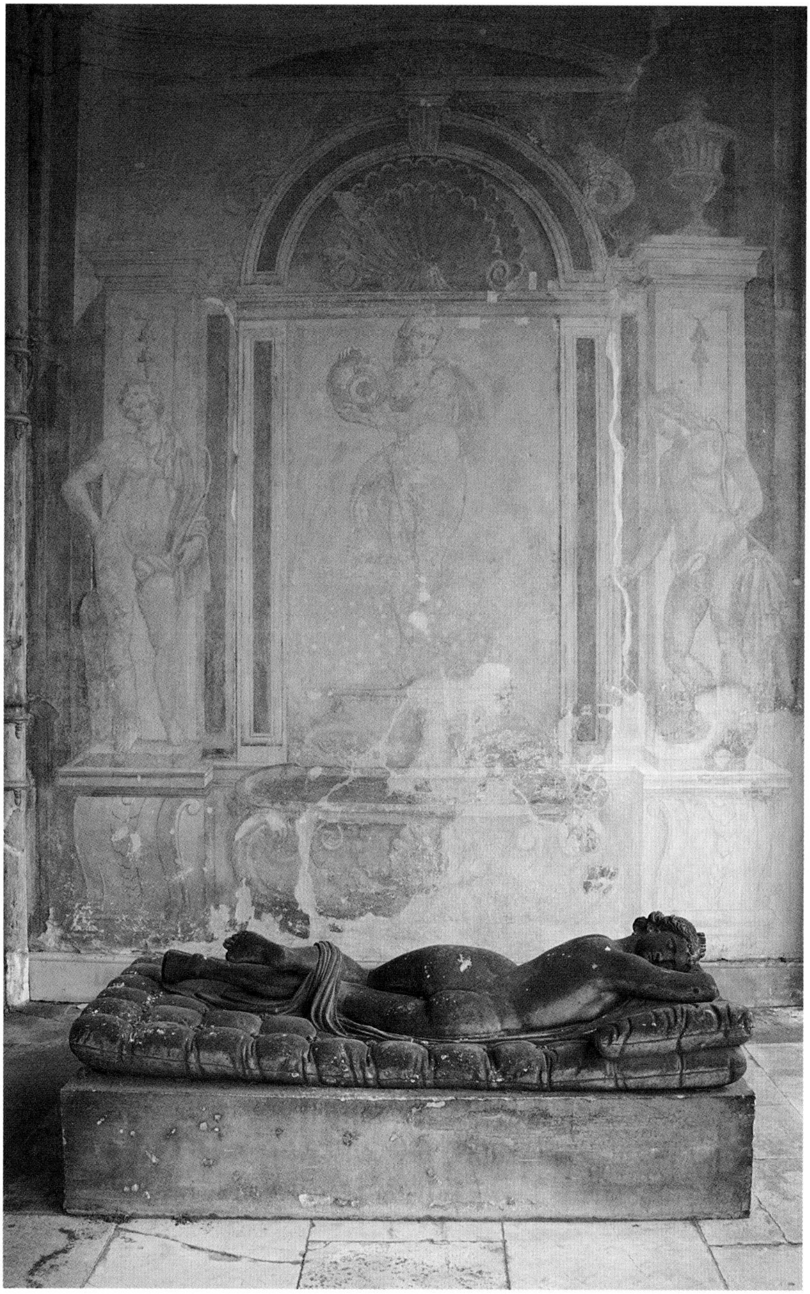

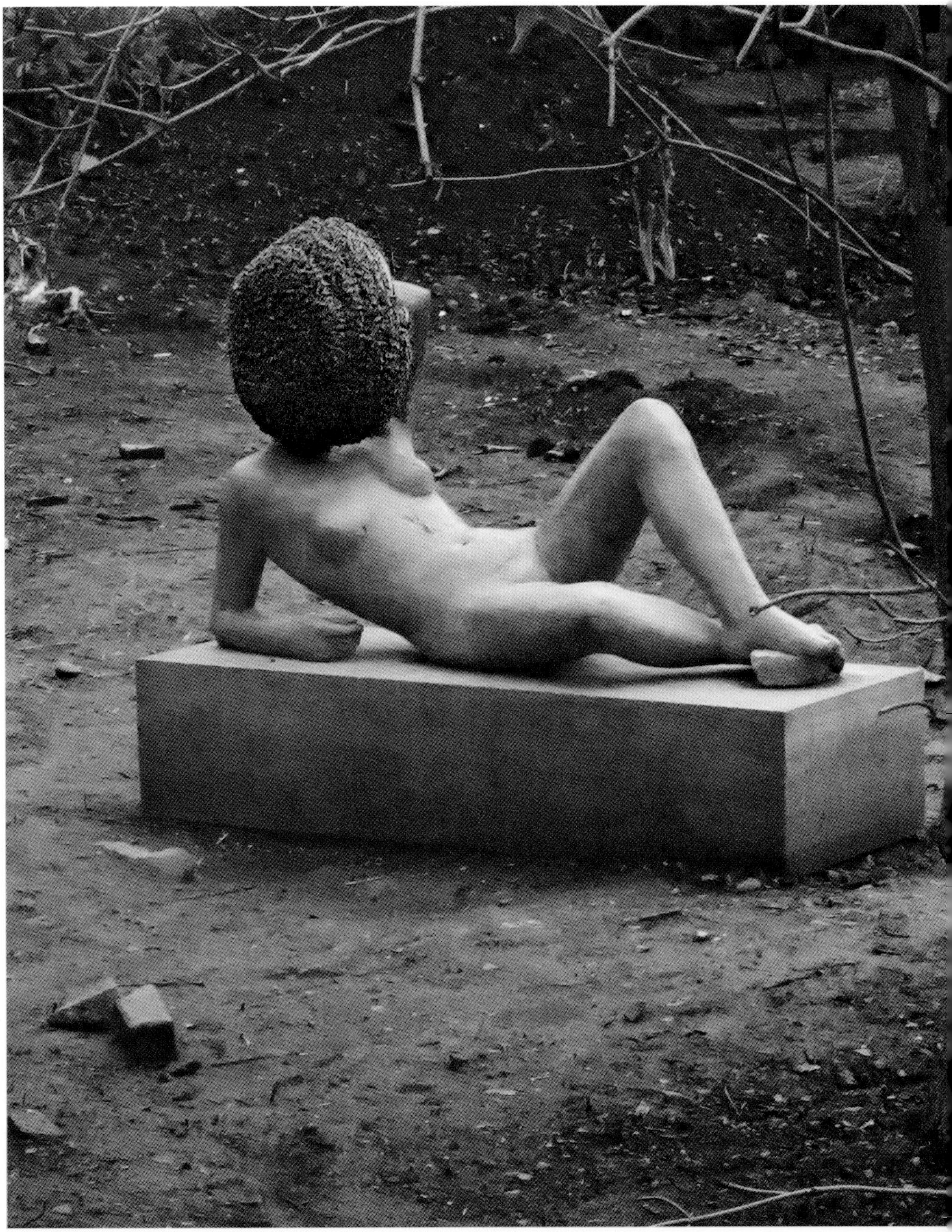

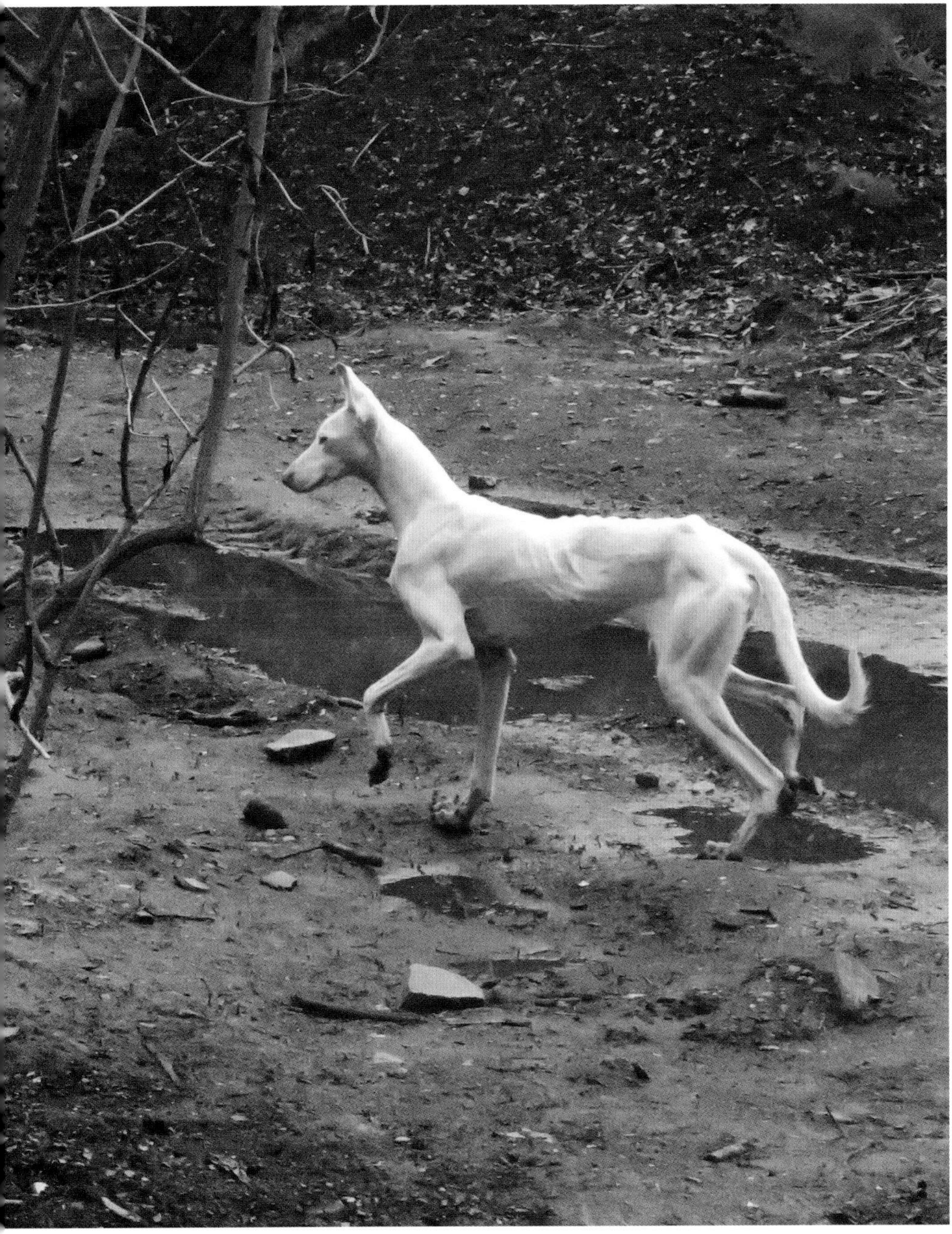

Such installations are animated by their viewers as well as by the sculptures, which disperse or condense the spatial environment around them. The coincidence of a single sculpture acting as a pivot within a defined space can be remarkable. The occupation of Mies van der Rohe's 1929 Barcelona pavilion[5] by Georg Kolbe's *Morning* extends this effect, but other such 'temples' – whether to Venus (as at West Wycombe),[6] to the **Three Graces** (as with Antonio Canova at Woburn); or even to royalty (as with Nicholas Hawksmoor's cupola for the figure of **Queen Caroline** at the new Queen's College, Oxford) – assert a similar fixity of purpose, and of circulation, around the female form, and are indeed usually circular. Making this purpose explicit in its title, the Temple to Female Virtue, by Joseph Wilton at Pusey House, is in fact essentially a tomb to the patron's wife, Mrs Brotherton, who stands at its centre.

Setting the ***Tinted Venus*** by John Gibson[7] in the pavilion by Owen Jones at the 1862 International Exhibition made its realism both more controversial and more confused. No longer merely provoking questions about the propriety of its coloration, the statue set now within a temple, rather than on a plinth, could be read not so much as human but as divine. This was an intriguing and complex juxtaposition of 'real woman' and 'sacred space'. This kind of protective setting is foreshadowed by the canopies that protect medieval tombs and the later 'tester' versions that literally echo the tester awnings of early modern beds.

The architecture that surrounds these sculptures makes them work, and makes the architecture work too. Both work harder, becoming more active. The way the figure is approached, and lit, the length of a direct or of a circuitous approach, the possibility of circumnavigation, all count. This may well be circumstantial, or cumulative, in a museum or church, but can be more deliberately managed within specific architectures or contexts. Individual monumental ensembles, especially the most complex, ensure spatial control. While many of those we have examined so far have been essentially pictorial, like frames or even frontispieces, here I want to return to ensembles that depend upon a more fully three-dimensional reading of the figure in space. In doing so, I will in fact return to the architecture of the church as an underlying spatial configuration.

– – –

257. Antonio Canova, *Three Graces*, 1814–17

258. Nicholas Hawksmoor, cupola (housing the statue of Queen Caroline by Henry Cheere), 1736

259. John Gibson, *Tinted Venus*, 1862

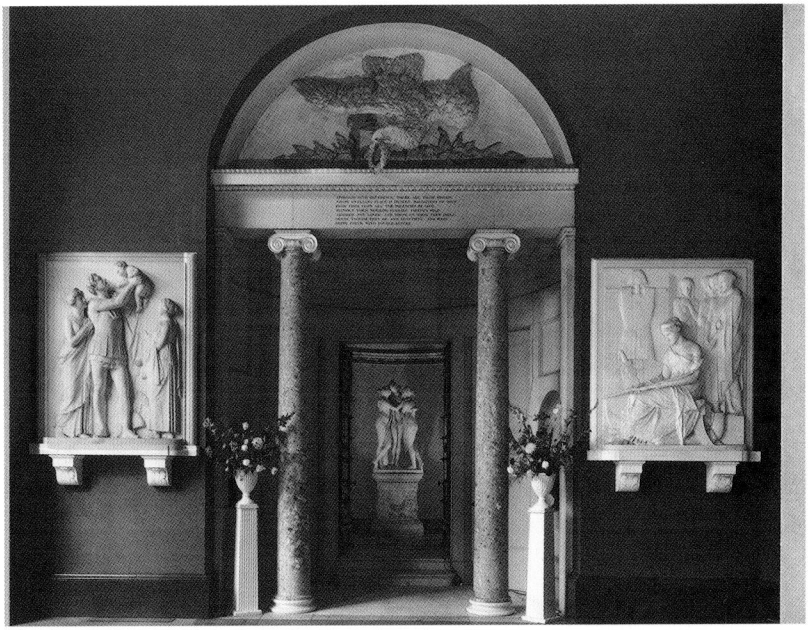

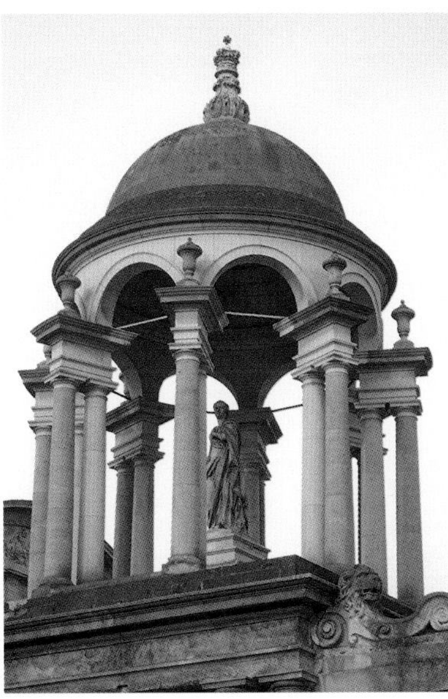

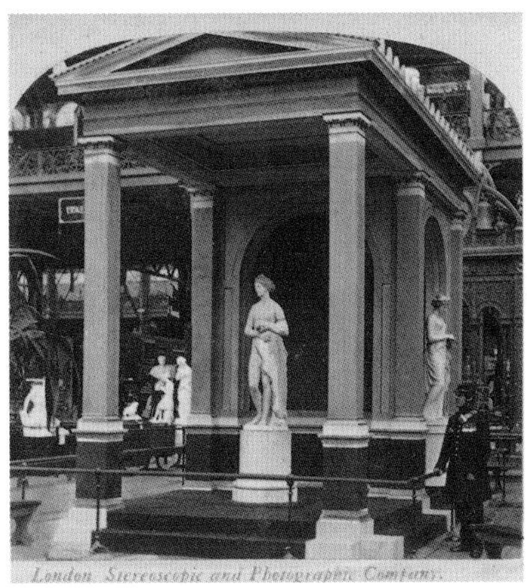
London Stereoscopic and Photographic Company.

One might say that the podium is a kind of equivalent for the pulpit, and Sean Dower's ***St Simeon's Drum Riser*** uses the language of the plinth/pulpit to speak of performance and of religion. St Simeon Stylites took his name as a pillar hermit from the column (north of Aleppo) that was effectively the saint's own plinth, on which he reputedly felt closer to god, and from which he preached to the pilgrims who came to hear him. Bill Woodrow's ***English Heritage – Humpty Fucking Dumpty*** goes further in suggesting the empty or rotten vaulting-box plinth, prised apart underneath its little dictator. We have touched already on speaking sculpture, and in these and other works Dower and Woodrow play on their interest in the object's projection by means of conjectural sound. But these figures are bereft of dignity, they represent instead hermits or idiots, effectively removed from the social space. Their isolation is striking, for they have no spatial referents.

...

260. Sean Dower, *St Simeon's Drum Riser*, 2012

261. Bill Woodrow, *English Heritage – Humpty Fucking Dumpty*, 1987

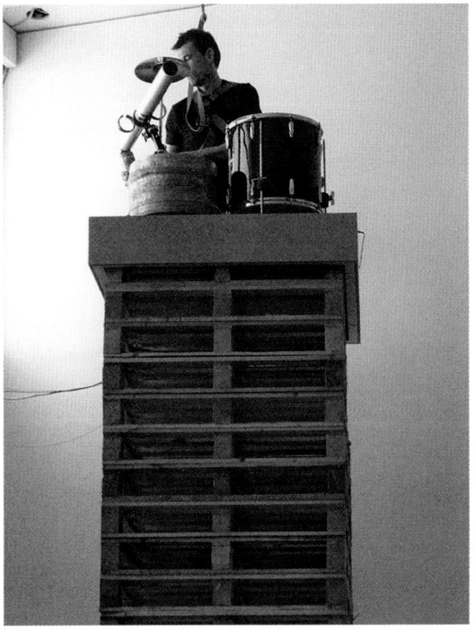

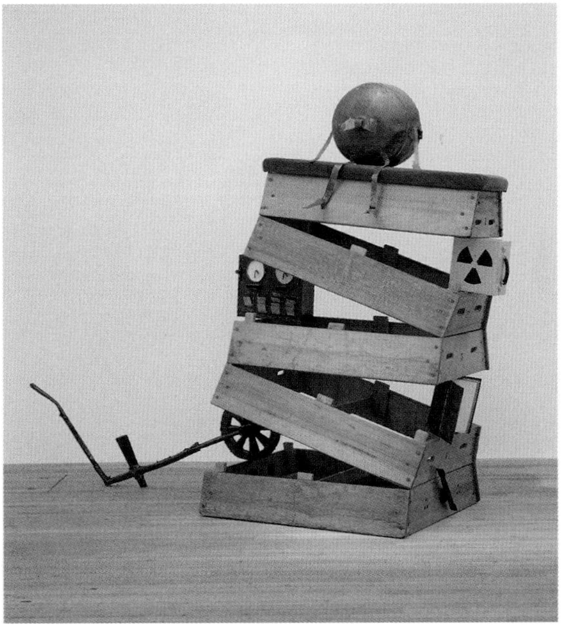

To a degree every still life might be said to relate both to the vessels on a table and to those that sit on an altar, and we find examples in sculptures by Lili Dujourie, Katharina Fritsch, Matthew Derbyshire, and in Rachel Whiteread's later works. More overt, if still implicit, is a work like ***Scape*** by Keith Wilson. But here we are still in the realm of the object, rather than the figure – the still life rather than the statue. This is perhaps the Protestant liturgy rather than the Catholic.

...

262. Keith Wilson, *Scape*, 1995

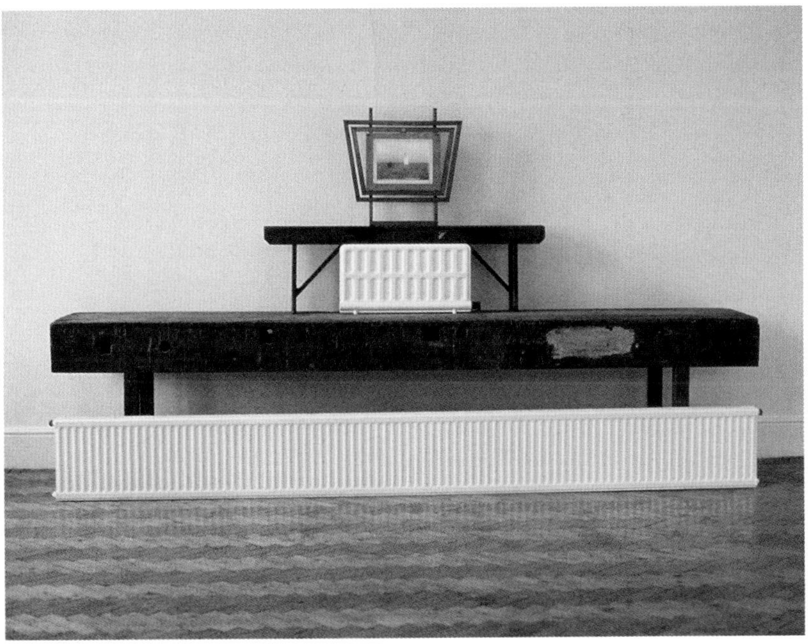

On another level are the table works of Sarah Lucas, in which she brilliantly tackles the terrain that lies between the still life and the figure, and thus brings us to the space between the table and the altar. In a sustained series of works, from ***Two Fried Eggs and a Kebab*** onwards, Lucas has confronted, head on, but nonetheless subtly, the intersection of these fields, sacred and profane.

Lucas's very stark use of the table can take us to the seminal question posed by Voltaire in his 1757 entry on 'Idole, Idolatre, Idolatrie' for his *Dictionnaire Philosophique* (1765). Voltaire quotes from Horace's *Satires* in which a statue muses on its origins as a fig tree, and a carpenter hesitates between making a god or a bench from its wood. The figurative choice is powerful beyond words, because the image will invariably overpower its medium.

La Fontaine's fable, 'The Sculptor and the Statue of Jupiter',[8] is similar.

> Un bloc de marbre était si beau
> Qu'un statuaire en fit l'emplette.
> 'Qu'en fera', dit-il, 'mon ciseau?
> Sera-t-il dieu, table ou cuvette?'
>
> A block of marble was so fine
> That a sculptor bought it.
> 'What should I make of it with my chisel?', he asked himself.
> 'Should it be a god, a table or a basin?'

The choice between god, a table or a basin is close to that posed by Voltaire, but the material, marble rather than wood, is different. However, the purpose of the story was the same for all three authors, Horace, Voltaire and La Fontaine: it was to warn against idolatry, and to point out the potentially dangerous elision of a wooden god with a piece of wood or stone. (Honoré Daumier reprised the verse to make his own salutary cartoon.[9])

...

263. Sarah Lucas, *Two Fried Eggs and a Kebab*, 1992

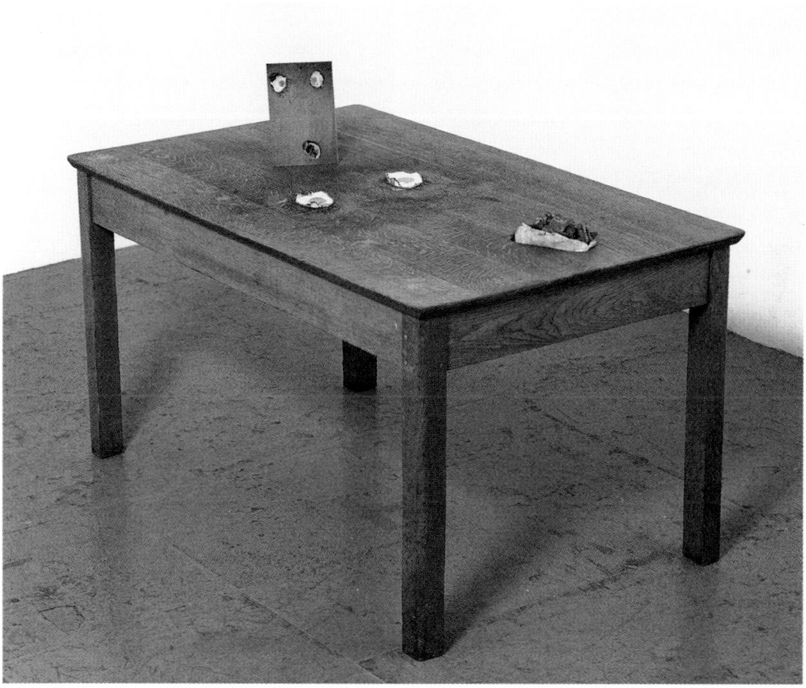

Another important difference between La Fontaine and Voltaire lies in the voice of their script. Whereas La Fontaine makes the sculptor the subject, for Voltaire, and Horace, the subject is the statue itself:

> Olim truncus eram ficulnus, inutile lignum, cum faber,
> Incertus scammum faceret[n]e Priapum, malvit esse deum.
>
> I was once a fig tree's trunk, a lump of useless wood, till the carpenter,
> uncertain whether to carve Priapus or a stool, decided on the god.[10]

The metaphor of tree as body or body as tree, which in Horace is embodied in the guardian figure of Priapus, comes together only more strongly in the form of the crucifix, which combines tree and body in one.[11]

The notion of the statue as fallen idol takes us, inevitably, back to the church. In Raphael's Vatican Stanze, Tommaso Laureti's ***Triumph of Christianity over Paganism*** on the ceiling of the Constantine Room illustrates the concept very well. The classical deity, apparently rendered realistically in stone or plaster, lies in fragments on the ground. The architectural interior is empty of objects other than the golden crucifix, which has replaced the statue on the plinth. The dead form lies on the ground, the 'living' form is upright.[12]

The same conflation between god and tree is what constitutes the strength of the Anglo-Saxon poem 'The Dream of the Rood', in which the tree/statue/god is again the narrator of the poem (see p. 38).

> It was as though I saw a wondrous tree
> Towering in the sky suffused with light,
> Brightest of beams; and all that beacon was
> Covered with gold.
> ...
> No felon's gallows that, but holy spirits,
> Mankind, and all this marvellous creation,
> Gazed on the glorious tree of victory.[13]

Here the body of Christ and the 'wondrous tree' are effectively interchangeable, and are further blended as the Rood makes reference to the 'felon's gallows', the 'beacon' and the 'tree of victory'. Its powerful first-person narrator oscillates between embodying the gallows and embodying the cross.

...

264. Tommaso Laureti, *Triumph of Christianity over Paganism*, 1585

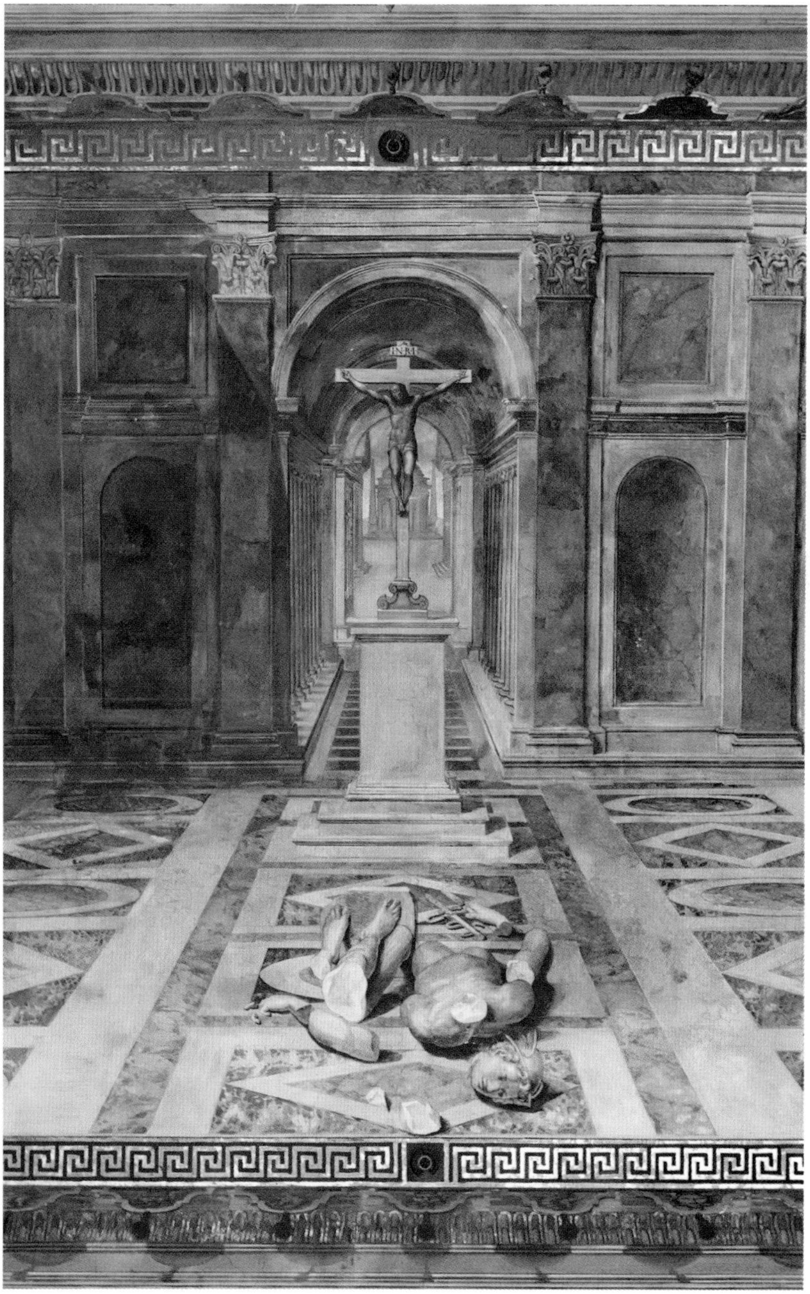

The tree is both a subject, bleeding from its right side, and an object, the Saviour's tree bedecked with treasure. The narrator listens to the cross speak, explaining how it was 'cut down at the copse's end, moved from my roots', how 'Upright I had to stand. A rood I was raised up', and how 'they pierced me with dark nails; the scars can still be clearly seen on me'. At first the Rood and Christ suffered together, but then his body was taken up and the Rood left standing, drenched with blood and wounded. The body was laid down and placed in a sepulchre made of stone. Later the Rood too was cut down and buried in a deep pit, but it was rescued from this place, decorated in gold and silver, set upright, and became 'the tree of glory'.

> The corners of the earth
> Gleamed with fair jewels, just as there were five
> Upon the cross-beam. Many bands of angels,
> Fair throughout all eternity, looked on.
> No felon's gallows that, but holy spirits,
> Mankind, and all this marvellous creation,
> Gazed on the glorious tree of victory.
> And I with sins was stained, wounded with guilt.
> I saw the tree of glory brightly shine
> In gorgeous clothing, all bedecked with gold.
> The Ruler's tree was worthily adorned
> With gems.[14]

The so-called **Drahmal Cross**, in the Cathedral of St Michael and St Gudula in Brussels, might represent, as it were, that 'tree of glory'. Thought to be part of the true cross, it was once covered in gold, and is still partly covered in silver. It is named for, and names, its maker, believed to be an English craftsman of the eleventh century and, like the Ruthwell Monument, it too quotes from lines in 'The Dream of the Rood'. If it has become the 'tree of glory' as dreamt of by the Emperor Constantine, the sign of his conversion and victory, it nonetheless remembers its brutal history. It declares:

> Rood is my name; of old I bore the mighty King, trembling, bedewed with blood.[15]

...

265. Drahmal Cross, 11th century

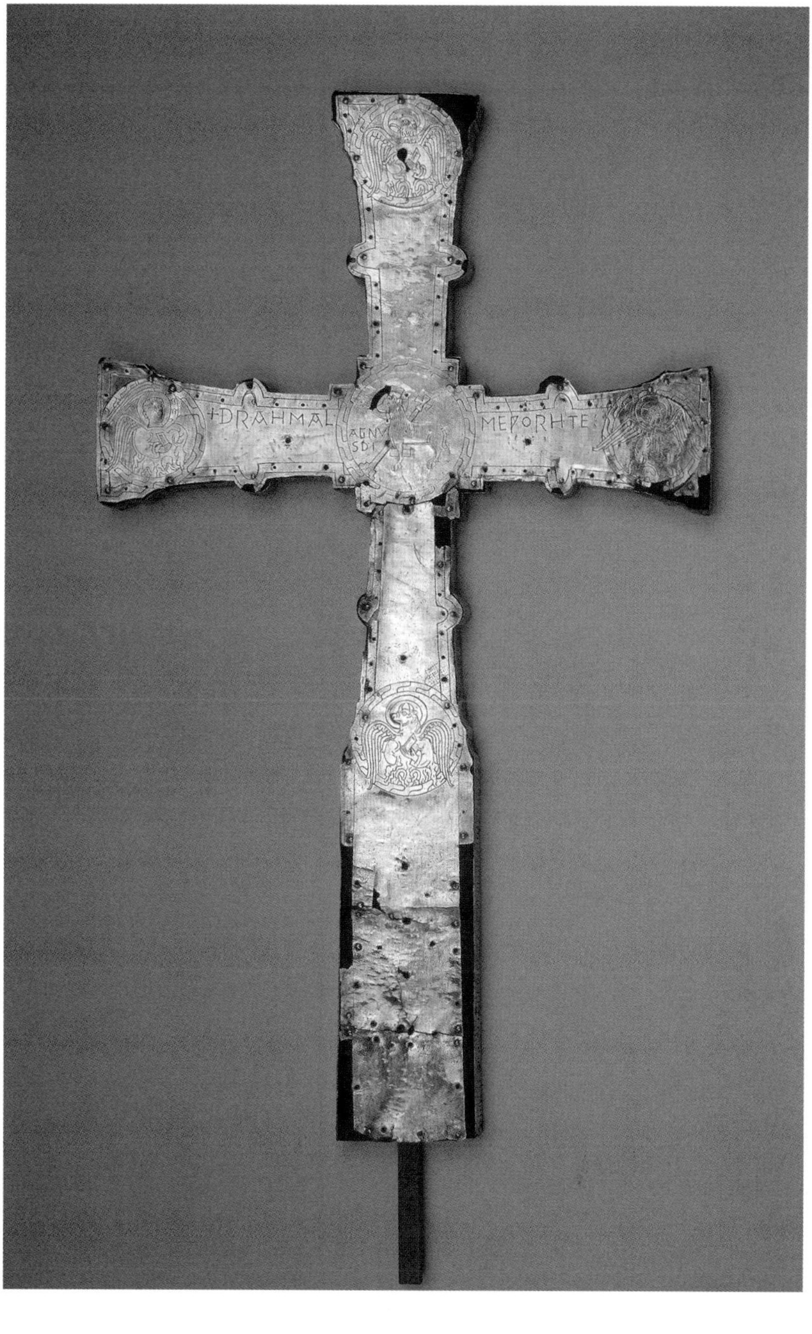
+DRAHMAL
AGNV
SDI
MEƿORHTE

The Chapman brothers' ***Great Deeds against the Dead*** seems to exploit this territory, allowing the tree to act as support for the crimes that have been committed against the human forms that depend upon it. It is both subject and support, medium and message.

- - -

266. Jake and Dinos Chapman, *Great Deeds against the Dead*, 1994

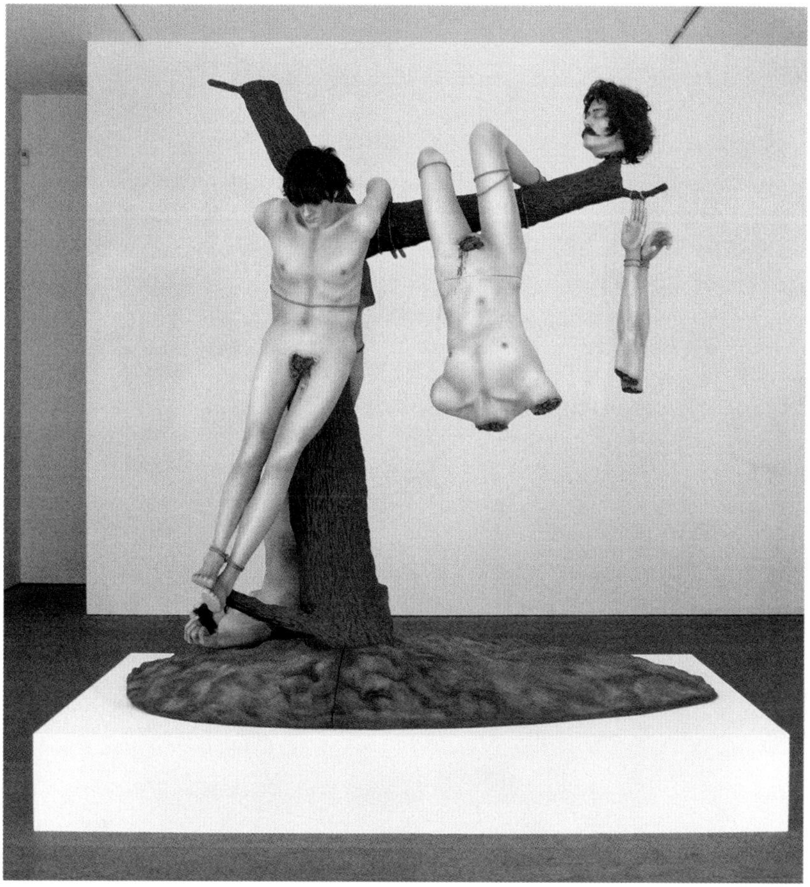

This kind of material and linguistic interchange, verbal and visual, operates across the classical and Christian worlds, notably in the examples of Daphne and of Saint Sebastian. Whereas Saint Sebastian might be figured almost as a tree, pierced with arrows, Gian Lorenzo Bernini's ***Apollo and Daphne*** goes one further, in translating into one piece of stone the foliage that is engulfing Daphne as she metamorphoses into the tree that bears her name:

> a thin bark closed around her gentle bosom, and her hair became as moving leaves; her arms were changed to waving branches, and her active feet as clinging roots were fastened to the ground.[16]

Thus, flesh becomes wood, wood becomes stone. The carving for which Bernini (or Giuliano Finelli) is celebrated in fact makes use of the joining struts of marble between the fingers much as traditional sculptures deployed the conceit of adding a carved tree trunk to conceal the fact that the marble was too fragile to support the body (as with Hercules figures in particular). Marble pretends to be wood. In Daphne, more than any other sculptural subject, the story itself lends enough ambiguity to suggest that the woman becomes tree, rather than that the sculptor needs to deploy deceptive technical devices.[17]

...

267. Gian Lorenzo Bernini, *Apollo and Daphne*, 1622–5

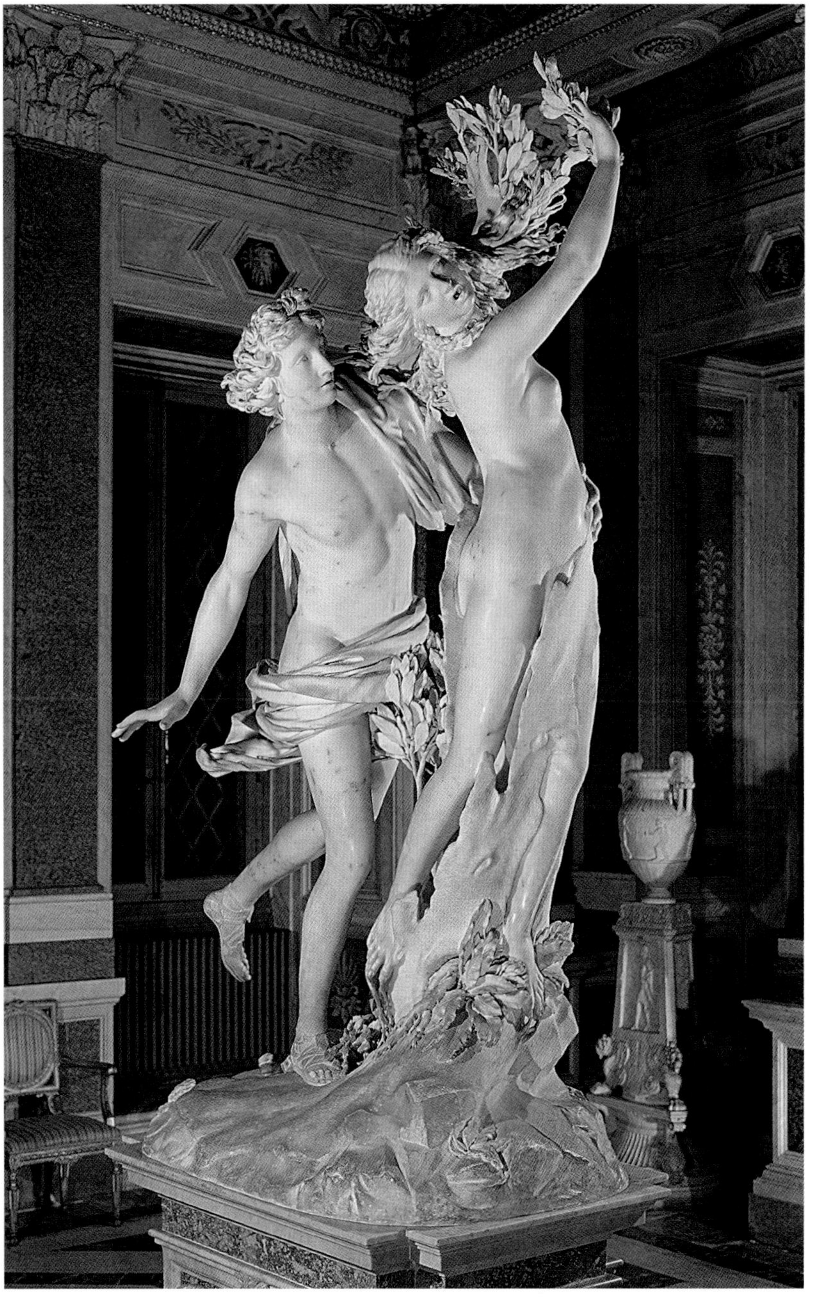

The coming together of tree and statue is a strikingly effective conflation, conceptually as well as visually. The gallows is a salutary reminder of the conflation of tree and body, and this lives on in the very name of the Tyburn Tree, commemorated by a **plaque** on the ground where the tree-cum-gallows had originally stood.

More powerful still is the rood, or crucifix, which combines figure and support in one. Surviving photographs from the Second World War emphasise this point, such as one of the **Church of St Lorenz** in Nuremberg, taken after the British and American bombing of 2 January 1945, with the altar cross appearing to be the last thing left alive.[18]

The crucifix form brings together much of what we have looked at in these chapters: the vertical combined with the horizontal, the figure within the frame, the upright human form of Christ integral to the wooden form of the tree. There is an underlying sense of the living form bound up with the inanimate, implicit as we have seen within the rood.

...

268. Tyburn Tree memorial plaque, erected 1965

269. Photograph of the Church of St Lorenz, Nuremberg, after the Allied bombing of 2 January 1945

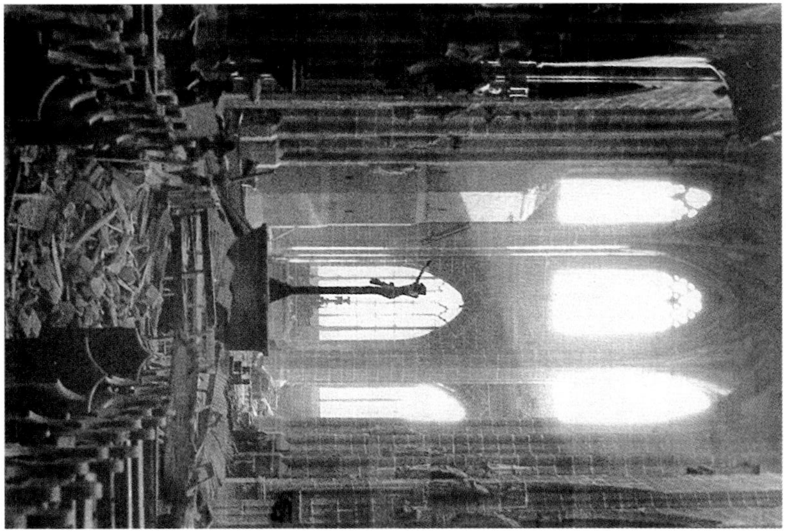

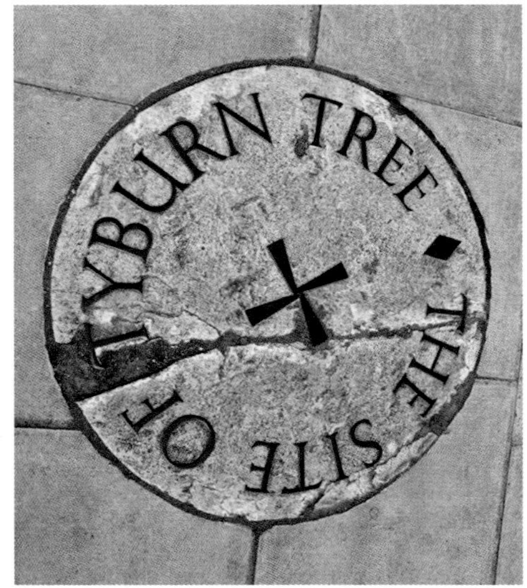
THE SITE OF TYBURN TREE

The rood represented the body of Christ, lifted up on the cross above the rood screen, flanked by Mary and Saint John, and was near ubiquitous in the English medieval church. Although some screens have survived the Reformation, no roods are left, and for a sense of what is missing we are thus consigned to a substitute image. This was painted in the reign of Mary Tudor, on a **tympanum board** within the chancel arch at St Catherine's, Ludham, in Norfolk, and equates more or less to what the congregation had been obliged to surrender because of the Reformation.[19]

British churches leave us then with the installation without its central figure, or rather, the installation echoes in broader lines the detail of this central nucleus. Whether in ground plan or in section, the church provides the cruciform casing, with its strong horizontal and vertical features, elements open and closed, but without their principal actor. My focus on the rood is less religious than curatorial: if this scene is missing something, something that combines the vertical force, downwards and upwards, and the horizontal pull at each side, its physical elements are nonetheless powerful and most focused at the transitional line marked by the rood screen. Its horizontality positions us at the threshold, under an open arch, the pavement strongly present beneath our feet. In front lies the altar, an enclosed table or box-like form representing the focal point of the composition and its staging.

...

270. Painted tympanum board, 16th century

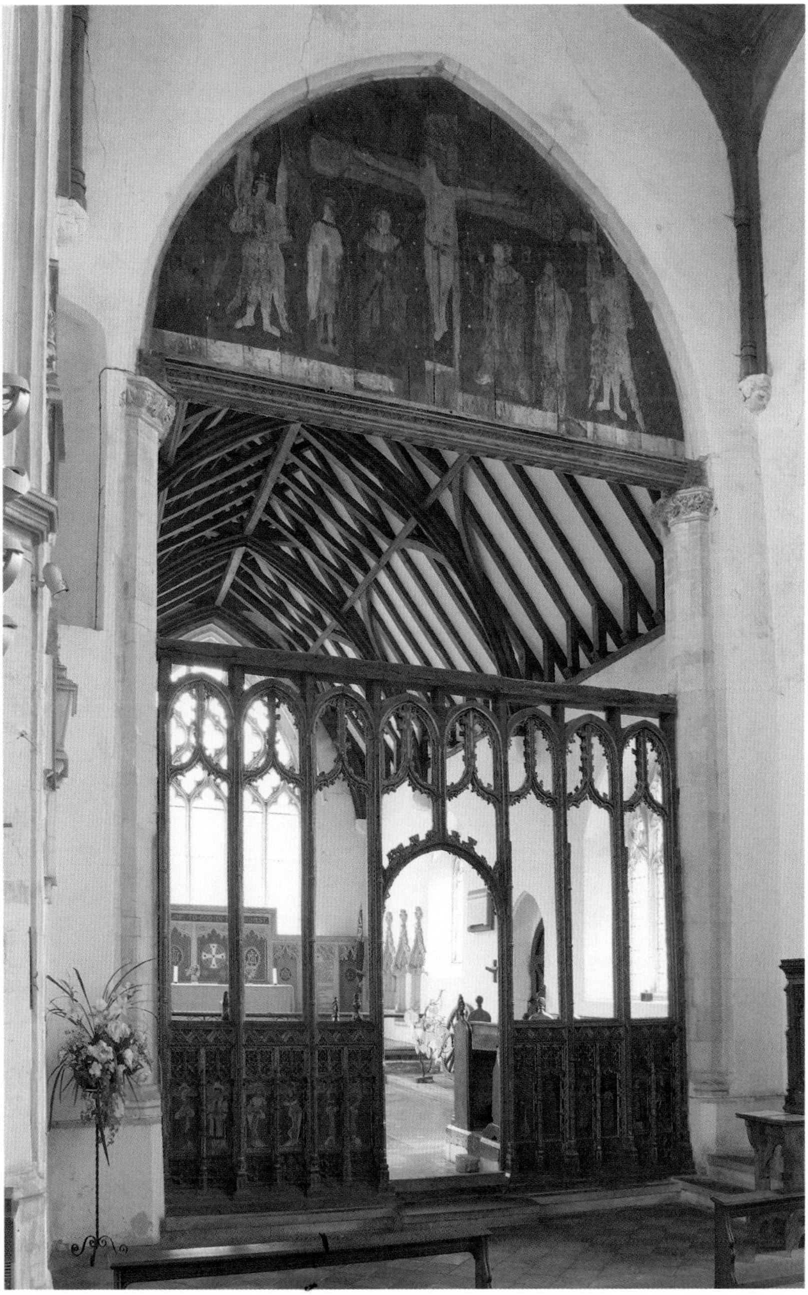

In many ways the tomb ensembles discussed earlier combine the same elements: their vertical and horizontal components represent the living and the dead, and often combine closed and open forms to suggest both past and future. A typical ensemble brings together, for example, the horizontal sarcophagus and the upright mourner, the closed urn or tomb with the open portal or arch. Such combinations hold good from provincial sixteenth-century examples through to the great compositions of Roubiliac, Rysbrack, Scheemakers and others in Westminster Abbey. A simpler, but contemporary example is the monument chamber for the **Lethieullier** family at Little Ilford, Essex, which comprises temple-like façade, podium, chest, sarcophagus and urns.

Not only death, but the church's physical limitations themselves, appear to be transcended by means of a flexible combining of closed symbolic objects and open framing devices. The threshold that stands between us and the deceased, half open, half closed, is perfectly illustrated by Roubiliac's **Nightingale Monument**, which itself must draw from the doorway motifs of classical ash-chests, altars and sarcophagi, as well as from cabinets and stoves.[20] Such monuments open themselves, almost literally, to a wider audience, to whom their vocabulary is equally relevant.[21] Indeed their involvement is demonstrated by the repeated usage of the moveable door, which looks like iron, because it is in black marble, but has real metal hinges and is supported by rollers.[22]

...

271. Monument to the Lethieullier Family, c.1737

272. Louis-François Roubiliac, monument to Sir Joseph and Lady Elizabeth Nightingale, 1761

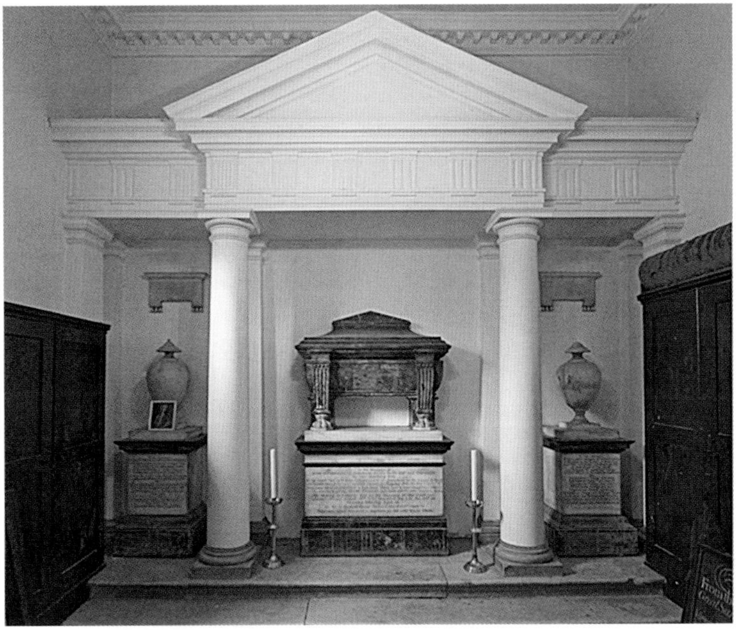

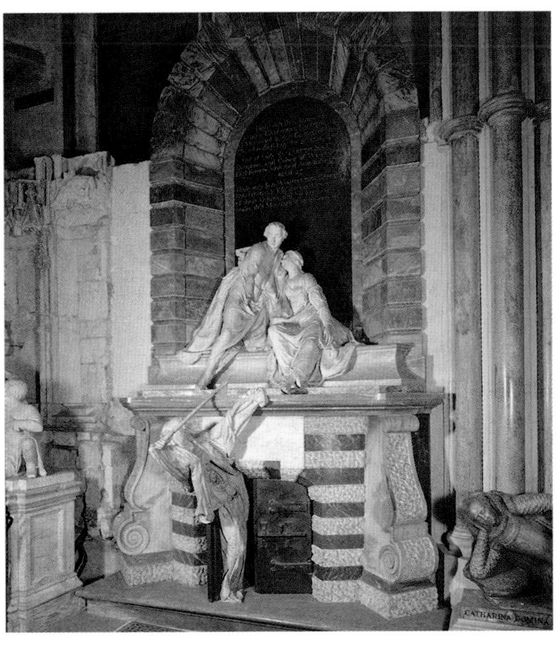

There is here a conflation of directional values or compass points, the elements and the senses, the amalgam suggesting the metamorphic moment at the threshold of the tomb or sanctuary. I suggest that this rich and pluralistic legacy still underpins the way we read sculpture today, even when it is ostensibly very distant from a commemorative or ecclesiastical context. It is now conceivable that we might look at Roger Hiorns's ***Untitled, 2005–2010***, with its bench, perpetual fire and mourner, in this light.

A good example of this is offered by Rosemarie Trockel's ceramic work. It is not just that her ceramic pieces have themselves gone through material transformation, it is her combining of doorway, fireplace and mirror motifs within one installation that speaks so strikingly to my subject. The way in which she suggested that the gallery wall be pierced or entered, by means of some of the transformational devices such as heat and light we have explored above, has inescapable roots in the lineage we have traced. Trockel's reinvention of a medieval world-view, exploring aspects of belief and sanctuary, is perhaps most clearly brought out in her altar text for St Peter's Church in Cologne: **'Ich habe angst'**.

- - -

273. Roger Hiorns, *Untitled, 2005–2010: Bench, fire and youth*, 2005–10

274. Rosemarie Trockel, *Ich habe angst*, 1993

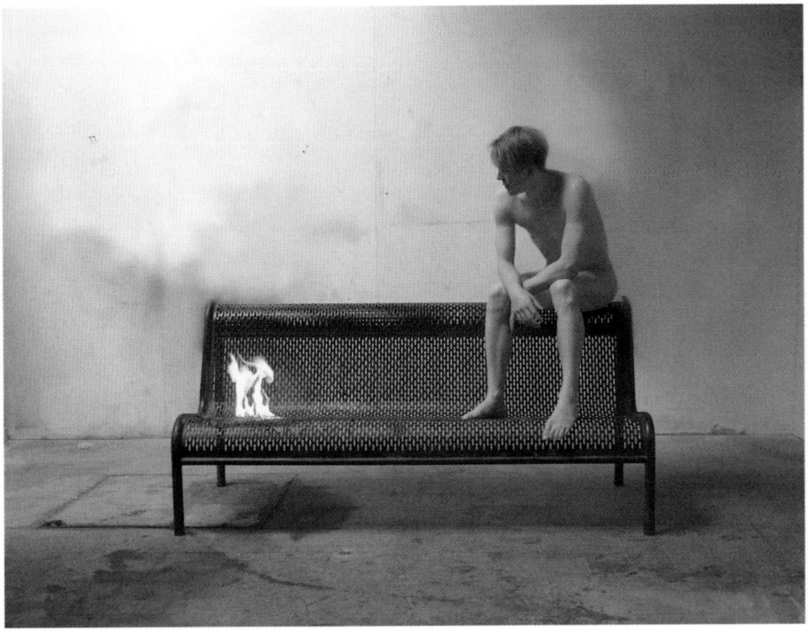

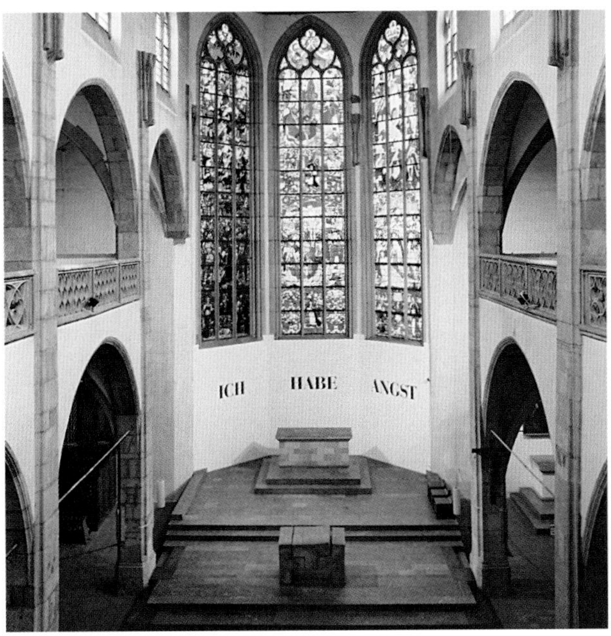
ICH HABE ANGST

We began with an excerpt from the lecture that **Rainer Maria Rilke** gave in Dresden. Rilke deliberately avoided mentioning the subject of his lecture for quite some time. Eventually he relented, saying:

> And now I venture to say to you the name which cannot be withheld any longer: Rodin. You know it is the name of countless objects. You ask to see them, and I am confused because I cannot show you any of them. But I seem to see one and another in your memory, and feel as if I could lift them out and place them here in our midst....[23]

This book has not been on Rodin, per se, partly because it has concentrated on British sculpture, but more pertinently because it is on no one artist, but rather on the forms of sculpture that we know, even if or because they are subliminal. This is why I have begun and ended with Rilke, for he attributed Rodin's power to the fact that we know these forms, and have always known them, even if we forget their names. This reticence, the modesty of objects, their stillness, was what Rilke lauded in Rodin. Even if the objects I describe, like those that Rilke described, are not here, they are in our memory, and we could almost imagine placing them here in our midst. Their titles are ultimately unimportant to us, because we know their forms more deeply. Rilke explained:

> my purpose is to awaken memories in you which are not yours, which are older than you; to restore connexions and renew relationships which lie in the distant past.[24]

I hope that I may have done something of the same, and by not trying too hard to remember names and titles, but rather returning to something that we have in common, may have touched on something rather simply physical, in front of us, below us, withheld from us or open to us. This brings us to the threshold of sculpture, the threshold that holds the promise of something beyond itself, because as sculpture is always close to death, it is also close to life.

275. Rainer Maria Rilke, 1908

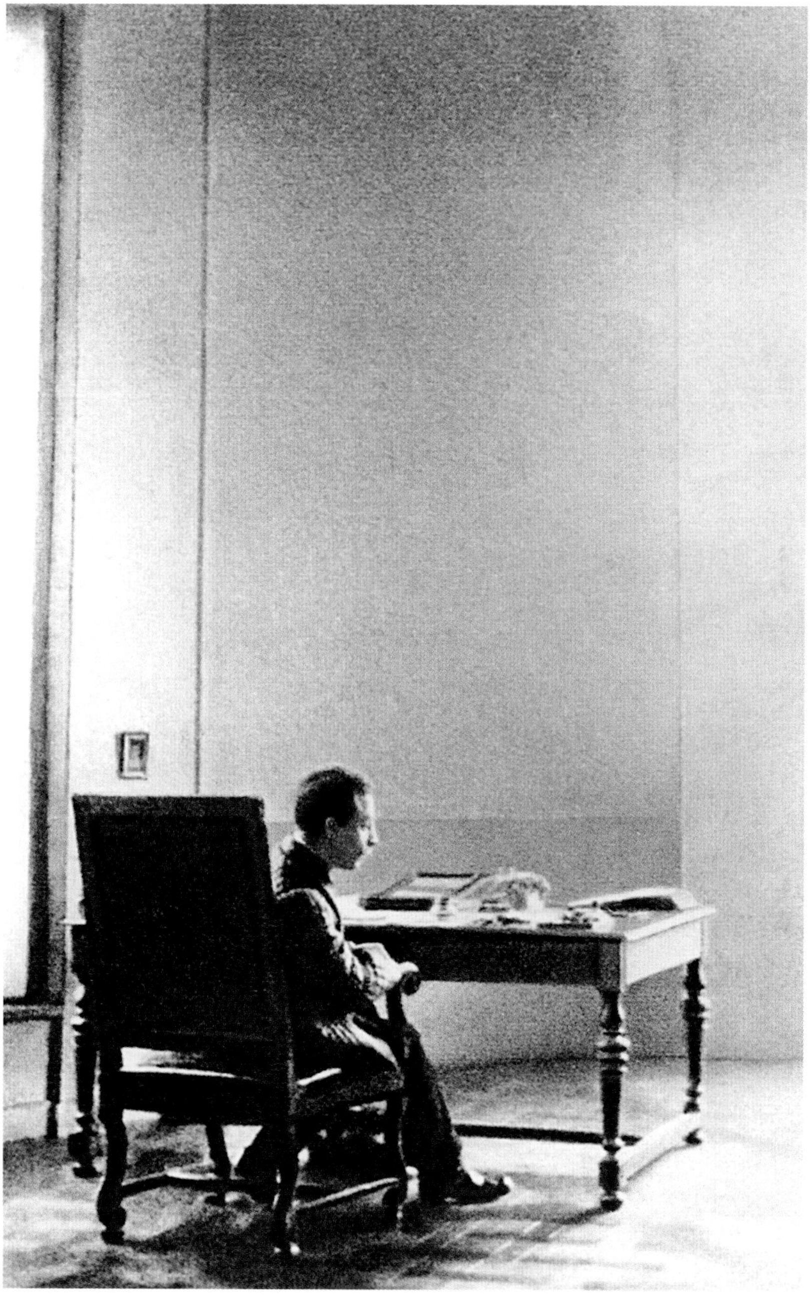

vertical

v1 'The Rodin Book' in *Rodin and other Prose Pieces*, with introduction by William Tucker, 1986, p. 45. Rilke met Rodin in September 1902, and published on him in 1903 and 1907 (parts I and II).

v2 Glasgow, 1806; Dublin, 1809; Great Yarmouth, 1815–17; the latter two both by or after William Wilkins.

v3 Interestingly another obelisk, the so-called Cleopatra's needle, was also intended to commemorate Nelson, and his victory at the Battle of the Nile (offered 1819, erected 1878).

v4 Another obvious example is the Duke of York Column, London, 1832–4. The view from its viewing platform was illustrated in magazines such as the Penny Magazine (1837), but the platform was closed to the public by the late nineteenth century.

v5 In Rome the second-century columns of Trajan and of Marcus Aurelius are both surmounted by later Christian figures, bronze added to stone, superimposing one ideological regime upon another. (Saint Paul and Saint Peter were added in 1587–8 by Pope Sixtus V.)

v6 Though plinths also had a practical protective role to play; on this see M. G. Sullivan in *Art Under Attack*, London, 2013.

v7 It is thought that Edward I may have been inspired by the Montjoie crosses that guided pilgrims, as well as by the crosses erected after the death of Louis IX between St Denis and Paris.

v8 After its eventual fall, ordered by Parliament and enacted around 1647, its loss entered popular folklore, cf. 'The Downfall of Charing Cross', one of the ballads collected by Bishop Percy and others (including Pepys and Johnson) and published in Percy's *Reliques* (1765). In it the iconoclasm is attributed to the belief that the cross was seditious, but the poet avers that it was never heard to speak a word, and indeed could neither write nor read, nor had ever gone to church.

v9 *Reliques of Ancient English Poetry*, London, 1846, 2: 248.

v10 See also *Henry VI*, Part 2, Act IV, Scene 6; line 2601, where Cade 'strikes his staff on London-stone'.

v11 The 1723 engraving by Henry Hulsberg after Nicholas Hawksmoor's drawing, showing Charles II as Colossus, is in the Victoria and Albert Museum. See Kerry Downes, *Hawksmoor*, London, 1969, p. 186. Hawksmoor went further in topping his churches with obelisk-steeples, raised high in the sky.

v12 Quoted by Philip Ward-Jackson in his entry on the Monument for his *Public Sculpture of the City of London*, Liverpool, 2003, pp. 260–68.

v13 In drawings in All Souls College, Oxford and the British Museum.

v14 Another famous sundial pillar is that by Edward Pierce for London's Seven Dials intersection (1693–4).

v15 For faceted: see e.g., Glamis and Holyrood House 1633, made by John Mylne for Charles I's coronation. For the lectern type see e.g., Culzean Castle, and for obelisks see e.g., Kelburn Castle and Drummond Castle, also by Mylne. Andrew Somerville counted 300 obelisk sundials in Scotland in his 1987 study for the Society of Antiquaries of Scotland (PSAS, vol. 117, pp. 233–64). Earlier studies by Margaret Gatty (London, 1872) and especially by Thomas Ross in the PSAS (1890), and by Ross and D. MacGibbon (Edinburgh, 1892) remain standard.

v16 The great horizontal dial at Drumlanrig Castle was made by the London clockmaker Henry Wynne in 1692, and is more sophisticated mathematically than most of the multifaceted dials, which appear to have primarily focused on their symbolism.

v17 And the octagon form was understood to represent regeneration.

v18 E.g., St Gregory's Minster, Kirkdale, and at St John, Escomb. The free-standing tradition is more often Welsh and Irish.

v19 See the rebus series on the A22, in Surrey and Sussex, which marks the distance from Bow Bells and includes the buckle of the Pelham family.

v20 Once the railway system was in operation, Welsh slate predominated and the last quarry in Swithland Wood, Leicestershire, was closed in 1887.

v21 Fifty miles west of Meadow View, West Drayton.

v22 Pyramid tombs became the norm by the mid-eighteenth century. Matthew Craske, *The Silent Rhetoric of the Body*, New Haven and London, 2007, p. 51.

v23 See here Craske, 2007, p. 10 and more generally.

v24 Ledward had founded the company Sculptured Memorials and Headstones. Headstones are generally vertical, and represent the head of the body. (Footstones would, on occasion, mark its foot.)

v25 The work was shown at the Whitechapel Gallery, placed on the South Bank, and transferred by the London County Council to the grounds of Kenwood House, Hampstead, in 1959.

v26 Patrick Eyres in *The Garden of Forking Paths*, ed. Heike Munder, Zurich, 2011, p. 68.

v27 It was a key work in the first LCC Outdoor Sculpture Exhibition, held in the park in 1948.

v28 A modern example of the flagpole is the weather-flag series by Rose Finn-Kelcey, *Variable Light to Moderate* (1971) and her *Windsocks* (1969).

v29 During the Commonwealth all regalia was destroyed and made anew for Charles II. The performances of artists such as André Cadere (1934–78), who carried his official status before him, in the form of a stick or rod, operate on this threshold.

v30 John Shute, *The First and Chief Groundes of Architecture*, London, folios iiii to xiiii. See the 1912 facsimile, published by Country Life.

v31 A further comparison is Auguste Rodin's *Age of Bronze*, first known, in the light of French defeat in the Franco-Prussian War, as *The Vanquished*. Its columnar quality suggests a plumb line running through a form that is in very slight contrapposto. The upright figure suggests past and future, defeat and survival. A wreath has been removed from its head and a spear from its upstretched hand. The potential signification is amplified if we remember that the broken column conventionally represents a life cut short.

v32 The book, *Vagmarken* (Stockholm, 1963) took the title *Markings* in the translation by Leif Sjoberg and W. H. Auden (New York, 1964).

v33 Richard Hamer, *A Choice of Anglo-Saxon Verse*, London, 1970, p. 161.

v34 Sixteen out of 156 in total.

v35 The poem was found among others in 1832 in the cathedral of Vercelli, Italy. See Margaret Jennings, 'Rood and Ruthwell: The Power of Paradox', *English Language Notes* 31.3, 1994, 6–12. See also Fred Orton in *Art History*, 21.1, 1998.

v36 Henry Duncan, *Account of the remarkable monument, in the shape of a cross, inscribed with Roman and Runic letters: preserved in the garden of Ruthwell Manse, Dumfriesshire*, Edinburgh, 1833.

v37 As at Dewsbury, Reculver, Masham and Wolverhampton, and at Cirencester, Catterick and York. See Fred Orton and Ian Wood, *Fragments of History: rethinking the Ruthwell and Bewcastle monuments*, Manchester, 2007.

v38 Henry Moore Foundation #1854–6, 1941–2; see J. Stallabrass in D. Mitchinson (ed.), *Celebrating Moore*, Aldershot, 2006, p. 246.

v39 See Frits Scholten, *Sumptuous Memories: studies in seventeenth-century Dutch tomb sculpture*, Zwolle, 2003.

v40 Reproduced courtesy of Michael Dean and the Herald Street Gallery.

horizontal

h1 Her viscera were interred in the Chapel of St Mary in Lincoln Cathedral, which was destroyed in the Civil War. A drawing by William Sedgewick in Sir William Dugdale's *Book of Monuments* (1641) records its similarity to the tomb in Westminster (and served as the basis for its restoration in 1892). Nigel Llewellyn reminds us of the closeness between the body on its bier beneath the hearse, and the tomb itself: *The Art of Death: visual culture in the English death ritual c.150–c.1800*, London, 1991, p. 115.

h2 In the following year Henry III was laid beside her body, his tomb marked also by William Torel.

h3 For examples of such specifications see Llewellyn, 1991, pp. 222–3. The term 'statue' appears by the 1620s.

h4 Kneelers appear by 1600; standing figures by 1626 according to Llewellyn, 1991, pp. 102–5.

h5 Royal effigies were used in funerals from the fourteenth century to 1625, helping to bridge the earthly and the divine, the real absence and the conceptual presence. On those stored in the Westminster Abbey Museum, see A. Harvey and R. Mortimer, *The Funeral Effigies of Westminster Abbey*, Woodbridge, 1994.

h6 In this, reprising the earlier convention for the burial of priests.

h7 Eoin Martin, *Queen Victoria, Prince Albert and the Patronage of Contemporary Sculpture*, University of Warwick, PhD, 2013, p. 220 et seq.

h8 The Crown Princess of Prussia asked for a 'recumbent statue', 'clothed in an armour of the middle ages'. Though he chose marble, Triqueti was clearly inspired by earlier representations of Albert as a Christian knight, as shown by Martin, ibid., p. 234.

h9 By contrast compare Francis Derwent Wood's Machine Gun Corps Memorial figure at Hyde Park Corner; naked and supporting an outsize sword.

h10 Later works by Wilding, including *Migrant* and *Rust*, play more overtly on sculpture's link with weaponry.

h11 And Archbishop Chichele in Canterbury in the previous decade, arguably the first in England. See also the Dean Colet tomb at St Paul's, 1519.

h12 The destroyed tomb to John Colet (d.1519) included a bust above the cadaver.

h13 See also Alison Wilding's *Vanish* and *Detail* (2004); Eric Bainbridge's *The Mind of the Artist (Exposed)* (2011); and, of course, the work of Mike Kelley.

h14 Ennio Quirini Visconti (1751–1818) was responsible for the new attribution.

h15 Jacob Epstein, *Let there be Sculpture*, London, 1940, pp. 155–6.

h16 *The Duchess of Malfi* (1614), IV, 2, quoted by Peter Sherlock in *Monuments and Memory in Early Modern England*, Aldershot, 2008, pp. 44–5.

h17 David Bindman and Malcolm Baker, *Roubiliac and the Eighteenth-century Monument*, New Haven, 1995, p. 39.

h18 By contrast the wounded fighter is a well-known trope in German twentieth-century figuration.

h19 The Westminster Abbey effigies had also involved death casts, and these skills were transferred to living subjects. In the late seventeenth century this led to a brief craze for life-casting, of which Pepys was a notable example.

h20 See also *I Morti di Bligny* (1935), which announces its own resurrection.

h21 Ed. John Butt, *The Poems of Alexander Pope*, New Haven, 1963, pp. 112 and 113.

h22 Though speaking sculptures are most commonly associated with Pasquino, more are horizontal than vertical. One might suggest that this informal aspect of the reclining figure made it especially appropriate for the English country seat, a place away from the constraints of the city, and for commemoration.

h23 See also Louis Nixon, *Untitled*, 1990, shown at *Space Explorations*, Beck Road, London.

h24 In a project somewhat akin to that of Mark Manders.

h25 See also Keith Wilson's *Trip Trap Flat Cap* (2002).

closed

c1 Pandora was the first woman, fashioned from clay by Hephaestus to punish Prometheus. Her name represents 'all the gifts', despite the fact that she carried all the ills, apart from Hope.

c2 A later example, from the V&A, is the mid-fifteenth-century casket that shows Saint George on its lid, with Saint Etheldreda of Ely on its sides, with other saints (V&A 634A–I–1870). The late fifteenth-century English brass chrismatory (V&A, M.108–1923) echoes the reliquary form.

c3 Created by the goldsmith Walter of Colchester and dedicated in 1220.

c4 And perhaps that double sense is inspired by the dual identity of Keats's 'Lamia'.

c5 See A. Harvey and R. Mortimer, *The Funeral Effigies of Westminster Abbey*, Woodbridge, 1994, p. 53.

c6 It was shown both recumbent and standing at Somerset House. Ibid., p. 73. The National Portrait Gallery has various versions of his death mask, one possibly contemporary and the others later. There is a further version in Florence.

c7 Quoted by Peter Sherlock in *Monuments and Memory in Early Modern England*, Aldershot, 2008, p. 64, from John Stow's *Survey of London*, 1633.

c8 The Easter Sepulchre at Heckington, Lincolnshire, is fourteenth century and in stone, set into the wall.

c9 Matthew Craske, *The Silent Rhetoric of the Body*, New Haven and London, 2007, p. 241. Exemplified in the 1730s by the Duchess of Buckingham.

c10 Whereas classical sarcophagi were often stacked together, seen primarily from the front, with their sides and back pushed in and up against others.

c11 Published by J. G. Wooding as a print, 1783 (British Museum 1864,0514.209).

c12 Michael Craig-Martin's *Four Identical Boxes with Lids Reversed* (Tate, 1969), though more delicate, also uses seriality, similarity and difference in a work that touches on the open/closed question.

c13 Harvey and Mortimer, 1994, p. 97.

c14 Works like Cragg's *Untitled* (1983, Kröller–Müller) show the grease-crayon scribble loosely but evenly all over the surface as if to emphasise the lack of materiality of the box, and its mere pictorialism.

c15 One might even argue that a work such as *Royal Ascot* by Mark Wallinger, which deploys a series of monitors, has its place in the procession of royal effigies.

c16 James I's effigy was shown in its 'mausoleum', and in 1678 Christopher Wren presented the project for a monument (described on the cover as a mausoleum) to Charles I; see Anthony Geraghty, *The Architectural Drawings of Christopher Wren*, Aldershot, 2007, pp. 193–5.

c17 E.g., the Adam mausoleum at Greyfriars, Edinburgh (1753), the Lyttelton monument/mausoleum at Hagley (1747) and the grandiose destroyed Colebrooke Mausoleum at Chilham, Kent (1755). Country churches can on occasion also be seen as mausolea, with an eye to their landscaping effect, as well as to dynastic preservation.

c18 It houses the remains of Sophia, wife of the 1st Baron Yarborough. John Soane's 1811 mausoleum to Sir Francis Bourgeois and Noel and Margaret Desenfans at Dulwich is inside the larger building, which to a degree gives the building its function, but makes the mausoleum more like the organ of a larger body and less like a container in itself.

c19 But also Annika Eriksson, Toby Paterson, Jorge Pardo, Job Koelwijn, Monika Sosnowska and Andrea Zittel.

c20 The V&A example comes from Compton Place, Eastbourne; another is at Kedleston.

c21 Izaak Walton, *The Complete Angler & The Lives of Donne, Wotton, Hooker, Herbert & Sanderson*, London, 1925, p. 234.

c22 Philip Cottrell's 2009 lecture, 'John Donne, Undone, Redone' is to be published. An earlier monument that portrays the shroud in a similar way is that to Sir Henry Slingsby, Knaresborough (1633–4).

c23 *Gentleman's Magazine*, vol. 90, Part 1, 1820, p. 113.

c24 Attributed by Katharine Esdaile to Roubiliac but by Malcolm Baker to Cheere. See Baker's catalogue of Roubiliac's funerary monuments in David Bindman and Malcolm Baker, *Roubiliac and the Eighteenth-century Monument*, New Haven, 1995, pp. 358–9.

c25 See Andrew Saint, 'Diary', *London Review of Books*, 20 Sept 2007 and the poem itself: 'All'ombra de'cipressi e dentro l'urne/Confortate di pianto e` forse il sonno/della morte men duro?', *Dei Seplocri, Carme di Ugo Foscolo*, Milan, 2010, p. 5.

c26 Epstein, *Let there be Sculpture*, London, 1940, p. 66.

c27 As given by Epstein as above, but not quite correct. Wilde has 'will fill' and 'mourners be outcast men'. A little later in his poem Wilde had indeed suggested: 'And every human heart that breaks/ in prison-cell or yard/ is as that broken box that gave/its treasure to the Lord'.

open

o1 The cloth might be understood as the parapetasma, separating the earthly from the celestial world.

o2 By Horace Jones, with statues of the monarchs (the last to pass through) by J. E. Boehm. See P. Ward-Jackson, *Public Sculpture of the City of London*, Liverpool, 2003, pp. 115–23.

o3 The Euston Arch, demolished c.1960, still has its pair at the other end of the London and Birmingham Railway in Curzon Street Station, Birmingham.

o4 It seems fitting that Robert Adam's 1760 design for a gateway to the Admiralty, his first commission in London, was indeed styled a 'screen'.

o5 It was designed as an arch, rather than a pedestal, despite the presence, in different periods, of two different sculptures atop it, firstly a statue of the Duke of Wellington by Matthew Cotes Wyatt (now in Aldershot), and then, as now, showcasing the Quadriga by Adrian Jones.

o6 Francis Legatt Chantrey's George IV was eventually installed on one of the empty plinths in Trafalgar Square.

o7 See, for example, Aachen, Hildesheim, Pisa and Monreale.

o8 See Tom Nickson, 'Moral Edification at Gonville and Caius College, Cambridge', *Architectural History*, 48 (2005).

o9 This piece, on slide and film, was never shown, but referenced in Tacita Dean's 2004 exhibition *An Aside*.

o10 Marx's eleventh commentary on Ludwig Feuerbach, found and published by Engels in 1888, mounted in the foyer by the ruling party of the GDR in 1953.

o11 Founded in 1784, and in Loughborough since 1840, the firm cast the Great Paul of St Paul's Cathedral, Britain's largest bell in 1880. It was sold to UK Bell Foundries in 2009.

o12 Epstein worked with Louis Osman to make the fittings for the Convent in Cavendish Square, used later also for Coventry Cathedral.

o13 A cast iron version is in the Graves Gallery, Sheffield.

o14 Similar herms by Rysbrack, probably representing Socrates and Plato, support a relief showing 'Britannia receiving the Riches of the East', suitable for its location, the headquarters of the East India Company.

o15 Werner Heisenberg (Uncertainty Principle) and Niels Bohr (Complementarity Principle) together (1927) produced what became known as the Copenhagen Interpretation, which led to a 'rethinking of the very idea of an outside world'. See Jackson Lears in his review of the *Life of J. Robert Oppenheimer*, *London Review of Books*, 20 December 2012.

o16 See Deborah Howard, *Architectural History*, 39 (1996). Howard suggests that the monument refers to Raleigh's *History of the World*, with its four columns citing Cicero in a translation by Ben Jonson. She also proposes the Mylne family, the royal master masons, and makers of the Holyrood House sundial, as the authors.

o17 Also *Country Life, New Ceramics and Pottery* at Barbara Gladstone Gallery, New York, 2006. *A Cosmos* was initiated in 2012 by the Reina Sofia, Madrid, and shown in the New Museum, New York, and the Serpentine Gallery, London.

o18 Coley's inspiration was reportedly a seventeenth-century story of the French village of Modseine, where miracles were being reported in such significant numbers that the authorities, in an attempt to curb the excessive religious fervour, put up a sign stating 'There will be no miracles here. By order of the king'; 'a place beyond belief' was how a New Yorker described her city on the radio just after the Twin Towers attack.

o19 In 1996 Massimo Bartolini, at the *Space Explorations* exhibition on 110 Euston Road, made *Mouse in the House*, a work that echoed this move in sound.

ensemble

e1 Bethan Huws in *Selected Textual Works 1991-2003*, Cologne, 2003, pp. 6 and 16.

e2 This room was the same room as that in which she first staged *Peeling the Apple*, discussed earlier.

e3 Rev. Richard Warner, *Excursions from Bath*, Bath, 1801, p. 107.

e4 G. B. Locatelli's 1780 reclining sculptural portrait of the dancer known as 'La Baccelli', at Knole, is a more mischievous version of this type.

e5 On this see my *Patio and Pavilion: the place of sculpture in modern architecture*, London/Los Angeles, 2007/8.

e6 Built by John Donowell for the second baronet before Donowell's dismissal in 1764, the temple figures in paintings of the estate by William Hannan. (It was recently rebuilt in 1982 to a design by Quinlan Terry.)

e7 Along with two other works by Gibson, and Harriet Hosmer's *Zenobia*, each on a different side.

e8 Jean de La Fontaine, *Fables*, Book IX, fable 6. Translation by the author.

e9 *Le Charivari*, 12 April 1869.

e10 Horace, Book I, Satire VIII, translated here by A. S. Kline, 2005.

e11 Consider also the Tree of Jesse, the divine genealogy, and potential links with the wooden effigy of the knight crusader. See Nigel Llewellyn, *The Art of Death: visual culture in the English death ritual c.1500–c.1800*, London, 1991, p. 307.

e12 Such images, reminiscent also of documentary photographs of early archaeological discoveries, such as the Delphi Antinous, now carry with them the idea of the fall of the idol, and its later rebirth and restoration as a complete and upright figure.

e13 Richard Hamer, *A Choice of Anglo-Saxon Verse*, London, 1970, p. 161.

e14 Ibid., pp. 161–3.

e15 This translation from A. S. Cook, 'The Date of the Old English Inscription on the Brussels Cross', *The Modern Language Review*, vol. 10, 2, April 1915, p. 157.

e16 Ovid's *Metamorphoses*, Book 1, chapter 6. This translation from http://www.theoi.com/Text/OvidMetamorphoses1.html#6,525.

e17 Ossip Zadkine (1939) and Julio González (1937) both made Daphne sculptures, the former in wood (and later in bronze), the latter again doubling the transformation by turning the wooden subject into iron (later cast in bronze).

e18 In Cologne the cathedral survived equally heavy bombing, as did the tenth-century cross commissioned by Archbishop Gero, which represents perhaps the oldest such form in Northern Europe.

e19 The image had been covered over by the canvas painting of the Elizabethan Royal Arms, and then blocked into the stairs. It remained there until 1879 when the Norfolk Archaeological Society discovered what the Arms covered. More generally, the constraints on religious activity that the Reformation entailed meant that tombs filled the gaps left by shrines.

e20 Malcolm Baker suggests that Roubiliac's likely time in Dresden introduced him to this more functional liturgical and domestic vocabulary: David Bindman and Malcolm Baker, *Roubiliac and the Eighteenth-century Monument*, New Haven, 1995, p. 230.

e21 Horace Walpole noted that it was 'more theatric than sepulchral' in his 1786 *Anecdotes*, p. 375; see Bindman and Baker, 1995, p. 35 and also p. 32.

e22 Another way of understanding this terminal form is as a vault that has been closed, particularly marking the end of a family line. See Craske, 1992 PhD, cited by Bindman and Baker, 1995, p. 101.

e23 'The Rodin Book' in *Rodin and other Prose Pieces*, with introduction by William Tucker, 1986, p. 49.

e24 Ibid., p. 45.

vertical

1 William Railton and Edward Hodges Baily, Nelson's Column, 1840–43. Trafalgar Square, London. Photo © John Bethell / Bridgeman Images

2 John Groves, Nelson Monument, 1807–8. Portsdown Hill, Portsmouth. Photograph by Tony Braime

3 Obelisk of Axum, c.3rd–4th century. Tigray, Ethiopia. Photograph by Ondřej Žváček, licensed under Attribution 2.5 Generic (CC BY 2.5) license

4 Queen Eleanor's Cross, c.1290/92. Hardingstone, Northamptonshire. © Bob Hunt / Alamy Stock Photo

5 Queen Eleanor's Cross, c.1290/92. Waltham Cross, Hertfordshire. akg-images / A. F. Kersting

6 Queen Eleanor's Cross, c.1290/92. Geddington, Northamptonshire. © Heritage Image Partnership Ltd / Alamy Stock Photo

7 London Stone, late 12th century. 111 Cannon Street, London. Early 20th-century photograph. Private Collection / The Stapleton Collection / Bridgeman Images

8 Christopher Wren, Monument to the Great Fire of London, 1671–7. City of London. Photograph by Beata May, licensed under Creative Commons Attribution-Share Alike 3.0 Unported license

9 Christopher Wren, Monument to the Great Fire of London, detail showing the gilt flames, 1671–7. City of London. © Sophie Kullmann

10 Charles Turnbull, Pelican Sundial, 1581. Corpus Christi College, Oxford. By permission of the President and Fellows of Corpus Christi College, Oxford / Photographer: Nicholas Read, 2014

11 Sundial, 1707. Kelburn Castle, Ayrshire. © Crown Copyright: Historic Environment Scotland

12 Sundial, 1671. Glamis Castle, Angus. © Historic Environment Scotland

13 John Mylne, obelisk sundial, 1630. Drummond Castle Gardens, Muthill, Perthshire. Photograph by Dennis Cowan

14 Sundial (detail from the Bewcastle Cross), late 7th century. Church of St Cuthbert, Bewcastle, Cumbria. © Stan Pritchard / Alamy Stock Photo

15 Robert Mylne, obelisk, 1771. St George's Circus, Southwark, London. © Simon Balson / Alamy Stock Photo

16 Milestone obelisk, late 18th century. Richmond Bridge, London. Photograph by Roger Redgrave, licensed under Attribution-NoDerivs 2.0 Generic (CC BY-ND 2.0) license

17 Sundial, 17th century. Pittodrie House, Aberdeenshire. Photograph © the author

18 Milestone, Markham Moor, Nottinghamshire. Photograph by B. Hilton

19 Stone boundary marker, Urra Moor, Yorkshire. © Michael Gamble / Alamy Stock Photo

20 Tombs along the Via Appia, Rome. akg-images / Bildarchiv Monheim / Schütze / Rodemann

21 Tyne Cot Commonwealth War Graves Cemetery, Belgium. Dorling Kindersley / UIG / Bridgeman Images

22 Gilbert Ledward, *Monolith*, 1936. Tate, London. © The Estate of Gilbert Ledward / Photograph © Tate, London 2017

23 Barbara Hepworth, *Monolith – Empyrean*, 1953. Kenwood House Gardens, Hampstead, London. Photograph: Studio St Ives, taken in 1948. © Bowness

24 Eric Kennington, signpost for Comet Inn, 1936. Hatfield, Hertfordshire. Photograph © Jonathan Black

25 William Ashurst, Ashurst Beacon, 1798. Ashurst Hill, Dalton, Lancashire. Photograph by Eddie J. Rodriquez

26 Reg Butler, final maquette for *The Unknown Political Prisoner*, 1951–2. On loan to Tate, London. © The Estate of Reg Butler / Photograph © Tate, London 2017

27 Henry Moore, *Three Standing Figures*, 1947–8. Battersea Park, London. Reproduced by permission of the Henry Moore Foundation

28 Herm, c.510 BC. National Archaeological Museum, Athens. Photograph © Bridgeman Images

29 Scene at Tyburn showing crowds gathered to watch a hanging, 1696. London Metropolitan Archives. © London Metropolitan Archives, City of London

30 The Gentleman Usher of the Black Rod at the State Opening of Parliament, 4 June 2014. © WPA Pool / Pool

31 John Shute, folio from *The First and Chief Groundes of Architecture*, 1563. Royal Institute of British Architects, London. © RIBA Collections

32 William Inwood, Caryatid porch, 1822. St Pancras Church, Euston Road, London. akg-images / David Borland

33 Hans Memling, *Martyrdom of Saint Sebastian*, c.1475. Royal Museums of Fine Arts of Belgium, Brussels. © Musées Royaux des Beaux-Arts de Belgique, Bruxelles

34 Andrea Mantegna, *Saint Sebastian*, 1481. Louvre, Paris. Photograph © Bridgeman Images

35 Pierre Puget, *Saint Sebastian*, 1663-8. Church of Santa Maria Assunta di Carignano, Genoa. © 2017. Photo Scala, Florence

36 Barbara Hepworth, *Torso*, 1930. Whitworth Art Gallery, University of Manchester. © Whitworth Art Gallery, The University of Manchester, UK / Bridgeman Images

37 Barbara Hepworth, *Single Form*, 1961-4. United Nations Plaza, New York. © Bowness

38 Runic alphabet and drawings of the Ruthwell Cross, c.1832. Canmore Collection. © Historic Environment Scotland

39 Drawn by Rev. Dr Duncan and engraved by W. Penny, *Runic Monument in the garden belonging to Ruthwell Manse*, c.1832. Canmore Collection. © Historic Environment Scotland

40 Henry Moore, *Upright Motive No. 1: Glenkiln Cross*, 1955-6. Hirshhorn Estate Garden, Greenwich. Reproduced by permission of the Henry Moore Foundation

41 Henry Moore, *Three Upright Motives*, 1955-6, cast 1965. Kröller-Müller Museum, Netherlands. Reproduced by permission of the Henry Moore Foundation

42 François Dieussart, monument to Charles Morgan, 1645-6. Great Church, Bergen op Zoom, Netherlands. From Frits Scholten, 'François Dieussart, Constantijn Huygens, and the Classical Ideal in Funerary Sculpture', *Simiolus: Netherlands Quarterly for the History of Art*, Vol. 25, No. 4 (1997), p. 305

43 Philista Stele, 2nd century BC. Ashmolean Museum, University of Oxford. © Ashmolean Museum, University of Oxford

44 Edwin Lutyens, Cenotaph, 1919. Whitehall, London. © Stan Pritchard / Alamy Stock Photo

horizontal

45 William Torel, effigy of Eleanor of Castile, 1291. Westminster Abbey, London. © Westminster Abbey, London / Bridgeman Images

46 Effigy of Edward III, 1377. Westminster Abbey, London. © Dean and Chapter of Westminster

47 D'Isigny family effigy, late 13th century. Norton Disney, Lincolnshire. Photograph by LeicesterPhoto LTD

48 Tomb to Anne, wife of Lord Bruce of Kinloss, 1627. Church of St Peter and St Paul, Exton, Leicestershire. Photograph by LeicesterPhoto LTD

49 Effigy of Lady Abigail Sherard and her husband, 1640. Church of St Mary Magdalene, Stapleford, Leicestershire. Photograph by LeicesterPhoto LTD

50 Monument to Sir Roger Smith, 1655. St Michael and All Angels Church, Edmondthorpe, Leicestershire. © Colin Underhill / Alamy Stock Photo

51 Carlo Marochetti, effigies of Queen Victoria and Prince Albert, 1867. Frogmore Mausoleum, Windsor Park. Royal Collection Trust / © Her Majesty Queen Elizabeth II 2017

52 Edgar Boehm, effigy to Elizabeth Dacre Howard, 1883. Lanercost Priory, Cumbria. Photograph by Rex Harris

53 William Goscombe John, Leverhulme tombs, 1913-25. Port Sunlight, Cheshire. © Conway Library, The Courtauld Institute of Art, London

54 Memorial to Bishop John Charles Ryle, 1900. Liverpool Cathedral. © Liverpool Cathedral

55 Alfred Gilbert, Duke of Clarence Memorial, 1894. Albert Memorial Chapel, St George's Chapel, Windsor.

56 Alfred Stevens, competition model for the Wellington Monument in St Paul's Cathedral, 1857. Victoria and Albert Museum, London. © Victoria and Albert Museum, London

57 Detail of the tomb of John Harington showing his head resting on a helmet, 1524. Church of St Peter and St Paul, Exton, Leicestershire. Photograph by LeicesterPhoto LTD

58 Detail of the tomb of John Harington showing gauntlets by his side, 1524. Church of St Peter and St Paul, Exton, Leicestershire. Photograph by LeicesterPhoto LTD

59 Tomb of Francis Hastings, 2nd Earl of Huntingdon, 1561. St Helen's Church, Ashby-de-la-Zouch, Leicestershire. Photograph by LeicesterPhoto LTD

89 Henry Moore, *Shelter Scene: Bunks and Sleepers*, 1941. Tate, London. © Tate, London 2017

90 Giuseppe Fiorelli, one of twenty plaster casts of preserved victims of the eruption of Mount Vesuvius in 79 AD, 1863. Pompeii, Italy. © Photograph William Starling

91 Arturo Martini, *La Sete*, 1934. Civic Museum of Contemporary Art (CIMAC), Milan. © 2017. DeAgostini Picture Library / Scala, Florence

92 John Cheere, *Sleeping Nymph (Ariadne)*, 1766. Stourhead, Wiltshire. © National Trust / David Cousins

93 *Marforio* (River God Fountain), 1st-2nd century. Capitoline Museums, Rome. Photo © Tarker / Bridgeman Images

94 Henry Moore, *West Wind* (in progress), 1928-9, for the London Underground Headquarters. Reproduced by permission of the Henry Moore Foundation

95 Richard Wilson, *Watertable*, 1994. Full-size billiard table, concrete pipe, ground water, electrics. Matt's Gallery, London. © Richard Wilson

96 Mark Boyle and Joan Hills, *Institute for Contemporary Archaeology: Holland Park Avenue Study*, 1967. Tate, London. © Boyle Family. All rights reserved, DACS 2017

97 Roger Hiorns, *Untitled*, 2008. Exh. Corvi-Mora Gallery, London. © Roger Hiorns. All rights reserved, DACS 2017. Image courtesy Corvi-Mora, London

98 Keith Wilson, *Puddle*, 1999. Flag Market, Preston, Lancashire. © Keith Wilson

99 Judith Dean, *Field*, 2005. Ragley Hall, Warwickshire. © Judith Dean

100 Coronation ogham stone and footmark, c.500 AD. Dunadd, Kilmartin Valley, Argyll. © Historic Environment Scotland

101 Stone of Scone, pre-840 AD. Edinburgh Castle, Scotland. Crown Copyright Historic Environment Scotland

102 Keith Arnatt, *Self-Burial (Television Interference Project)*, 1969, photographs. Tate, London. © Keith Arnatt Estate. All rights reserved, DACS 2017

103 Keith Arnatt, *Invisible Hole Revealed by the Shadow of the Artist*, 1968. Photograph: gelatin silver print on paper, exhibition copy for *Seven Exhibitions*, Tate Gallery, 1972, image: 60.8 x 75.6 cm. Tate, London. © Keith Arnatt Estate. All rights reserved, DACS 2017

104 Brass commemorating Geoffrey Sherard and his wife, 1490. St Mary Magdalene Church, Stapleford, Leicestershire. Photograph by LeicesterPhoto LTD

105 Rubbing of brass commemorating John Claymond, 1537. Chapel at Corpus Christi College, Oxford. From Peter Sherlock, *Monuments and Memory in Early Modern England* (Farnham: Ashgate, 2008)

106 Floor plaques marking the lying-in-state of King George V and Queen Mary. Westminster Hall, London. ©UKParliament

107 Path made of headstones. Leeds General Cemetery. © Sophie Kullmann

108 Design by Lionel Budden with bronze reliefs by Tyson Smith, Liverpool Cenotaph, 1926-30. St George's Plateau, Liverpool. © Historic England

109 Richard Long, *Untitled*, 1968. Exh. Konrad Fischer Gallery, Düsseldorf. © Richard Long. All rights reserved, DACS 2017

110 Bethan Huws, *Riverside Piece*, 1989. Oak parquet floor with oil. Exh. Riverside Studios, London. Photograph: John Riddy, London / © Bethan Huws and VG Bild-Kunst, Bonn 2017

111 Richard Long, *A Line Made by Walking*, 1967, photograph. Tate, London. © Richard Long. All rights reserved, DACS 2017

closed

112 Harry Bates, *Pandora*, 1890. Tate, London. © Tate, London 2017

113 Harry Bates, lid of the ivory casket from *Pandora*, 1890. Tate, London. © Tate, London 2017

114 Harry Bates, frieze on the ivory casket from *Pandora*, 1890. Tate, London. © Tate, London 2017

115 John Gibson, *Pandora*, 1856. Victoria and Albert Museum, London. © Victoria and Albert Museum, London

116 Monymusk reliquary, c.8th century. National Museums Scotland. Image © National Museums Scotland, acquired with the aid of the Art Fund

117 Reliquary casket with scenes from the Martyrdom of Saint Thomas Becket, c.1173-80. The Metropolitan Museum of Art, New York /

Gift of J. Pierpont Morgan, 1917 / Photograph by Schecter Lee

118 Becket Casket, c.1180–90. Victoria and Albert Museum, London. © Victoria and Albert Museum, London

119 Pilgrim's badge of the shrine of Saint Thomas Becket at Canterbury, 1350-1400. The Metropolitan Museum of Art, New York / Gift of Dr and Mrs W. Conte, 2001

120 Detail of monument to Robert Kelway and the Harrington Family, 16th century. Church of St Peter and St Paul, Exton, Leicestershire. © Conway Library, The Courtauld Institute of Art, London

121 Alfred Gilbert, model for tomb of Prince Albert Victor, Duke of Clarence and Avondale, 1892. Victoria and Albert Museum, London. © Victoria and Albert Museum, London

122 John Latham, *Art & Culture*, 1966. The Museum of Modern Art, New York. © 2017. Digital image, The Museum of Modern Art, New York / Scala, Florence

123 Saint Eustace Head reliquary, 1180-1200. British Museum, London. © Trustees of the British Museum

124 George Frampton, *Lamia*, 1900. Royal Academy of Arts, London. © Royal Academy of Arts, London / Photo: RA / Paul Highnam

125 Antony Gormley, *Natural Selection*, 1981. Lead tools, fruits, weapons, vegetables and objects. Length: approx. 10 metres. Tate, London. © The artist / Photograph © Tate, London 2017

126 Henry VII's death mask, 1509. Westminster Abbey, London. © Dean and Chapter of Westminster

127 Benjamin Robert Haydon, plaster cast of the life mask of John Keats, 1816. National Portrait Gallery, London. © National Portrait Gallery, London

128 William Cumberland Cruikshank and James Hoskins, plaster cast of a bust incorporating the death mask of Samuel Johnson, 1784. National Portrait Gallery, London. © National Portrait Gallery, London

129 Death mask cast in plaster of Thomas Lawrence, 1830. National Portrait Gallery, London. © National Portrait Gallery, London

130 Lynn Chadwick, *Inner Eye (Maquette III)*, 1952. Tate, London. © The estate of Lynn Chadwick. All rights reserved 2017 / Photograph © Tate, London 2017

131 Eric Bainbridge, *Sugar*, 1989. Leeds Art Gallery. Image: Workplace Gallery, London. © Eric Bainbridge

132 Reliquary figure of a Benedictine monk with a heart-shaped orifice in its breast for a relic, 15th century. British Museum, London. © Trustees of the British Museum

133 Easter Sepulchre, c.1500. St Mary's, Coity, Wales. From the collections of the National Monuments Record of Wales: B. C. Clayton

134 Sarcophagus, early 4th century. British Museum, London. © Trustees of the British Museum

135 Tomb chest monument to Sir Thomas Moyle and his wife Katherine, 1560. Victoria and Albert Museum, London. © Victoria and Albert Museum, London

136 Tomb of Francis Hastings, 2nd Earl of Huntingdon, 1561. St Helen's Church, Ashby-de-la-Zouch, Leicestershire. Photograph by LeicesterPhoto LTD

137 Monument to Robert Lord Willoughby, 1738. St Michael's and All Angels Church, Edenham, Lincolnshire. © Conway Library, The Courtauld Institute of Art, London

138 Charles Francis Greville, frontispiece to accompany a set of five engravings commemorating Sir William Hamilton bringing the Portland Vase to England, 1786. British Museum, London. © Trustees of the British Museum

139 Robert Adam, monument to Major John Andre, 1780. Westminster Abbey, London. © Dean and Chapter of Westminster

140 John Sell Cotman, *Sarcophagus in a Pleasure Garden*, c.1806. British Museum, London. © Trustees of the British Museum

141 Edward Godwin, monument to James McNeill Whistler, 1912. St Nicholas Church, Chiswick. Photograph by Patche99z, licensed under Creative Commons Attribution-Share Alike 3.0 Unported license

142 Jacob Epstein, W. H. Hudson Memorial (Rima), 1923–5. Hyde Park, London. © Estate of Jacob Epstein / Photograph © Courtauld Institute of Art

143 Robert Morris, *Untitled (Box for Standing)*, 1961. Museo Nacional Centro de Arte Reina Sofia, Madrid. © Robert Morris / Artists Rights Society (ARS), New York / DACS, London 2017

144 Rachel Whiteread, *Monument*, 2001. Fourth Plinth Project, Trafalgar Square, London. **© Rachel Whiteread. Courtesy the artist and Gagosian**

145 Joseph Beuys, *Das Paar* [*The Couple*], 1952/53. Plaster, wax, wood. Installed in vitrine: 164 x 160 x 72 cm. Collection of Céline and Heiner Bastian, Berlin. Photo by Jörg von Bruchhausen, Berlin. © DACS, 2017

146 146. Wax memorial figure of Charles II (with, left, the Duke of Buckingham), 1685. Westminster Abbey, London. © Bishopsgate Institute

147 Damien Hirst, *A Thousand Years*, 1990. Glass, steel, silicone rubber, painted MDF, insect-o-cutor, cow's head, blood, flies, maggots, metal dishes, cotton wool, sugar and water, 207.5 x 400 x 215 cm. Exh. Saatchi Gallery, London. © Damien Hirst and Science Ltd. All rights reserved, DACS 2017. Photo: Roger Wooldridge

148 Darren Almond, *Terminus*, 1999. Exh. White Cube Gallery, London. © Darren Almond / image courtesy of White Cube, London

149 Joseph Beuys, *Dumb Box*, 1982. Tate, London / National Galleries of Scotland. © DACS, 2017

150 Tony Cragg, *Axehead*, 1982. Tate, London. © DACS 2017

151 Bill Woodrow, *Untitled (Telephone)*, 1979. Rob Tufnell Gallery, London. © Bill Woodrow. All rights reserved, DACS 2017

152 Bill Woodrow, *Tape Recorder*, 1979. Künstlerhaus, Hamburg. © Bill Woodrow. All rights reserved, DACS 2017

153 Rachel Whiteread, *Untitled (Orange Bath)*, 1996. Rubber and polystyrene, 80 x 207 x 110.2 cm. Exh. Saatchi Gallery, London. **© Rachel Whiteread. Courtesy the artist and Gagosian**

154 Nicholas Hawksmoor, mausoleum, 1729. Castle Howard, Yorkshire. Photograph © Bridgeman Images

155 Thomas Espin, summerhouse, 1819. Louth, Lincolnshire. Photograph by LeicesterPhoto LTD

156 Theophilus Fairfax Johnson, Johnson Mausoleum, 1843. Spalding Cemetery, Lincolnshire. Photograph by LeicesterPhoto LTD

157 Rachel Whiteread, *Detached 1*, 2012. Concrete and steel, 200 x 172 x 109 cm. **© Rachel Whiteread. Courtesy the artist and Gagosian.** Photography by Mike Bruce for Gagosian Gallery

158 Mike Nelson, *Coral Reef*, 2000. Tate, London. Courtesy of the artist and Matt's Gallery, London / Photograph © Tate, London 2017

159 Rose Finn-Kelcey, *God Kennel - A Tabernacle*, 1992. Exh. documenta IX, Kassel, Germany. Image: Courtesy the Estate of Rose Finn-Kelcey

160 Rose Finn-Kelcey, *The Royal Box*, 1993. Exh. Saatchi Gallery, London. Image: Courtesy the Estate of Rose Finn-Kelcey

161 Rose Finn-Kelcey, *Steam Installation*, 1992. Exh. Chisenhale Gallery, London. Image: Courtesy the Estate of Rose Finn-Kelcey

162 Robert Adam (designer) and Carron Iron Co. (maker), stove cast in the shape of an urn, c.1780. Victoria and Albert Museum, London. © Victoria and Albert Museum, London

163 Alfred Gilbert, *Mors Janua Vitae*, 1905-9. Royal College of Surgeons of England, London. Courtesy of the Hunterian Museum at the Royal College of Surgeons of England

164 Nicholas Stone, monument to John Donne, 1631. St Paul's Cathedral, London. © Conway Library, The Courtauld Institute of Art, London

165 Monument to George Villiers, Duke of Buckingham, 1628. Chapel of St Thomas, Portsmouth Cathedral. Photograph by Paul Watt / Simpler-life photography

166 Thomas Browne, dedicatory spread from *Hydriotaphia, Urne-Buriall; with an account of some urns found at Brampton in Norfolk*, 1658. Image courtesy of Chris Mullen, fulltable.com

167 Grinling Gibbons, monument to the 3rd Viscount Campden, 1686. Church of St Peter and St Paul, Exton, Leicestershire. © Conway Library, The Courtauld Institute of Art, London

168 Attributed to Henry Cheere, monument to the 2nd Duke of Ancaster, 1741. Saint Michael's Church, Edenham, Lincolnshire. © Conway Library, The Courtauld Institute of Art, London

169 John Michael Rysbrack, urn featuring the portrait of the widow of the 9th Earl of Huntingdon, Selina Countess of Huntingdon, 1746. St Helen's Church, Ashby-de-la-Zouch, Leicestershire. Photograph by LeicesterPhoto LTD

170 John Michael Rysbrack, monument to Sir John Dutton, 1749. St Mary Magdalene,

Sherborne, Gloucestershire. © Conway Library, The Courtauld Institute of Art, London

171 Louis-François Roubiliac, monument to Richard Boyle, Viscount Shannon, mid-1750s. St Mary's Parish Church, Walton-on-Thames, Surrey. © Conway Library, The Courtauld Institute of Art, London

172 Louis-François Roubiliac, monument to George Lynn, 1758. St Mary, Southwick, Northamptonshire. © Conway Library, The Courtauld Institute of Art, London

173 Joseph Nollekens, monument to Lieutenant General Bennett Noel, 1787. Church of St Peter and St Paul, Exton, Leicestershire. © Conway Library, The Courtauld Institute of Art, London

174 Carlo Marochetti, tomb of Ugo Foscolo, 1827. St Nicholas Church, Chiswick. Photograph by Peter Hammond

175 Jacob Epstein, tomb of Oscar Wilde, 1914. Père Lachaise Cemetery, Paris. © Estate of Jacob Epstein / Photograph by JHvW, licensed under Creative Commons Attribution-Share Alike 3.0 Unported license

176 Barbara Hepworth, *Helikon*, 1948. The Museum of Modern Art, New York. Photograph: Studio St Ives, taken in 1948. © Bowness

open

177 Ceal Floyer, *Welcome*, 2011. Exh. Esther Schipper Gallery, Berlin. Image courtesy of the artist and Esther Schipper, Berlin. Photo: © Andrea Rossetti / © DACS 2017

178 Martin Creed, *Work No. 203: EVERYTHING IS GOING TO BE ALRIGHT*, 1999. White neon, 1300 x 50 cm. © 2017 Martin Creed. Courtesy of the artist and Hauser & Wirth / Photo: Hugo Glendinning

179 Maximilian Colt, monument to Robert Chamberlayne, 1615. St Bartholomew the Great, Smithfield, London. Photograph by Sarah Cocke

180 Louis-François Roubiliac, monument to Thomas Myddelton and Arabella Myddelton, c.1756. Wrexham Parish Church, Clwyd, Wales. © Conway Library, The Courtauld Institute of Art, London

181 Louis-François Roubiliac, monument to Richard Children, 1753. St Peter's and St Paul's, Tonbridge, Kent. Photograph by Michael Sheppard

182 Charles Mabey, *Time and Fortune Draw a Curtain Over Temple Bar*, 1880. Temple Bar Memorial, Paternoster Square, London. Photograph by William Hall

183 Christopher Wren, Temple Bar Gate, 1672. Paternoster Square, London. Photograph by Andreas Praefcke, licensed under Creative Commons Attribution-Share Alike 3.0 Unported license

184 Horace Jones, Temple Bar Memorial, 1880. Royal Courts of Justice, London. Eric Nathan / Alamy Stock Photo

185 Decimus Burton, Green Park Arch, (now Wellington Arch), 1826–30. Green Park, London. © Historic England / Bridgeman Images

186 John Nash, Marble Arch, 1826. Junction of Oxford Street, Park Lane and Edgware Road, London. akg-images / A. F. Kersting

187 Henry Wilson, bronze doors, 1905. St Mary's, Nottingham. Image courtesy of St Mary's, Nottingham

188 Eric Gill, *Prospero and Ariel*, 1933. BBC Broadcasting House, Portland Place, London. Photo © Stefano Baldini / Bridgeman Images

189 James Woodford, bronze doors, 1934. Royal Institute of British Architects, London. © Nick Fielding / Alamy Stock Photo

190 Gates of Humility, 16th century. Gonville and Caius College, Cambridge. Photograph by J. D. Forrester, licensed under GNU Free Documentation License

191 Martin Creed, *Work No. 1432: Gold leaf on door* (MC 031), 2012. Dimensions variable. Johnen Galerie, Berlin. Courtesy of the artist and Johnen Galerie

192 John Frankland, *You Can't Touch This*, 1992–3. © John Frankland. All rights reserved, DACS 2017

193 Rose Finn-Kelcey, *Pearly Gate*, 1997. Exh. Camden Arts Centre, London. Image: Courtesy the Estate of Rose Finn-Kelcey

194 Barbara Hepworth, *Four Square (Walk Through), in situ* at the Trewyn Studio in 1966. Barbara Hepworth Museum and Sculpture Garden, St Ives. © Bowness. Photograph © Jorge Lewinski

195 Nathan Coley, *Untitled (Threshold Sculptures)*, 2007. 8 cm-high plank of wood on the floor. Doggerfisher, Edinburgh. © Nathan Coley

196 Adam Chodzko, *Untitled Stile (Teenage Version)*, 1992. Arts Council Collection, Southbank Centre, London. © Adam Chodzko. All rights reserved, DACS 2017

197 Lucy Gunning, *Gate*, 1996. © Lucy Gunning

198 Ceal Floyer, *Vorsicht Stufe*, 2009. Humboldt University, Berlin. Image courtesy of the artist and Esther Schipper, Berlin. © DACS 2017

199 A. K. Dolven, *Out of Tune*, 2011. Sound installation (Folkestone, Kent) with bell; steel columns; wire and spliced rope; Scraptoft Tenor, 14th-century Anglican church bell. 20 x 30 metres. Courtesy of A. K. Dolven / Wilkinson Gallery London and OSL Contemporary Oslo. Photograph: Thierry Bal

200 Fiona Banner, *Tornado*, 2010. Exh. Newcastle. Courtesy of Fiona Banner and Frith Street Gallery, London

201 Sanctuary Ring knocker, copy of 12th-century bronze original. Durham Cathedral. © Clearview / Alamy Stock Photo

202 Alfred Stevens, doorknocker, *c.*1865, originally designed for Westonbirt House. Victoria and Albert Museum, London. © Victoria and Albert Museum, London

203 Keith Wilson, *Football in Railings*, 1998. V22 Collection, London. © Keith Wilson

204 Chichester Grille, *c.*1250. Victoria and Albert Museum, London. © Victoria and Albert Museum, London

205 Wrought-iron grille, 1480–1500. Victoria and Albert Museum, London. © Victoria and Albert Museum, London

206 John Tresilian, gates to Edward IV's chantry chapel, 1477–84. St George's Chapel, Windsor. Royal Collection Trust / © Her Majesty Queen Elizabeth II 2017

207 Alfred Gilbert, Queen Alexandra Memorial, 1926–32. Marlborough Road, London. Photograph by Ellacott

208 Alfred Gilbert, Sam Wilson Chimneypiece, *c.*1908–14. Leeds Museums and Galleries. © Leeds Museums and Galleries (Leeds Art Gallery) / Bridgeman Images

209 Charles Sargeant Jagger, *Scandal* relief and firebasket, 1930. Victoria and Albert Museum, London. © Victoria and Albert Museum, London

210 Rose Finn-Kelcey, *Just Minus*, 1994. Exh. British School at Rome. Image: Courtesy the Estate of Rose Finn-Kelcey

211 Anna Barriball, *Draw (fireplace)*, 2005. Exh. MK Gallery, Milton Keynes. Courtesy of Anna Barriball and Frith Street Gallery, London

212 Fireback, 1735–40. Duff House, Scotland. Photograph by Michelle Tones. © Historic Environment Scotland

213 *Annunciation* fireback, 17th century. Bessie Surtees House, Newcastle. © Historic England

214 Fireback depicting Protestant martyrs being burnt at the stake, *c.*1600. Anne of Cleves House Museum, Lewes. Photograph © the author

215 Fireback depicting the Burning Fiery Furnace, 1636. Anne of Cleves House Museum, Lewes. Photograph © the author

216 Fireback depicting firedogs, date unknown. Anne of Cleves House Museum, Lewes. Photograph © the author

217 Anthony Hatch, firedog, 1650–80. Victoria and Albert Museum, London. © Victoria and Albert Museum, London

218 Firedogs, date unknown. Ty Mawr Wybrnant, Conwy, Wales. © National Trust / Boris Mollo

219 Charles Rennie Mackintosh, fireplace, *c.*1904. Victoria and Albert Museum, London. © Victoria and Albert Museum, London

220 Geoffrey Clarke, *Woman* (a pair with a welded steel sculpture *Man* of the same date), 1953. Tate, London. © Geoffrey Clarke / Photograph © Tate, London 2017

221 Attributed to Joseph Wilton, chimneypiece, *c.*1775. Victoria and Albert Museum, London. © Victoria and Albert Museum, London

222 William Collins and Henry Cheere, *Shepherd and Shepherdess*, *c.*1761. Victoria and Albert Museum, London. © Victoria and Albert Museum, London

223 Anne Seymour Damer, *Two Sleeping Dogs*, 1784. Goodwood, Sussex. © Country Life Picture Library

224 *Sacrifice of Isaac*, 1783. St Mary Magdalene Church, Stapleford, Leicestershire. © Photograph Groenling

225 Lucy Gunning, *Peeling the Apple*, 1996. Exh. City Racing. © Lucy Gunning

226 Thomas Johnson, mirror frame, 1750–60. Victoria and Albert Museum, London. © Victoria and Albert Museum, London

227 By or after Thomas Chippendale, mirror, *c.*1765. Victoria and Albert Museum, London. © Victoria and Albert Museum, London

228 John Frankland, *Untitled Brown Work*, 2005. Matt's Gallery, London. © John Frankland. All rights reserved, DACS 2017

229 Convex mirror, *c.*1800. Victoria and Albert Museum, London. © Victoria and Albert Museum, London

230 Hermione Wiltshire, *Puff*, 1996, Exh. Bowes Museum. © Hermione Wiltshire

231 Helen Chadwick, *Vanitas II*, 1986. National Portrait Gallery, London. © Estate of Helen Chadwick

232 Anish Kapoor, *Turning the World Upside Down*, 1995. Stainless steel, 120 × 120 × 120 cm. Exh. Fondazione Prada, Milan, 1995. Photograph: Attilo Marazano, Sienna / © Anish Kapoor. All rights reserved, DACS 2017

233 Cerith Wyn Evans, *Inverse Reverse Perverse*, 1996. Exh. White Cube, London. © Cerith Wyn Evans / image courtesy of White Cube, London

234 Anish Kapoor, *Double Mirror*, 1998. Stainless steel, dimensions variable. Exh. Hayward Gallery, London, 1998. Photograph: John Riddy / © Anish Kapoor. All rights reserved, DACS 2017

235 Mark Leckey, *Made in 'Eaven*, 2004. Looped 16 mm film. Tate, London. Courtesy the artist and Cabinet, London / Photograph © Tate, London 2017

236 Mirror, *c.*1720. Victoria and Albert Museum, London. © Victoria and Albert Museum, London

237 Easter Sepulchre, 14th century. St Andrew's Church, Heckington, Lincolnshire. © Conway Library, The Courtauld Institute of Art, London

238 Monument to Richard Bertie, 1582. St James Church, Spilsby, Lincolnshire. Photograph by Julian P. Guffogg

239 Kinnoull Monument, 1634. Old Parish Church, Perth, Scotland. © Historic Environment Scotland

240 Frontispiece from *The History of the World* by Sir Walter Raleigh (London: William Stansby, 1614). © The Master and Fellows of Trinity College, Cambridge

241 Monument to Lord Sherard, 2nd Baron Sherard of Leitrim, 1640. St Mary Magdalene Church, Stapleford, Leicestershire. Photograph by LeicesterPhoto LTD

242 Charles Harris, monument to the 3rd and 4th Dukes of Ancaster, *c.*1793. St Michael's Church, Edenham, Lincolnshire. © Conway Library, The Courtauld Institute of Art, London

243 Giorgio Sadotti, *Fire*, 2012. © Giorgio Sadotti. All rights reserved, DACS 2017. Photo: Giorgio Sadotti

244 Rosemarie Trockel, *A Cosmos* exhibition, 2012. © DACS 2017

245 Nathan Coley, *Heaven is a Place where Nothing ever Happens*, 2008. Illuminated text / scaffolding. Exh. Folkestone, Kent. © Nathan Coley

ensemble

246 Bethan Huws, *The Lake Writing* exhibition at the Institute for Contemporary Art (ICA), London in 1991 (installation view). Photocopies of manuscripts, 24 pages, 29.7 x 21 cm. Tate Collection / Photograph: Steve White, London / © Bethan Huws and VG Bild-Kunst, Bonn 2017 / © ADAGP, Paris and DACS, London 2017

247 Bethan Huws, *The Lake Writing* exhibition at the Institute for Contemporary Art (ICA), London in 1991 (text). Tate Collection / Photograph: Steve White, London / © Bethan Huws and VG Bild-Kunst, Bonn 2017 / © ADAGP, Paris and DACS, London 2017

248 Lucy Gunning, *Mirror Event* - Grasmere, Cumbria, 2007. © Lucy Gunning

249 Lucy Gunning, *Climbing Around my Room*, 1993, film still. © Lucy Gunning

250 Martin Creed, *Work No. 227: The lights going on and off*, 2000. Dimensions variable, 5 seconds on / 5 seconds off. © 2017 Martin Creed. Courtesy of the artist and Hauser & Wirth / Photo: Martin Creed

251 John Vanbrugh, Temple of the Four Winds, 1724. Castle Howard, Yorkshire. © Steve Morris / Alamy Stock Photo

252 Nicholas Hawksmoor, Four Faces Monument, *c.*1720s. Pretty Wood, Castle Howard, Yorkshire. Courtesy of Castle Howard

253 John Cheere, *Sleeping Nymph (Ariadne)*, 1766. Stourhead, Wiltshire. © National Trust Images / David Cousins

254 View across the lake from the position of *Ariadne*, Stourhead, Wiltshire. © National Trust Images / David Noton

255 *Borghese Hermaphrodite*, 18th-century copy. West Wycombe Park, Buckinghamshire. © National Trust Images / John Hammond

256 Pierre Huyghe, *Untitled*, 2011–12. Exh. documenta 13, Karlsaue Park, Kassel, Germany. © ADAGP, Paris and DACS, London 2017

257 Antonio Canova, *Three Graces*, 1814–17, in its original setting in the sculpture gallery at Woburn Abbey, Bedfordshire. © Conway Library, The Courtauld Institute of Art, London

258 Nicholas Hawksmoor, cupola (housing the statue of Queen Caroline by Henry Cheere), 1736. Queen's College, Oxford. Photo by Rex Harris

259 John Gibson, *Tinted Venus*, 1862, shown in a contemporary photograph of the International Exhibition. The Metropolitan Museum of Art, New York. © 2017. Image copyright The Metropolitan Museum of Art / Art Resource / Scala, Florence

260 Sean Dower, *St Simeon's Drum Riser*, 2012. Courtesy of the artist (Sean Dower) and De La Warr Pavilion 2012

261 Bill Woodrow, *English Heritage – Humpty Fucking Dumpty*, 1987. Tate, London. © Bill Woodrow. All rights reserved, DACS 2017

262 Keith Wilson, *Scape*, 1995. Leeds Art Gallery. © Keith Wilson

263 Sarah Lucas, *Two Fried Eggs and a Kebab*, 1992. Table, photo, fried eggs, kebab. 151 x 89.5 x 102 cm. © Sarah Lucas, courtesy Sadie Coles HQ, London

264 Tommaso Laureti, *Triumph of Christianity over Paganism*, 1585. Detail of the ceiling in the Constantine Room, Vatican Museum, Rome. © Nick Fielding / Alamy Stock Photo

265 Drahmal Cross, 11th century. Cathedral of St Michael and St Gudula, Brussels. Courtesy of St Michael and St Gudula Cathedral, Brussels

266 Jake and Dinos Chapman, *Great Deeds against the Dead*, 1994. Exh. Saatchi Gallery, London. © Jake & Dinos Chapman. All rights reserved, DACS 2017

267 Gian Lorenzo Bernini, *Apollo and Daphne*, 1622-5. Galleria Borghese, Rome. Photograph © Bridgeman Images

268 Tyburn Tree memorial plaque, erected 1965 near Marble Arch, London. © Chris Dorney / Alamy Stock Photo

269 Photograph of the Church of St Lorenz, Nuremberg, after the Allied bombing of 2 January 1945, showing the crucifix still standing.

270 Painted tympanum board, 16th century. St Catherine's Church, Ludham, Norfolk. Photograph by Paul Hurst

271 Monument to the Lethieullier Family, c.1737. Church of St Mary the Virgin, Little Ilford, Essex. Photograph by Brian Lewis

272 Louis-François Roubiliac, monument to Sir Joseph and Lady Elizabeth Nightingale, 1761. Westminster Abbey, London. Photograph © Bridgeman Images

273 Roger Hiorns, *Untitled, 2005-2010: Bench, fire and youth*, 2005-10. © Roger Hiorns. All rights reserved, DACS 2017. Image courtesy Corvi-Mora, London

274 Rosemarie Trockel, *Ich habe angst*, 1993. St Peter's Church, Cologne. © DACS 2017

275 Rainer Maria Rilke at the Hotel Biron in Paris, 1908. © akg-images

Page numbers in *italics* indicate illustrations.

acknowledgements

This book was initiated with an invitation to give the 2015 Mellon Lectures in London and New Haven. Entitled 'Sculpture on the Threshold', they were given at the National Gallery and the Yale University Art Gallery. I was pleased to be asked by Mark Hallett to give the lectures and thank him for his confidence in the project throughout. Seeing the potential in a series to allow one to create something consecutive, and cumulative, but in which each part had its own subject, I developed the structure of the book, in which each chapter has an individual identity, but helps to build a larger whole. The Mellon link necessarily defined the geographical focus of the project, but I contend that the examples hold good much more generally.

I was enormously lucky to have Sophie Kullmann as my original picture researcher; her work ensured the lectures were properly visual. I should like to thank my audience for their regular attendance and response, some of it written and in detail, as well as Martina Droth, who chaired the final plenary session at Yale. I am grateful to Gillian Malpass for persevering with the possibility of publishing the lectures with Yale. The process of preparing the book for publication has been ably managed by Emily Lees and Maisoon Rehani at the Paul Mellon Centre, with William Hall, my designer.

My thanks go to Richard Wrigley, with whom I travelled to see many of the sculptures in Lincolnshire and Leicestershire, to Hugh Blythe for discovering with me the sundials of Aberdeenshire and Ayrshire, and to Peter St John, for his encouragement. The place where I found my way into thinking about sculpture was Leeds, at the Henry Moore Institute, and it was a process that was shared with colleagues there, and with artists.

It was only as the series took shape that I realised too how much it owed to the enthusiasms of my father, who took us as children to see stones and structures, man-made and natural, mostly in Argyllshire. Those trips were clearly formative.

Designed by William Hall
Layout by Marine Fanet and William Hall

Printed in China

Library of Congress Cataloging-in-Publication Data

Name: Curtis, Penelope, author.
Title: Sculpture: vertical, horizontal, closed, open / Penelope Curtis.
Description: New Haven : Yale University Press, 2017. | Includes bibliographical references and index.
Identifiers: LCCN 2017008588 |
ISBN 9780300227222 (cl : alk. paper)
Subjects: LCSH: Sculpture.
Classification: LCC NB1140 .C87 2017 |
DDC 730-dc23
LC record available at https://lccn.loc.gov/2017008588

A catalogue record for this book is available from the British Library